The Short Guide Series

UNDER THE EDITORSHIP OF

Sylvan Barnet

Marcia Stubbs

A Short Guide to Writing about Literature by Sylvan Barnet

A Short Guide to Writing about Art by Sylvan Barnet

A Short Guide to Writing about Biology by Jan A. Pechenik

A Short Guide to Writing about Social Science by Lee J. Cuba

A Short Guide to Writing about Film by Timothy Corrigan

A Short Guide to Writing about History by Richard Marius

A Short Guide
to Writing
about History

A Short Guide to Writing about History

RICHARD MARIUS
Harvard University

SCOTT, FORESMAN AND COMPANY
Glenview, Illinois Boston London

Library of Congress Cataloging-in-Publication Data

Marius, Richard.
  A short guide to writing about history.

  (The Short guide series)
  Includes index.
  1. Historiography.   2. History—Methodology.
  3. History—Research.   4. Authorship.   I. Title.
  D13.M294   1989   907'.2   88–33712
  ISBN 0–673–39998–2

    2   3   4   5   6   7   8   9   10—KPF—94   93   92   91   90   89

Printed in the United States of America

Acknowledgments appear on pages 255–256, which are considered an extension of the copyright page.

For my sons
Fred and John.
For the miles we have
biked together
following history
under the soft skies of France.

Preface

For most people history is a jumble of facts held together by vague impressions. The seemingly infinite number of facts can be overwhelming. Once when I was teaching the European history survey at the University of Tennessee in the 1960s, a bright student told me in deep frustration, "I have to learn more facts in this course than I do in anything else but organic chemistry." I had always loved to read history and to talk about it and think about it; the comparison of my beloved discipline with a subject as mysterious and complex as organic chemistry seemed shocking, irreverent.

Yet my student had a point. Any history course involves a mass of factual information. Teachers and students alike are sometimes tempted to suppose that history is nothing but facts and that knowing history is simply a matter of listing the facts one after another. Facts in history are essential; no one can doubt that. I agree with E. D. Hirsch, Jr., that part of what he calls "cultural literacy" is the ability to recognize a great many "facts" or "terms" if we are to understand either what we read about history or what we see in the daily news. The facts give us a frame of reference that allows us to relate new knowledge to old and fit what we know into a context.

But every working historian knows that the joys of history lie beyond *mere* fact. Historians have to decide first what is fact and what is fiction, and that is no easy task. Many charming stories that pretend to be history are pleasant fictions; they did not happen. Martin Luther did not nail ninety-five theses to a church door in Wittenberg, Germany, to start the Reformation, and he did not say "Here I stand, God help me, I can do no other" when he stood before the Emperor Charles V at the Diet of Worms. Paul Revere did not stand on the opposite shore "waiting to ride and spread the alarm" when the two lanterns were posted in the belfry of Old North Church; he was still in Boston when his friend Robert Newman posted the lanterns to alert others across the Charles River that the British were on their way to seize military supplies stocked by the Patriots in Concord. Revere did not make it all the way into Concord as Longfellow has it in his famous poem; he was captured by the British near Lexington, and although he escaped, the British took his horse, and others had to carry the warning deeper into that chilly April night. Looked at closely, the "facts" in history may dissolve. Or they may change their shape, taking on more or less meaning.

Even when the facts are fairly certain, historians must still make sense of them. How are facts related to each other? Historians wrestle with cause and effect—always a complicated business. What caused the enormous national interest in the Scopes Monkey Trial in Dayton, Tennessee, in 1925? What part did radio play in causing the college football boom of the 1920s and the 1930s? What have been the effects of Watergate on American journalism and on the American psyche? What have been the effects of the Civil Rights movement of the 1960s? The answers to questions like these require more than filling in the blanks. They require discovery, debate, reasoning, and careful conclusions. All these needs are best met by writing. Historians write; they think by writing. Other historians challenge them or build upon their ideas by writing. Without writing, history would dissolve into legend.

In most history courses, students are required to write papers to demonstrate both a command of the facts and the ability to think about them. They are seldom given any formal instruction in how to do the special kind of writing that the study of history demands. They are expected to pick up this skill almost by osmosis. For years history teachers have ritually complained that their students do not write well. Only recently have we begun to understand that helping our students write acceptably about history is part of our responsibility in teaching them the discipline itself.

In the following pages I offer some simple and practical advice to help students write better history papers. In so doing I have tried to help students think of themselves as real historians—not merely parrots who repeat only what they have heard from their teachers. I would like them to think of themselves as detectives, exploring the evidence of the past to resolve its mysteries—or at least to make plausible suggestions about how the mysteries might be resolved. I hope that the book will not only help them write and think better about historical evidence but also give them confidence to believe that they can study the sources for themselves and write essays that are thoughtful and original.

Before I came to my present job as director of the Expository Writing Program at Harvard, I spent sixteen years in the classroom teaching history, first at Gettysburg College in Pennsylvania and then at the University of Tennessee, Knoxville, my alma mater. My students wrote and wrote and wrote; I spent much time helping them use their writing to learn the discipline I wanted them to love. I owe my greatest debts to that long procession of students who not only studied history and writing under my direction but who by their patience, good humor, and enthusiasm taught me how to be a better teacher, both of writing and of the glorious discipline that tries to make sense—however transitory—of the ever shifting past.

Many people have read various versions of this manuscript and have commented upon it, and I have much appreciated their efforts to make this a better book. Among them are Ned Landsman, SUNY Stonybrook; Frederick Blue, Youngstown State University; Bruce Wheeler, University of Tennessee, Knoxville; and Maury Klein, University of Rhode Island, Kingston. I have often gratefully agreed with their suggestions but sometimes not. Mention of their names is not to say that they have certified the contents of the book.

I am deeply grateful to my wife, Lanier, and to my sons and others close to me whose love and friendship sustain the life out of which I write.

Contents

Introduction

Students struggling over an essay in history often say that they know the subject but cannot write about it. They usually mean that they have a jumble of facts in their heads but cannot tell a story about them. Their complaint reveals a discovery, that history is a special kind of storytelling and that facts are not enough. You can have a big, bad wolf, a little girl named Red Riding Hood, an old grandmother, a basket of cakes, and a dark woods without having a story. You can even know the date of the wolf's birth, the color of Red Riding Hood's hair, and the grandmother's mailing address without having a story. To create a story you have to put the facts together in a special way, making sense of what you know. You have to make readers want to know the story you have to tell them.

All this telling involves science and art. Science is a synonym for knowledge. History is far from being an exact science, but it does involve data—evidence, facts, bits of information gathered from many, varied sources. The art lies in putting those facts together to tell a story accurate in detail and interesting in presentation.

History means "story" in most languages. We might say that the past is a collection of millions of stories. Some of them are legends, based merely on what people have told others about the past but without solid information. Some of the stories are flawed by inaccuracies and downright lies. Some of them are more than half hidden in the obscurities of time. Some have been forgotten altogether. Historians try to resurrect stories about the past, set them in order, and tell them for their own time; they try to tell the truth.

The "truth" is complicated, contradictory, and usually obscure. What happened? Who was responsible? Who was affected? Why did it happen? Where and when did it happen? The evidence that allows us to frame answers to these questions is like pieces of a jigsaw puzzle washed out of a shipwreck and cast upon a rocky beach by the waves. Many of the pieces are lost. Many that remain are faded and warped. Historians fit the pieces together as carefully as possible and discover holes in the picture. They do their best to fill in the gaps with some design which seems plausible and which fits the available facts—a sensible conjecture or inference. We will change the metaphor slightly: The historian resembles the artist called upon to restore a badly damaged painting done hundreds of years ago. The work that appears after such restoration may come close to the original, but one is never quite certain just how close.

The historian's paintbrush is the written word. History as we have known it for centuries is the past reconstructed by historians' writing about it. We cannot know history well unless we can write about it. Like the story of Little Red Riding Hood, we can know some things about history without knowing history itself—a few dates, some names, fragments of biography, interesting anecdotes, a general sketch of time when things happened. That fragmentary knowledge is not history, for history is more than a list of facts. It is not to be memorized like the multiplication table or the irregular verbs in a foreign language. To write history, we apply the mind to studying, ordering, and understanding data that are vast and complicated, the relics people have left behind them from life. It involves making connections, deciding who is to be believed and who not, what happened and what did not, what might have happened and what could not have occurred, why things turned out as they did and not in some other way, when things happened, where they happened, who caused events and who was affected by them.

STUDYING HISTORY AS A WAY OF THINKING

The good historian is a thinker, and the best measure of the historian is the way in which he or she writes.

Writing requires us to develop our ideas, to be precise, to say what we mean. The good talker can touch on first one idea and then another, sometimes using body language to stress a point, being loud and overbearing when the argument is weak. He may depend on someone else in the group to help out when his logic or his facts fail. The good writer performs a much more daring act: developing an idea with logic and clarity and with the boldness that arises from the confidence that readers can study the words again and again and discover that they add up to a plausible statement, if the evidence is adequate. The good writer cannot hide his thoughts. If we are illogical or unfair or untruthful or confused or foolish, our words are there on the page to be discovered by anyone with the care and the interest to look. The good talker can contradict himself, waffle, and weasel and, on being called to task, can claim that his hearers misunderstood him. Because our short-term memories are so fallible, we may think that we have indeed misunderstood. Because we are usually polite in groups, we may allow the talker to escape from his own confused expression by a dexterous shifting of words.

The writer enjoys no such emergency exit. Once it is said, it is there for all to see again and again. Socrates complained to Phaedrus in a dialogue by Plato that "writing is unfortunately like painting; for the creations of the painter have the attitude of life, and yet if you ask them a question they preserve a solemn silence." He meant that writing cannot talk back. Writing is only the words there on the page. If written words "are maltreated or abused," says Socrates, "they have no parent to protect them; and they cannot protect or defend themselves." Socrates thought that speaking was much superior to writing—though we know everything that we know about him from dialogues written down by his disciple Plato. At the least we can say that writing a strong essay is much more difficult than casual talking about history or anything else; writing must be much more precise and orderly if it is to carry a point with reasonable clarity.

Clear writing goes hand in hand with a sense of human possibility and limitation. No wonder that in some societies, such as ancient Israel, historians were priestly figures. Those historians wrote immersed in their beliefs about the relation of God to humankind and therefore with a specific definition of human nature. Today in a secular world, historians explicitly or implicitly still deal with human nature, and their sense of what the human being is determines what they can believe about the past. Can we be heroic?

Can we be selfless? Does human history move in response to leaders? Or are leaders thrust up by the society that in fact leads them? Are our strongest motivations economic or sexual? Do we have a natural aggressiveness, or are we naturally peace-loving?

As important as any other question about human nature is this: Do we have any freedom of choice? Is history a sequence of decisions that could have gone either way? Or is it a masquerade, a perpetual series of predestined events that no human will can control? Did Robert E. Lee have to fight the battle of Gettysburg in the way he did, or did he have a choice? Did President Harry Truman have a choice about how he might have responded to the Soviet Union after World War II? Or was he compelled by events to become a cold warrior? Historians have usually written as if the people they write about had the freedom to choose. Herbert Butterfield, a philosopher of history, wrote, "History deals with the drama of human life as the affair of individual personalities, possessing self-consciousness, intellect, and freedom."[1] Yet in his novel *War and Peace,* Tolstoy wrestled with the idea of freedom and observed that "to conceive a man perfectly free, not subject to the law of necessity, we must conceive a man *outside of space, outside of time, and free from all dependence on cause.*[2] He wrestled with the problem of just how much freedom we have and what part of life is constrained by necessity. His clearest conclusion was that leaders only seem to lead, that in fact they symbolize the collective working of a power inherent in the masses of people.

Historians, asking questions about the past, may not say explicitly that their answers depend on their view of human nature. Yet the answers depend on assumptions, sometimes unexpressed, about what is possible for human nature and what is not.

We are formed by the past. How we think, how we react to the occasions in daily life, the vocabulary we use in speaking about the past—all are legacies. Studying the past may help us understand better how we came to be who we are. These discoveries in turn help us decide that which we want to retain from the past and that

---

[1]Herbert Butterfield, *Christianity and History,* New York, Charles Scribner's Sons, 1950, p. 26.

[2]Leo Tolstoy, *War and Peace,* trans. Constance Garnett, New York, Modern Library, n.d., p. 1131.

which we want to reject. By discovering that our lives are historically conditioned, we find some freedom. We know that what *is* does not have to be this way.

Every moment in the past has a unique quality. Every event we study in history existed in its own network of cause and effect, its own relationships between people and events, its own modes of thought, often taken for granted by the societies themselves. A thunderstorm roars over the Kansas prairie today, and the television news meteorologist in bright suit and hair spray explains it as caused by a collision between a cold front and a warm front. In ancient Mesopotamia, the Babylonians heard the thunder as the voice of their storm god Marduk and thought that he was throwing lightning bolts at earth. In these and in countless other ways, spontaneous responses in the past to many experiences differed from our own. Part of our task is to work our way back into that early mind set so that we think about experience as people in different times thought of it. Yet we can never fully abandon our own perceptions; we cannot recover the past exactly as people at another time thought of life and the world.

Sometimes historians endeavor to perceive the unique qualities in events and the qualities that seem to repeat themselves in one way or another. They look for patterns. The earliest great empires in Western civilization were made possible by domestication of the horse shortly after 2000 B.C. The horse allowed armies and imperial emissaries swift passage from place to place, and armed horsemen struck terror into soldiers assaulted amid terrible noise and motion by such swift and mighty animals. Those empires rose swiftly and swiftly collapsed. The Roman Empire rose and endured for centuries. What circumstances made the empires of the Babylonians and the Assyrians, the Hittites, the Persians, and the Greeks of Alexander the Great rise and fall with such bewildering speed? Why did Rome endure for so long? In answering questions such as these, historians ponder the relations between influences that seem unique to one historical epoch and other influences that seem to endure in all kinds of human communities.

Because of this changing fusion between the unique and the repetitious, studying history does not help us predict the future; the old cliché that history repeats itself is not true. Some broad patterns do repeat—empires, countries, and cultures rise and fall. Protests against a dominant culture often show up in the way people—especially young people—dress and wear their hair. Some feel that these repetitions lock the whole of human history in invariable cycles of repetition. History becomes a treadmill on which human beings must toil endlessly without getting anywhere.

On close investigation, the swirls and waves of history do not appear to move in predictable patterns. Those who assume that learning about the past will allow them to avoid mistakes in the future underestimate the continuous flow of the new—of change—into human events. New inventions or new ways of thinking or new combinations can upset all predictions. Both the German and the French general staffs in 1914 thought that a European war at that time would be like the war between Germany and France in 1870 and 1871. In that earlier war, the Germans moved swiftly by railroad and on horseback, outmaneuvered the French, and determined the outcome of the war within three months. Though Paris did not fall to the Germans until 1871, the French were beaten in the field by September 1870 in a war that began in July. It was a war of motion, dramatic, soon over, with little damage either in destroyed property or in human deaths.

The generals on both sides in 1914 expected a short war, not realizing the power in a new weapon—the machine gun—that slaughtered advancing soldiers in unimaginable numbers, a daily massacre that quickly turned the conflict into a four-year stand-off in opposing lines of trenches that ran from the Swiss border across France to the English Channel. In this long, hard war, millions died, and the north of France was devastated. In 1940 the French, learning from World War I, built concrete forts called the Maginot Line across northern France, anticipating another war in which armies would face each other until one dropped from exhaustion. They planned without the new technology, the airplane and the swift armored tank used by the Germans to defeat the French army in forty days of *Blitzkrieg*—lightning war—in the summer. At the very least, experiences such as these teach us to be cautious in suggesting what history can predict.

What about leadership? The current mood in historical studies is to be skeptical about how much individual leaders may accomplish on their own. We have moved closer to Tolstoy than to Butterfield. Historians know that any event in history is brought into being by a huge network of contributing forces, some clearly visible, some difficult to find. What caused the American Revolution? The traditional answer has been oppression of American colonies by Britain, the mother country, and most of us can probably call off events in that oppression which we learned in grade school: the Stamp Act, the Boston Massacre, the Boston Tea Party, and finally the skirmishes in Lexington and Concord on April 19, 1775, when someone fired "the shot heard 'round the world." Individual leaders such as John Hancock, Sam Adams, John Adams, James Otis, and others in Massachusetts long appeared to have been leaders, rallying an almost unanimous populace by their oratory and their example to resist the oppressor. That, at least, was the history of the American Revolution as many of us learned it in grade school and in popular mythology spread by Fourth of July oratory.

On examination, British "oppression" seems much less severe than was once commonly supposed, support for the Revolution much less than unanimous, and leadership of the patriot forces much more ambiguous. Historians have been searching for deeper causes that provoked a substantial number of Americans to want their independence from Great Britain enough to fight for it. Orators are nothing unless they have an audience, and our experience in the present may show us that orators do not so often persuade people to change their minds as they provide words for feelings that people already have. Which groups were dissatisfied and willing to listen to the patriot orators? Why? Which groups were content under British rule, and why? What role did American women and the American clergy play? To what degree was the American Revolution a class struggle within colonial American society? How much of the Revolutionaries' success did they fall into because the British were busied by their war with France? Here is a puzzle with many more pieces than "leaders" and "followers." Here are two complex populations, Americans and British, in continual flux with not only different motivations but different intensities of feeling and different resources, and somehow out of this confused conglomeration, the American Revolution happened.

Historians nowadays do not reject the notion that individuals make a difference. Biography remains the form in which the general American public most often reads history, and biographies emphasize the individual. Still, a mood among historians sees the individual working under more complicated restraints, with more ambiguity and with both less success and less abject failure than biographers once admitted. For a very long time biographers attempted to provide heroes to be imitated or villains whose acts were to be avoided. Now the emphasis is much less judgmental, and the biographer's motive is to tell a balanced story and to explain rather than to condemn or praise.

Historians now study sources and deal with issues that once drew little attention. For centuries, history was written almost entirely about what men did. If women entered the story, it was because they did things male historians generally expected men to do: they ruled countries, as did Queen Elizabeth I of England; they refined radium, as Madame Curie did in France; they wrote novels, as a great many women have done for several centuries. Historians usually neglected women in all fields, but they were willing to give limited attention to women who, the historian felt, acted like men. Now historians are turning to many other areas with historical interest—women in the home, the woman laborer in factories and on farms, styles of motherhood, women in settlement houses, women as immigrants, women's voting patterns, and so on. Black history, immigrant history, labor history, sexual history, the history of fashion, the history of sports—all interest modern historians working away at uncovering as much of the human experience as possible and leading the profession of history itself away from the notion that to understand the past we need only understand the personalities and the decisions of a few important male leaders.

Whatever its subject, the study of history is an unending detective story. Historians are detectives, seeking to solve mysteries in the evidence and to tell a story that will give order to the confusion of facts that we can know about the past. Historians make connections, assign causes, trace effects, make comparisons, uncover patterns, locate dead ends, and find influences that continue through the generations until the present.

We encounter most of the history we know by writing. We read books and articles, and slowly we gain some understanding about the shape of the past, the general framework within which events took place. When we study history in college, we write about the past using the methods that professional historians have used. Writing helps us think about what we know, and of course it helps our teachers see what we know and how we are thinking.

This little book will guide you through the major steps in writing papers in history for college undergraduate classes. Inevitably in such a book we must discuss some of the issues historians face in historical study when they write. We must also deal with some issues in writing that writers confront in all disciplines. This is a book both about methods in historical study and about methods in writing. It should give you some understanding of general problems underlying all historical study, and it should help your writing in all courses that you take in college or university. It should make you a better detective, and a better teller of some of the innumerable stories that together make up the study of the past.

1
The Essay in History

In history courses, students write essays: research papers, book reviews, examinations, or reports. As a graduate student you may write a thesis or dissertation, each an essay in longer form.

Because the essay is your goal, we describe some of its qualities at the beginning so that we will know where we are going.

The essay is an almost universal form in Western culture, a tool used in all disciplines and familiar to us in popular magazines and newspapers. In fact it is so common that we seldom try to define it. We recognize an essay when we read one. The moment we start reading, the familiar form creates expectations in us. We do not think much about those expectations unless they are not met.

In this chapter we are going to walk through several common features of the essay, especially the essay about history. We call to mind things you already know. The numbered items are a checklist to help you understand the essay form. When you write essays about history or about another subject, you can measure them against these criteria. Read the chapter quickly, and come back to it when you are writing papers for your course.

1. The essay has an argument.

We write essays to tell readers something we want them to know, but not everything we know. Teachers of English composition say that the essay should have a *thesis,* a subject that can be expressed in one or two sentences. The word "argument" helps convey one of the major purposes in writing an essay: we write to persuade readers to believe something.

"Why am I writing this essay?" "What do I want to tell my

readers?" "What do I want them to believe?" Ask yourself these questions and answer them every time you write.

I want people to believe that Robert E. Lee was chiefly responsible for the Confederate defeat in the battle of Gettysburg.

I want people to believe that the highly praised eleventh edition of the *Encyclopaedia Britannica* reveals many prejudices against blacks and women.

I want people to believe that many historians have disagreed with one another on why Rome fell and that their opinions were related to broader cultural influences in their own times.

I want people to believe that opinions have steadily changed about the value of Arthur Schlesinger, Jr.'s *The Age of Jackson,* published in 1945.

I want people to believe that the conspiracy between gamblers and players on the Chicago White Sox baseball team to throw the 1919 World Series happened in the following way.

I want people to believe that Woodrow Wilson shared many white American prejudices about blacks and that these prejudices caused him to approve of racial segregation in the federal civil service.

Everything in your essay should contribute to your thesis. Don't meander. Don't put in interesting information merely because it is interesting. If you write about historians' opinions about the fall of Rome, don't digress into describing Roman temple architecture. If you write about Woodrow Wilson and racial segregation, don't give us long pages about the history of the Presbyterian Church, in which Wilson's father was a minister. Readers unconsciously expect every detail in an essay to contribute to the topic the author has announced. When they start reading unrelated information, they become confused. Stick to the point.

2. Good essayists get to the point quickly.

This advice may translate into this dictum: Keep your readers informed. Let them know what you are doing as soon as you can. Don't postpone stating your purpose. Don't try to surprise your readers by hiding your intentions until the very last so that they will say, "Oh, so *that's* what you are doing." It's almost always a mistake to try to pull off a surprise ending in an essay about history. At the beginning of your paper your readers should know the subject you are treating and the general direction you take in treating it.

Titles can help you get to the point. Devise a title for your work that helps readers understand your purpose. Popular journals—and some professional journals as well—use subtitles to help get articles' purposes up front so that readers can tell immediately what the writer has in mind. An article in the December 1987 *Smithsonian* carries this title and subtitle:

Title:

> *Could Canada Have Ever Been Our Fourteenth Colony?*

Subtitle:

> *Well, probably not. But in 1775 an astonishing two-pronged assault, one heroically led by Benedict Arnold, nearly took fortress Quebec.*

Some history teachers frown on such an informal style for title and subtitle, though historians in more recent times have loosened up their ideas on what is proper. Informal titles are more and more common in historical journals and in conventions in which historians present papers about their work. The advantages given by the title and subtitle here are obvious: A browsing reader knows immediately what the article is about. Readers can't read everything; a title helps them choose. If your title is interesting enough, some previously uninterested readers may look at your work. If that happens, you have won a great victory.

Academics often use the title split by a colon to achieve the same effect as a subtitle. An influential article by Hanna Holborn Gray in the 1963 *Journal of the History of Ideas* was entitled:

> *Renaissance Humanism: The Pursuit of Eloquence*

Readers knew immediately that the article was about renaissance humanism, defined here as "the pursuit of eloquence."

A title in the summer 1987 issue of *Albion,* a journal devoted to British history, was, "Evangelical Thought: John Wesley and Jonathan Edwards." We know at once that the author intended to study evangelical thought as it was expressed by John Wesley and Jonathan Edwards, who led great religious revivals at the same time, Wesley in England and Edwards in America.

Go from a clear title to your purpose in the paper as quickly as you can. In the opening paragraph, plunge right in. Certainly by the end of the second paragraph readers should know your subject. Here is a good beginning to an article about a historical topic:

> For thirty years J. E. Neale's portrait of the Elizabethan Parliaments was the stuff of textbooks. Highly political and bedeviled by puritanical proto-bolsheviks, the Virgin Queen's parliaments were painted as the nursery in which the modern parliamentary system, characterized by an organized Opposition, was born. In the last decade, however, Neale's interpretations have been challenged and overturned, making obsolete most of the histories of Elizabethan England available to students. The purpose of this article is to assess the new research on Elizabethan Parliaments, to summarize what we now know about the role Parliament played in governing England, and to suggest what remains to be done.[1]

In one paragraph the author sets the problem and tells us what he is going to do about it. He presents information; we know that he will develop some ideas that arise from what he gives us here.

The more striking the information at the beginning, the greater the interest that may be provoked among readers. Here is an essay in historical science. Notice the title, the subtitle, and the first two paragraphs. (The subtitle here serves as an abstract, a summary of the article. This technique is often used in professional journals about history.)

The Bubonic Plague

A bacterial disease carried by fleas that feed on rats, it has afflicted human beings for more than 1,000 years. The factors responsible for its alternate rise and fall remain a mystery.

---

[1] Norman L. Jones, "Parliament and the Governance of Elizabethan England: A Review," *Albion,* Fall 1987, p. 327.

In the year 1346 Europe, northern Africa and nearer parts of the Middle East had a total population of approximately 100 million people. In the course of the next few years a fourth of them died, victims of a new and terrifying illness that spread throughout the area, killing most of those unfortunate enough to catch it. The disease put an end to the population rise that had marked the evolution of medieval society: within four years Europe alone suffered a loss of roughly 20 million people. The disease responsible for such grim statistics was the bubonic plague, and this particular outbreak, lasting from 1346 to 1352, was known as the Great Dying or the Great Pestilence. Later it was appropriately referred to as the Black Death, a name that has come down through history.

Although the effects of the Black Death may have been particularly catastrophic, striking as it did after a long period in which the disease had been unknown in the West, this was not the first time the plague had ravaged Europe. Some 800 years earlier, during the reign of the emperor Justinian in the sixth century, there was an epidemic of similar proportions. There were also repeated, if less widespread, epidemics in the two centuries following the plague of Justinian's time, and for four centuries after the Black Death. The disease has undergone a precipitous decline since that time, but it still occurs sporadically in various parts of the world today, including the U.S.[2]

The news that one hundred million people died in a plague is both appalling and fascinating. We want to know more. We learn in the first paragraph that the subject in this essay will be a history of Black Death outbreaks. We are hooked. But what would we do if we were to come upon a lead paragraph like this?

From earliest times human beings have been affected by many things. Often some of the things that have affected human beings have been death and disease. Disease is always with us, and some people die from it. Everybody eventually dies from something. At times when some people die in great numbers, we say

[2]Colin McEvedy, "The Bubonic Plague," *Scientific American,* February 1988, p. 118.

```
that there is a plague. The meaning of the word
"plague" comes from a Latin word meaning "blow" or
"misfortune." The dictionary today says that "plague"
can be "anything that afflicts or troubles; calamity;
scourge" or "any contagious epidemic disease that is
deadly." One of the most deadly of all plagues was the
Bubonic Plague of the fourteenth century. It killed
people right and left, and this paper is going to be
about it.
```

Teachers read this rambling beginning with foreboding. That which follows is almost certain to be disorganized and difficult to follow. Students write such beginnings because they are not confident enough about the ideas they have to share. You may have to ramble around in a rough draft to define your topic. But by the time you get to your final draft, you must have a sharper beginning, one that delivers concrete information and lets readers know that you are going to make something of it. Otherwise they will skip to something else—or if they have to read what you have written, they will not do so with pleasure.

Begin your essays with something direct, concise, and interesting. How do you know what is "interesting"? Listen to your own mind. What do *you* find interesting in the information you have? Start with that. Are you interested in rambling statements like this: "From earliest times families have been important in the history of humankind"? Don't you know that already? Isn't it boring? Then don't start with a vague and empty statement. Open with some of the information which drew you to the subject in the first place, which made you think this topic would make a good paper. If you are interested in something, you can get your readers interested in it, too.

What about a story? People love stories or anecdotes. Start with a good story, and you may woo readers into following it to the end—by which time they will be well into your essay. The anecdotal beginning is common in popular magazines; it often appears nowadays in scholarly journals as well.

On April 21, 1922, an explorer named Roy Chapman Andrews topped the summit of Wanchüan pass outside of Kalgan (today Zhangjiakou), China. Standing at the Great Wall, he gazed out over the western horizon. "Before us lay Mongolia," he wrote later, "a land of painted deserts dancing in mirage; of limitless grassy plains and nameless snow-capped peaks; of untracked forests and roaring streams. . . . The hills swept away in the far-flung graceful lines of a panorama so endless that we seemed to have reached the very summit of the earth."

For Andrews, this moment marked the beginning of one of the most remarkable expeditions in the history of science. In a sense he had reached the summit of the Earth, since what lay ahead—Outer Mongolia and the Gobi Desert—was one of the last scientifically unexplored areas on the globe. The maps he carried showed little more than wavering dotted lines indicating ancient caravan routes (the major ones were missing), vague indications of mountain ranges and a few wrong landmarks and oases.

The expedition's caravan of motorcars started down the rough, boulder-strewn track into the great Asiatic interior basin that is Mongolia. For the first hundred miles they bumped and slid on a muddy road alongside the rolling, cultivated fields of Inner Mongolia, settled by the Chinese. Slowly the fields gave way to a more arid landscape.

After many miles they passed a small temple, which was deserted. Dozens of soldiers' uniforms and monks' robes were scattered about, many of them containing weathered human bones. Well-fed feral dogs slunk among the ruins. The expedition quickly passed by.

Here and there a low escarpment began to interrupt the monotonous horizon. Several expedition members stopped to inspect an outcrop of sedimentary rock while Andrews, in the lead car, continued on. A half-mile west of the tiny settlement of Iren Dabasu, Andrews stopped to make camp at the base of some gray-white ridges. He had just finished pitching the tents when the last two cars roared into camp. Andrews hurried to meet them. "I knew that something unusual had happened," he wrote, "because no one said a word. Granger's eyes were smiling and he was puffing violently at his pipe. Silently he dug into his pockets and produced a handful of bone fragments; out of his shirt came a rhinoceros tooth, and the various folds of his upper garments yielded other fossils."

Andrews was stunned and could say nothing. Walter Granger, chief paleontologist of the expedition, stuck out his hand. "Well, Roy," he said, "We've done it. The stuff is here."

It was one of the great moments in paleontology.[3]

The first two paragraphs tell us that this is a story about an exploration of Mongolia, a land then little known to the outside world. Those interested in early explorations and adventure may read on, asking this question: What does this story mean? Once you have told a good tale, you have to tell your readers why you told it. The explanation makes your essay.

The anecdotal beginning may make you take a little longer to get into the body of your argument. This article is helped along by its subtitle: "Larger than life, Roy Chapman Andrews led a mammoth expedition into Mongolia to seek the Missing Link—and found fossil treasure." Even without the subtitle, one already interested in Andrews or in early explorations in remote parts of the world may read on. The story draws us on by its details and by its suggestion of tension and difficulty and challenge. Finally we see that this is a special kind of adventure story—the discovery of fossils in Mongolia by Roy Chapman Andrews. Though the story is a bit long, it still performs the general service of an introduction:

It quickly announces the subject of the paper.

It provides the direction in which the paper will go, letting readers know something of what is in store for them.

It sets the tone for the paper.

Tone is a vital if intangible part of any essay. How do you want to sound to readers? What voice of yours do you want them to hear? In this introduction we hear the writer's voice. We know that the article will be serious without being pedantic, that it will emphasize story over abstraction, and that it will provide many concrete facts, which will be described in language using the senses: things we see, hear, touch, taste, and smell. Every piece of writing

[3]Douglas J. Preston, "A Daring Gamble in the Gobi Desert Took the Jackpot," *Smithsonian,* December 1987, p. 94.

has an implied author, a person readers can imagine standing behind the printed text on the page.

3. A good historical essay is built on evidence.

Anyone writing about history needs to know the power that evidence confers. How can you make readers believe you? The subject may be open to several opinions. How can you make yours persuasive?

You won't succeed merely by saying, "In my opinion things happened in the way I say they did." Unsupported opinions carry little weight in a historical essay unless you are a world-renowned authority whose previous work makes your opinions matter. Writing about history is much like proving a case in a court of law. An effective lawyer does not stand before a jury and say, "My friends, I firmly believe my client is innocent. You must believe he is innocent because I believe he is innocent. I feel totally convinced that he is innocent. You may think he looks guilty. I disagree. In my opinion he is innocent, and I want you to rule that he is not guilty because I think he is not guilty. Take my word for it." Clients who have such lawyers should prepare themselves for prison. Lawyers that limited may repeat themselves again and again. They may shout or weep or whisper or swear to the truth of their feelings. But the jury will not believe them unless they can produce some evidence.

So it is with the historical essay. You may have opinions about how something happened, why it happened, who was most responsible and who was most affected, when it happened, where it happened. Unless you present evidence, no one will pay much attention to your opinions. Your readers are your judge and jury. You are the lawyer arguing your case. It's all very well if readers think you are sincere; you gain much more by convincing them that you are right.

What is evidence? The issue is more complicated than it may seem at first glance. Evidence is detailed factual information that may give readers reason to believe what you tell them. Are you writing a paper about Woodrow Wilson? Evidence may be a book, an article, or a speech by Wilson. Evidence may be a book or an article about him written by a historian whose work is recognized as authoritative. Evidence may be a book or article written by one of Wilson's contemporaries who knew him well. It may be the book or article written by a colleague at an occasion such as the Paris Peace Conference in 1919 after World War I.

Are you writing a paper about Ralph Waldo Emerson, the nineteenth-century New England philosopher? Evidence would include all of Emerson's works—his lectures, his books, his many articles in journals. It would include the books and articles written by his friends and foes during his lifetime and the books and articles written about Emerson since his death. It would also include the large, comfortable house where he lived in Concord, Massachusetts, a house lovingly preserved as a museum by citizens of his town. In walking about that house, looking at its library, its spacious rooms, its furniture, we get an idea about Emerson's tastes and his style of life.

You write, that is, from knowledge. To gain it, you must study the past. You must put details together. You must think about what you have studied. Historians construct their work by carefully fitting evidence together to create a story, an explanation, or an argument.

4. Writers of formal essays in history document their sources and avoid plagiarism.

Readers want to know where you got your facts. Later in this book we'll discuss ways of documenting sources. In this checklist we emphasize that you must always let readers know the sources from which your information comes. It is dishonest to take either facts or interpretations from others without letting readers know that you have done so. Plagiarism is the act of presenting others' thoughts as your own. It is the ultimate dishonesty in writing.

Always put material you copy from your sources in quotation marks if you use it in your essay word for word as you found it in the sources.

Always tell readers when you summarize or paraphrase a source.

Always give credit for the ideas you get from someone else, even if you express those ideas in your own words.

5. Essays end simply and cleanly.

Endings are difficult for some writers. You can end with a quotation expressing the main point in your essay. You can summarize the significance in the information you give readers: What did it mean at the time? How did it affect events that came later? How does it affect us still today? You can sometimes come to the end of a series of events and stop with a concluding episode: "On July 5, 1863, Lee fell back toward the Potomac. The battle of Gettysburg was over."

Avoid preaching a sermon at the end, making moral judgments on what you have told readers. Avoid introducing significant new information that should have come earlier in your essay. It's usually best to avoid rhetorical questions at the end.

6. Most good essays about history are written in a dispassionate tone.

History excites passions. We identify with the people and the times we are writing about. Often we seek to praise heroes and condemn villains, but it is a mistake to extol them or condemn them in emotional language. You don't have to prove that you are on the side of the angels. When you write about people, it is enough to report what they have done and to try to explain their actions. Don't waste your time preaching to the dead. You can trust your readers. If characters you describe did terrible things, your readers can see that. If the characters did noble things, your readers can see that, too. If you spend your time telling them your feelings about Hitler or Stalin or some other villain from the past, you detract from the point you are trying to make, and your passion may be embarrassing.

A simple recounting of the facts is usually enough to elicit the appropriate reaction. Describing the British retreat from Concord and Lexington on April 19, 1775, historian Louis Birnbaum lets the facts speak for themselves:

> The mood of the British soldiers was murderous. They surged around houses along the route, instantly killing anyone found inside. Some of the regulars looted whatever they could find, and some were killed while looting by Minutemen who had concealed themselves in the houses.
>
> Houses with fires in the hearth were burned down simply by spreading the embers about. Generally, those homes without fires on the hearth escaped destruction because it was too time-consuming to start a fire with steel and flint.

As the column approached Menotomy, the 23rd Regiment was relieved of rear-guard duty by the marine battalion. Colonial fire reached a bloody crescendo in Menotomy, and again British troops rushed house after house, killing everyone found inside, including an invalid named Jason Russell.[4]

The author could have said, "The British soldiers acted horribly in what they did to these poor people," or "So does war bring out the worst in us," or, "The wicked British soldiers who were killed while they were looting houses got what they deserved." Readers don't need such coercive comments, and they often resent them. They can see for themselves what happened, and they can make up their own minds about the wickedness or the goodness or the sadness or the horror of it all. Trust them.

7. An essay should include original thoughts of the author; it should not be a rehash of others' thoughts.

Essays are examples of reasoning. The most respected essays demonstrate an author carefully setting things in order and making sense of them. Don't disappoint your readers by telling them only what other people have said about your subject. Try to show them that by reading your work they will learn something or see something with a special vision.

This advice does not mean that your paper should make astonishing revelations. Few historians make fundamentally new interpretations or discover revolutionary new information.

New information does turn up, and some historians are lucky enough to be in the right place at the right time to make use of it. The detailed journals made by James Boswell, the eighteenth-century companion and biographer of Samuel Johnson, were a remarkable discovery. They turned up in a Scottish castle where they had been scattered about like so much waste paper. The capture and opening of German archives following World War II has been an even more momentous discovery, allowing us now to trace German political and military policy through this century. The Freedom of Information Act has opened many FBI and other government files that were long secret, and much historical information

---

[4]Louis Birnbaum, *Red Dawn at Lexington,* Boston, Houghton Mifflin, 1986, p. 184.

has been gained from this source. Local historians often turn up new information in studying old records in courthouses and churches and other places. You, too, can turn up new information for some papers that you write in college.

Even if you do not find completely new facts, you can think about the facts at your disposal. You can see new relations. You can see causes and effects that others may have missed. You may reflect on motives and influences. You can present conclusions that are your own. Don't be satisfied with writing a paper as you might be satisfied with building a model plane you bought in kit form from a hobby shop. In building such a model, you stick together parts that someone else has designed until you have an airplane that looks like the picture on the box. Some students go to the library and take a piece of information from this book and another piece of information from that book and so on until they have a sort of kit for a paper. Then they stick it all together without contributing anything of their own except manual dexterity. Try to contribute some interpretation that is your own to these assembled facts. Be willing to take risks by asking questions about the information that others may not have asked, and by trying to answer those questions sensibly.

8. Authors of essays consider their audiences.

No one can write to please or interest every possible reader. Different articles are intended for different audiences. Every beginning history student should spend a few hours in the library looking at the many periodicals devoted to history. It is fairly easy to distinguish between publications meant for a popular audience and those for specialists. *The American Historical Review,* official journal of the American Historical Association, is intended for specialists—usually professors of history—who know the subject fairly well. *American Heritage* and *History Today* are aimed at those many readers who are interested in history but not necessarily knowledgeable about the subjects treated in the articles. Studying these journals, trying to analyze the reasons for their differences, will help you see how different the intended audiences may be.

Your first audience will be your instructor and the other students in your class. Tell them something that you have learned or thought about, giving enough information for them to understand what you are telling them. Don't give them needless or irrelevant facts. Don't spend a lot of time telling them things they already know. Avoid falling into the trap of providing so much background for your paper that you never get to the subject itself. If you write about the civil rights movement in the 1950s and 1960s, don't provide a detailed history of slavery before the Civil War. Your readers know that slavery held American blacks in bondage; you need make no more than passing reference to slavery, if you mention it at all. If you write about some aspect of sports history such as the fans' frenzy for their favorite baseball teams, don't start by giving the history of baseball. Your readers do not need that information.

What you think about your audience will help you decide which words to define. What do your readers know before they read your work? If you write a specialized paper in a history course on the Protestant Reformation, you do not have to explain the Catholic doctrine of transubstantiation though you mention it in passing. You are writing for readers who know a great deal about the subject; they certainly know the meaning of transubstantiation.

> Luther rejected transubstantiation because he thought that it made an idol out of the eucharist and because he believed that it was not scriptural.

But if you write about Luther for a more general audience who are not well versed in religious doctrines, you may provide a definition, for some of those readers may not know the meaning of the word.

> Luther rejected transubstantiation. This was the Catholic doctrine of the eucharist, the service Protestants call "the Lord's Supper," to commemorate the death of Christ. Catholics believed that when the priest lifted the bread, called the "host," before the altar and pronounced the words in Latin, "Hoc est enim corpus meum," a miraculous transformation took place. The bread became the actual body of Christ; the wine in the chalice became the actual blood of Christ. By the miracle no bread was left and no wine was left, although the elements continued to taste as they had before the transformation. God knows we would be revolted if we had all the sensations that would come if we were eating ordinary human flesh and drinking ordinary blood.

No writer can be entirely sure about what an audience knows or does not know. Just as we convey to our readers an "implied author," so we always write with an implied reader in mind, someone we think may read this work. Think carefully about that reader, and write accordingly.

9. An honest essay takes contrary evidence into account.

Good historians try to express the truth about what happened. If you study any issue long and carefully enough, you will begin to form opinions about it. You will think you know why something happened, or suppose that you understand a personality clearly. Yet the evidence in history seldom stacks up entirely on one side of an issue, especially in the more interesting problems about the past. Different parts of the evidence contradict one another; you must face such contradictions squarely.

Do you want to argue that President Lyndon Johnson was a failure as president because of his efforts to win the Vietnam War? Fair enough. But how do you interpret his efforts to make "war on poverty" and his struggle to get the Civil Rights Act of 1964 through the Congress? Looking at the records, you will find that Johnson did accomplish some major goals. Were these sufficient to make him a successful president? Perhaps not. But they are evidence that you must take into account when you seek to judge Johnson's term in office.

Different historians often interpret the same facts in very different ways. On highly controversial issues, you must take into account views opposed to your own. If you should argue that Robert E. Lee was chiefly responsible for the Confederate defeat in the battle of Gettysburg, you must consider the argument by a number of historians that the blame should be laid at the feet of General James Longstreet, one of Lee's subordinates. You may still argue that Lee was the major cause behind the defeat (although remember too that the Union army had something to do with it). You do not weaken your case by recognizing opposing views; you strengthen your own argument by letting readers know that you are aware of other ways of looking at the facts you present. They know then that you have studied the matter, that you have read more than one book or article, that you have surveyed the various opinions, and that you have arrived at your own argument.

Never give informed readers the impression that you are hiding information because you think it might reduce their belief in your case. This advice translates into a simple principle: Be honest. Nothing turns readers off so quickly as to suppose that the writer is not being fair with the facts.

10. Essayists use standard English and observe the common conventions of writing.

Sometimes student writers feel abused when teachers require them to spell words correctly, to use correct grammar and punctuation, and to proofread their papers. In fact it is a terrible distraction to try to read a paper by a writer who does not observe the conventions. Readers should be following what a writer is saying. They should not be asking themselves questions like these: "Is that word spelled correctly?" "Why has he not put a comma here?" "Why has she used this word?" Reading is hard work, especially when the material is dense or complicated, as it often is in history courses. A careless attitude toward the conventions may not bother the writer, who presumably knows what he or she wants to say. But lack of attention to detail continually throws us as readers off because we do not know what the writer wants to say until we have carefully absorbed what he or she has written.

Students who complain when teachers enforce the conventions do themselves a great disservice. In the world beyond college, few things about your writing will be more harshly judged than careless disregard for the conventions. "Look at this letter; it has three misspelled words in it. How can we have confidence in anybody like this?" We all would like to believe that our ideas in our writing are so compelling that no one can resist them, no matter how sloppy our use of the conventions may be. The world of readers who do not know us will judge otherwise.

Never hand in a paper without proofreading it carefully. Read it over and over to find any misspelled words, lapses in grammar, typographical errors, places where you may have inadvertently left out a word (a common error in these days of writing with the computer).

These are qualities essays have. Keep them in mind as you write your own.

2

Thinking about History

===

Studying history raises difficult problems. To write history is to write about the past, people and events that are gone and cannot be recovered. We are not able to put the past in a laboratory to examine it, test it, and observe it again and again as we may see an instant replay of a close play at second base when we're watching a World Series game on television. Real life has no instant replay. Things happen in the present; we remember them later on. We cannot make them happen again exactly as they happened before. History does not repeat itself. When we write about history, we reconstruct a story from the past. When we read about history, we have to remind ourselves that we are reading a reconstruction.

The problems in working with history resemble our problems with memory. What were you doing a year ago today? If you keep an appointment book, you can look in it and see a list of people you saw on that day. But what did you say when you saw them? If you keep a journal, you have a better tool for memory. Even so, the journal does not tell you everything. You went to a movie. What was the plot, and who were the stars? Someone says to you, "I remember when we sat on the beach at Pawley's Island, South Carolina, year before last, and talked about Elvis Presley." "Oh," you may say. "I thought that was three years ago, and was it Pawley's Island or was it in Charleston?"

We resurrect our own memories by the records we keep ourselves and by the memories and records that other people keep about us. If by some misfortune we get involved in a legal case about something we did or witnessed some time ago, we may have a lot of trouble producing a coherent, plausible record about the past. Legal cases picked up by the newspapers and television news often involve government servants, and an exciting case may involve the whole country in speculating about what did or did not happen. After all that has been written about the Watergate scandal and the later resignation of Richard M. Nixon from the presidency, we still do not know exactly what happened. Burglars broke into the Democratic headquarters in the Watergate building in Washington on June 17, 1972. They were discovered by a night watchman and arrested. It turned out that some of them had worked in the White House. Investigators discovered that very early in the affair President Nixon worked with members of his staff and cabinet to cover up White House involvement.

What did the burglars want? Why did they break into the Democratic headquarters? Did Nixon know about it before it happened? An often-repeated question asked by Senator Howard Baker of Tennessee during congressional investigation of the burglary and the cover-up was, "What did the president know, and when did he know it?" We still cannot answer those questions precisely. Who was "Deep Throat," the person who told reporters Carl Bernstein and Bob Woodward so much about the inner workings of the White House during those days? We do not know that either; we may never know the answers to these questions, despite countless books and articles on the subject and interminable probing by the Congress and law enforcement officials.

The Watergate case exemplifies a familiar problem in knowing history. What happened in the past? That question in turn involves another: What can we believe about the past, knowing all we do of human experience in the present? What, in other words, is plausible? Legends of the saints told in the Middle Ages are filled with miraculous happenings. St. Denis was said to have been beheaded in Paris while preaching to the pagan Gauls; he walked with his head in his hands to the site of the later monastery named for him outside the city and set his head down there to mark the place where he should be buried. The kings of France were later buried in the monastery church built on the site. A statue of the saint, holding his head in his hands, is now on the front of Notre Dame Cathedral in Paris. Just now we don't see people walking about, head in hands. Our inexperience with such phenomena makes us doubt that they ever happened. We respect this story only as a charming tale, not literal truth; it is not plausible.

What to do with the story about St. Denis and his head seems easy. Other questions are not so simple. Why did Hitler go to war in 1939? He seemed to have everything Germany could want in Europe. France, Britain, and even the Soviet Union showed him in dozens of ways that they did not want to fight him. He must have had some inkling of how horrible modern war with its mass destruction could be. Did he go to war because he miscalculated? Or did he go to war because he loved war and wanted war no matter what peace terms the allies were willing to give him and no matter what price he and Germany had to pay? Historians have lined up on both sides of this question. The theory that he simply miscalculated arises in part because rational people—among them historians—cannot believe that anyone would deliberately lead his people into the horrors of modern war on the scale of World War I and World War II. Just as we cannot believe that St. Denis walked across Paris carrying his head in his hands, we cannot believe that even a Hitler would be so irrational as to seek the war he got. Yet we also recognize in this post-Freudian world that human motives are complex, mysterious, and often absurd.

Studying history thus involves us in some kinds of thinking common in daily life. We must weigh evidence, deciding what to believe and what not. We must interpret evidence, deciding not whether we will believe something but how we understand it. We must try to put all we know together to make a coherent and plausible story.

How do we make sense of evidence? How do we read the records? Often we have so much evidence that we can't tell everything. A friend of mine is writing a biography of President Harry S. Truman. Thousands of letters written by Truman survive, as do thousands of letters written to him. Hundreds of books have been written by eyewitnesses to events during Truman's life. Thousands of people saw Truman and spoke to him and could give impressions of him were they asked to do so. He was president during the infancy of television. Even so, he lived on until 1972, well into the television age, and reporters, scholars, and others conducted innumerable interviews with him. Films and tapes of these interviews are stored in the television-network archives and in the vast

Truman Library in Independence, Missouri. How does one sort through all this material to write a biography? Obviously, one selects. But how? What are the standards for selecting evidence? These are unending problems.

PRIMARY AND SECONDARY SOURCES

By talking about evidence, we have made a slight leap in this chapter. Where does evidence come from? Historians say that evidence comes from *sources*. The letters Harry Truman wrote are sources for his life; accounts by people who knew Truman are also sources, as are books written about him.

Historians classify sources of evidence under two general heads—primary and secondary. These sometimes overlap, but the classification is useful. Primary sources are those closest to the topic you are studying, the sources that provide our nearest information about the people and events we choose to write about. They are first in time, the earliest sources we can find. Primary sources may be written down by participants in events you write about in a paper. Many soldiers on both the British and the American side wrote accounts of the battles in Lexington and Concord, fought on April 19, 1775, to begin the American Revolution. Those accounts are primary sources for anyone wishing to write a book or article about those battles. Suppose you want to write about some aspect of English law. Your primary sources will include legal decisions made by judges and statutes passed by Parliament. If you write a study about immigration to the United States after the Civil War, primary sources will include census records, records from the ports to which the immigrants came, and letters, diaries, and memoirs written by the immigrants themselves. Primary sources for a paper about President Woodrow Wilson would include the vast collection of his papers being edited at Princeton University, including just about every scrap that Wilson ever wrote, including the class notes from which he taught when he was a professor of history at Bryn Mawr College.

Secondary sources interpret primary sources. Louis Birnbaum's *Red Dawn at Lexington,* a detailed account of the fighting at Lexington and Concord, is a secondary source for the battles. So too is *Patriots: The Men Who Started the American Revolution,* by A. J. Langguth, who devotes a chapter to the battles. *The Transcript of the Record of the Trial of Nicola Sacco and Bartolomeo Vanzetti in the Courts of Massachusetts and Subsequent Proceedings 1920–27* is a primary source for the Sacco-Vanzetti case that stirred America in the years between their trial and execution for murder. Francis Russell's study of the case, *Sacco and Vanzetti: The Case Resolved,* published in 1986, is a secondary source.

Secondary sources for a study of English law would include works by legal historians. Secondary sources for the history of immigration to the United States would include books written by historians about the immigrants, books such as *World of Our Fathers* by Irving Howe, who studied Jewish immigrant culture, especially in New York City. Secondary sources for a paper about Woodrow Wilson would be works written by historians and others about Wilson, including the five-volume biography of Arthur Link about Wilson's presidency.

Defining which are primary sources and which secondary depends on the historian's purposes. If you are writing a paper on the New England Puritans, your primary sources will include Puritan sermons, books of theology, and anything else that the Puritans themselves wrote. Your secondary sources for a paper on the Puritans will include works by historians such as Sydney Ahlstrom and Perry Miller. But suppose you want to write a paper on the changing attitudes toward the Puritans taken by American historians. This kind of essay is a history of history, and then your primary sources will be works by historians such as Ahlstrom and Miller. Your own work about their attitudes will then become a secondary source. You could easily write an essay about the various and often contradictory attitudes of biographers who have written about Woodrow Wilson—or almost any other president. Then the biographies would be your primary sources—not works Wilson himself wrote. Your aim is to study the biographers, not Wilson.

The primary sources used by historians are usually written records of some sort, but other relics from the past may inform historians. Anyone writing about the battle of Gettysburg should walk over the battlefield. If you are writing about more recent wars, you have a wealth of photographs, films, sound recordings of various kinds, and often recordings of reminiscences by eyewitnesses and participants. If you are writing art history, you have the paintings and sculpture about which you write. If you are writing about the extravagance of King Louis XIV of France, you can visit the Château of Versailles, built by the Sun King outside Paris, and you can see that extravagance for yourself. If you are writing about American popular culture you might want to visit a place like Pioneer Village in Nebraska, where the founder, Harold Warp, and his successors have assembled an amazing collection of commonly used items from their first models through successive changes—gas pumps, washing machines, sewing machines, automobiles, farm equipment, and so on. Robert Caro, biographer of President Lyndon Johnson, went to the hill country in Texas to see what the land was like there in the place where Johnson was born and where he grew to manhood. Caro got an elderly woman to show how it was to draw water by hand out of a deep well, pulling a rope attached to a bucket up hand over hand again and again to get enough water to do a wash. In that way Caro got a direct view of the literally back-breaking labor in such a task. That woman was to Caro a primary source, a witness to the hardship and poverty that, he saw, helped form Lyndon Johnson's character.

Things have changed. The Gettysburg battlefield does not now look like the fields Confederates and Union soldiers fought over more than a century ago. It is not quite the same to see automobiles in a museum as it was to see them on the roads. Still, one can see something, and items like these are primary sources of a sort. Sources such as these lend a quality of vivid life to the work of good historians, and you should use them when you can.

Use primary sources whenever you can as the basis for your papers. They enrich your work and allow you to make some claim for originality in your conclusions. Secondary sources have obvious value; they quickly supply you with facts that might take you years to accumulate if you had to dig them all out on your own. They point you toward the debated issues. They exercise your mind by leading you through the scholars' mental wrestling on a subject that interests you. Read as many secondary sources as you have time to read while you are writing a paper. But never be content to write a paper on Woodrow Wilson by consulting only books about Wilson and not materials that Wilson wrote himself. Never write a paper about humanism in the renaissance without reading some of the works by renaissance humanists. Never write an essay on development of Impressionist painting without spending a great deal of time looking at Impressionist art and reading all the letters and essays by the Impressionist artists that you can find.

Primary sources are exciting. As you study them carefully, the past seems sometimes very near, the people who made history very human in their impulses, their inconsistencies, their passions, the influences they felt, their changing values, their failures, and their successes. When we read primary sources, we can feel that history was made by real people and not by robots with human names moving around according to dictates by some great computer program in the sky. To read primary sources is to discover how leaders saw the decisions they had to make with all their difficulties and ambiguities; it is to see choices; and it is to see how even those who seem successful, society's winners, have failures and how they lose. Studying primary sources about more ordinary people—peasants obligated to give a set number of days' work to their lords on medieval manors, children in the 1950s watching popular television shows, students with grievances in the France of the 1848 revolution—brings us in contact with the levels in society who must follow if leaders are to lead. Reading letters by Swiss historian Jacob Burckhardt enables us to see his discouragement over the reception given his 1860 classic, *The Civilization of the Renaissance in Italy,* and helps us understand something about the pessimism that informs the book. Should you write about the changing opinions on the renaissance, not only Burckhardt's great book but also his correspondence would be primary sources for your work.

THE JOURNALISTIC QUESTIONS

In any paper about history, this question arises: What do we emphasize, and what do we discard? Where do we focus our attention, and what do we ignore?

We begin by asking some questions about our material. The questioning helps us sort things out, decide what is important, what is unimportant, what truly signifies the man or the woman and what does not. In this chapter we explore ways of questioning the sources we read and the papers we write. The questions help us organize our own approach to the subject. They provide a means for scanning material with an active mind.

I call the following questions the "journalistic questions" because young reporters and would-be journalists learn them early in their careers. The questions correspond to a seemingly natural and almost universal way in which literate people respond to information. By thinking about these questions in a systematic way, you may help yourself both ask and answer questions in your reading and your writing.

The journalistic questions are these: Who, What, When, Where, Why? They may serve as tools of analysis in any discipline. When you approach any body of evidence or any issue in history, you can ask who the people involved were, what happened, when it happened, where it happened, and why it happened. The questions often overlap: it may be impossible to separate a *what* question from a *why* question. To explain *what* happened is sometimes to explain *why* it happened. We can scarcely separate a *who* question from a *what* question; to talk about someone is to discuss what that person did. The overlap among the questions is the very reason journalists have always used them. A complex event is like an elaborate tapestry tightly woven of many different-colored threads. The threads are distinct, but they are difficult to sort out. The journalistic questions help us keep our eyes on this or that thread so that we can see how it contributes to the whole. They help us analyze human actions. To analyze means to "break down," to separate into parts. Analyzing human events helps us to see them in subtly different ways helpful in writing or reading about history or any other discipline.

The question, "Who committed the murder?" combines a *who* and a *what,* because what happened—the murder—calls up the question, "Who did it?" Yet they are very different questions. In police investigations (and in mystery stories), detectives look for motives. *Why* was the murder committed? Suspicion falls on the people who had some reason to do in the victim. Yet establishing a motive does not prove that the person with a clear motive was the killer. The victim may have had lots of enemies, and therefore lots of people may have had an answer to the question, "Why kill this person?"

Racial segregation in the federal civil service—including the United States Post Office—came about during the administration of President Woodrow Wilson shortly after he took office in 1913. That is *what* happened. But *who* was responsible? And *who* was affected? And *why* was segregation installed? *When* was it installed? *Where* was it installed?

The emphasis we place on this or that journalistic question may determine what approach we take to a historical event. Suppose we study the assassination of President John F. Kennedy on November 22, 1963, a murder that threw the United States and much of the rest of the world into trauma. One may ask a *what* question and a *who* question in almost the same breath: What happened, and who was responsible? What happened was that President Kennedy was murdered. Were two or three shots fired? Who killed him? Was there one killer? Were there perhaps two or three? Was the assassin Lee Harvey Oswald? Enough discussion has been raised about the event to make an interesting topic for a paper that might be titled "Theories About the Kennedy Assassination," a paper that could dwell on the question, *what* happened?

You can ask another *what* question: "What happened because of the Kennedy assassination that might not have happened had he lived?" Here the question about who killed President Kennedy would be unimportant. The *what* question turns us rather to consider what happened and what might have happened—perennial discussions about many events in history. You can see that you may combine the *what* question and the *who* question, or your inquiry may lead you to distinguish between the two.

The journalistic questions can help you work through writer's block. All of us experience writer's block at one time or another. We can't get started, or we can't continue, or we can't finish a piece of writing we are working on. The journalistic questions may give our minds a little push that enables us to overcome inertia. When you start writing down the answers to these questions, you free your mind in surprising ways that may lead to original thought and exciting inquiry into a topic.

Multiplicity of the Questions

Always remember that each of the questions can be posed in many ways. You will find not one *who* question or *what* question or one *why* question. You may find dozens. Ask as many of them as you can. Push your mind.

Who was Martin Luther?

Whom did he oppose?

Who opposed him?

Who protected him?

Who supported him?

Who wrote about him?

Who were his associates?

What did he do?

What did he believe?

What did he want?

What did his opponents do?

What did his supporters do?

What did his associates do?

What did indifferent Germans do?

Why did he do these things?

Why did he gather such a following?

Why was he not put to death?

Why did his supporters rally to his side?

Why did his enemies take the attitude toward him that they did?

When did he live?

When did he arrive at the ideas that made him break with the Catholic Church?

When did he stop believing in purgatory?

When did he realize that he had started a new movement and that he would not reform the Catholic Church?

When did he think the world would end?

When did he sanction armed resistance to Catholic authorities?

Where did he live?

Where did he have greatest influence?

Where did he have least influence?

Where have his works been most studied?

Where have most biographies about him appeared?

Where did Luther travel?

Writing these questions down will start ideas pouring through your mind. Suddenly the relations between questions may become extremely important. You may push yourself to ask a dozen or more "where" questions. That effort may make you ask, "Where did Luther travel?" This question in turn may be related to the question, "What did he believe?" Some scholars have argued that because Luther left German lands only once in his life and after 1522 seldom left the little town of Wittenberg, he did not have to meet the sort of stern questioning from independent minds that might have made him modify his assertions or resolve some of the contradictions in his thought. Because his world was relatively enclosed, he could so dominate his own small circle that he rarely changed his mind in response to colleagues' arguments. Here a *what* question and a *where* question and perhaps a *why* question are all linked.

Jot down as many *what* questions as you can think of, even if some of them seem frivolous. Then ask as many *why* questions as possible, and so on. The questions shape your thinking. Asking one of the questions helps you ask another, and you may discover that almost without knowing how it happened, you have come on a question that may make a good subject for a paper.

Now let's look at the questions one by one.

Who?

When we ask the question "who," we often seek biographical information. Who exactly was Ronald Reagan? Who were his parents? Who were his early influences? Who were his friends in Hollywood? Later on, who were his friends in politics and in business?

The *who* question makes us think of character. What kind of person was one of the great figures in history? A character sketch, drawn from a number of sources and expressing good and bad, consistencies and contradictions, can make an excellent history paper. Of course you can always write on other historians' divergent opinions about a character they have all written about. Each of them has a different view of the *who* question; those different views are worth studying and comparing.

The *who* question makes us think about responsibility. Who was most responsible for the outbreak of World War I? Who was the most effective leader in the civil-rights movement in the 1950s and 1960s? Who has been most influential in gaining civil rights for women in recent years?

The *who* question may make us think of who was first in performing some act. Who first understood what was required to make an airplane fly? Who first thought that a communist society might solve most social problems? Who were the first communists to reject Joseph Stalin's terrorism in Russia? Who was the first person killed in a car crash? Who first flew across the Atlantic Ocean? Who made the first practical tin can? Who invented dynamite? Who invented the paper towel? Who developed the first workable technique for cleaning woollen clothes? Who invented modern lipstick?

The *who* question may also turn our attention to those affected by events in history. Who died in the medieval plague called the Black Death? Who has been most helped by federal civil rights legislation? Who has been least helped? Who is most likely to be influenced by newspaper editorials? Who are the most common victims of drug abuse? Who were the supposed beneficiaries of William Jennings Bryan's campaign for free coinage of silver when he ran as Democratic nominee for the presidency in 1896? Who was most helped and who was most harmed by the western railroads built in the nineteenth century?

Sometimes the *who* question will help us satisfy simple curiosity. Who knew about the planning behind the Watergate burglary in 1972? Who was involved in the English Bloomsbury group of writers early in this century? Who were the people most interested in passing a Prohibition amendment to the United States Constitution? Who were women writers in Colonial America?

It is a good idea to avoid putting entire responsibility for great happenings on one person's shoulders. Yes, people do make a difference. We can legitimately wonder if World War II would have taken place as it did without Adolf Hitler, just as we can ask what would have happened to the American civil-rights movement without the Rev. Martin Luther King, Jr. The bad guys and the good guys in history have changed the course of events, often in dramatic and radical ways. Yet influential historical figures appear on the scene when people are ready to receive them. Hitler's rise to power in Germany and the consequent horrors that he brought on

Europe were not his accomplishments alone; he had helpers, followers, indifferent ones willing to accept his leadership though they
might have preferred someone else. Who were his supporters? Who
were his foes within Germany? Who went along indifferently? The
Rev. Martin Luther King, Jr., found both a black and a white community in the United States ready to respond to his powerful voice.
Try, that is, to consider historical characters within their context.

What?

The *what* question may require careful examination of the evidence to help us weed out the legends or the misunderstandings
and see just exactly what someone did or what happened. Deciding
what happened may be extremely difficult, making us put together
bits and pieces of evidence, with which we can construct a mosaic,
a picture that gives a rough idea of what happened, though it may
have many holes. Sometimes we can fill in those holes only by
conjecture.

What questions may involve the historian in thinking much
like a detective. What happened on the night Luther died, February
18, 1546? Did he have a chance to make a pious exit in his friends'
arms, uttering brave and faithful last words? Or did he die in his
sleep? The questions have been debated frequently. What was the
British ocean liner *Lusitania* carrying when it was torpedoed by a
German submarine and sunk, costing 1,500 lives, in 1915? Some
scholars say that the ship was carrying not only passengers but mu-
nitions, and that the Germans knew about its dual cargo. What
happened on Lexington Green in Massachusetts early in the morning of April 19, 1775, when British soldiers of the "King's Own"
Regiment faced a ragged line of American colonials? The sources
are immensely confused and contradictory.

Another *what* question is, "What does this fact mean?" How
we use words influences our way of thinking about our evidence
and the judgments we make about it. Words change meaning, and
yet they often carry forward connotations. Always aim to use
words about the past as people in the past used them. Try to understand what people meant when they used words that may seem
common today.

In the nineteenth century the word "liberal" was used in England to describe businessmen who wanted to make a place for themselves in a country that had been dominated by an aristocracy whose power was based on land holding. The liberals were capitalists who thought government should keep its hands off business. In general, they were opposed to any efforts to help working people. In the twentieth century the word "liberal" has been used in America to describe support of government aid to the poor, to education, to farmers, and so on. What is the relation between use of the words in these two ways that seem radically different? The main similarity is in the root of the word "liberal," which comes from a Latin word meaning "liberty." Liberals in both the nineteenth and the twentieth century have advocated liberty for citizens; the citizens to whom liberty would be granted were of different classes. Anyone writing about liberalism has to be sure to see both the similarities and the differences in the two uses of the word.

Such problems arise throughout the study of history. Be on guard to keep yourself from reading today's definition into yesterday's words. Don't rely on simple dictionary definitions of words. Words are defined by their context in time and place, and you must be sure to understand that context. "What does this word mean?" The question opens a rich field of historical investigation that never dries up.

Why?

Sometimes we know *what* happened. But *why* did it happen, and why did it have the influence that it did? These questions about cause and effect have an eternal fascination for historians and readers alike. Keep in mind several considerations about cause and effect.

First, always distinguish between the *precipitating cause* and the background causes of a great event. You might call the precipitating cause the *triggering* cause, the cause that sets events in motion. The background causes are those which build up and create the context within which the precipitating cause works. Precipitating causes are often dramatic and fairly clear-cut; background causes are more difficult to sort out and often ambiguous.

The precipitating cause behind the Civil War was the bombardment and capture of Fort Sumter by South Carolina forces on

April 12, 1861. Immediately afterward, Lincoln called for 75,000 volunteers to suppress the rebellion, and soon afterward fighting began.

No one would say that the incident in Charleston Harbor by itself caused the Civil War. Behind the events on that Friday morning lay the tangled issues of American sectionalism—slavery in the Southern states; different economies, cultures, values, political philosophies, religious expressions, educational systems, histories; and finally the 1860 election of President Lincoln—known to oppose extending slavery into states yet to be formed from territories west of the Mississippi River. These were the background causes of the war, and ever since historians have been trying to sort them all out and tell a sensible story explaining why we fought America's bloodiest war.

Background causes supply rich and complex possibilities for writing about the *why* of history. They give writers scope for research, analysis, and conjecture. They often figure in newspaper reports meant to explain events that suddenly make headlines. When Arab demonstrators began provoking the Israeli army to violence in winter 1987–1988, newspaper reporters rushed to write about the many years of conflict on the land called the West Bank of the Jordan River, taken over by the Israelis in the 1967 war with the Arabs. In effect these reporters were trying to explain the *why* behind the triggering causes that provoked weeks of violence. Those causes would have triggered nothing unless something had been there to provoke. If you pull the trigger of an empty pistol, you get only a snap from the firing pin. The gun has to be loaded before the pistol will fire. Background causes are, in effect, the cartridge loaded into the gun that makes the trigger do something.

Historians write books and articles on such subjects. Why did the religious fundamentalist controversy break out in America during and after World War I? The precipitating cause may have been a little religious-book series called *The Fundamentals*. Why did those little books have such an audience? What was happening in America that made them popular? These *why* questions probe into background causes.

Precipitating or triggering causes can be worthwhile subjects in themselves. Exactly what happened at Fort Sumter or Pearl Harbor or during the Watergate scandal will make an interesting story, perhaps more complicated than we usually suppose. Part of the story involves the reasons explaining why the incident at Ft. Sumter on April 12, 1861 did precipitate war. Why were passions so greatly aroused on that day in that year? The *what* question and the *why* question come together, as they often do.

Second, always remember that historical causation is complex. It is almost always a mistake to lay too much responsibility for a happening on only one cause. (This is another form of the caution against putting too much responsibility on the shoulders of one human being in history.) Rebecca West, in her remarkable 1942 book about Yugoslavia, *Black Lamb, Grey Falcon,* tells in detail the story about the assassination of Archduke Franz Ferdinand of Austria-Hungary in Sarajevo on Sunday, June 28, 1914—the precipitating cause of World War I. The Archduke was heir to the throne of the Austro-Hungarian Empire. When he was murdered, leaders of the Empire decided they must punish Serbia, the Balkan country the Austrians believed responsible for the terrorists who killed Franz Ferdinand and his wife. Russia defended Serbia because it was made up of Slavs, kin to the Slavs in Russia. Germany defended Austria against Russia. When the Archduke perished, a chain of events was set dragging across Europe that pulled the continent into war. West tells the assassination story in novelistic detail.

She also goes deeply into all the centuries of conflict between Austria and Serbia, parent of the modern Yugoslav state. She tells a complex story about grievances that the two peoples built up against each other, culminating in the assassination and the subsequent war. By gradually building up the many sources of friction, West shows how easy it was for the Archduke's death to precipitate the war.

Good historical writing covers many different but related causes for a great happening. Studying history helps us see how many influences flow into the making of any great event. Causes in history are like the tributaries to a great river. Although a bad historian sees only the main channel in the largest stream, a good historian looks at the entire watershed, trying to map the smaller streams that contribute to the whole. Good historians see things in context—often a large context including people and events surrounding the event they seek to describe. Thinking in context means that we try to sort out and weigh the relative importance of various causes when we consider any major happening.

The sense of context is especially valuable now that historians have discovered the masses. The common people were usually neglected by historians, who supposed that all history was made only by leaders. Do you want to understand sixteenth-century England under Queen Elizabeth I? Then study her life, and you will know her England. Do you wish to understand the American Civil War? Study the strategies, tactics, and personalities of the generals on both sides. Do you want to study the Protestant Reformation? Study the thought expressed by the leading Reformers. Do you wish to understand Jewish culture in the middle ages? Study sayings by Jewish scholars such as Moses Maimonides. These ideas fueled most nineteenth-century historical writing in the West.

We realize more fully than ever before that leaders cannot lead unless they have followers. And so we ask questions like these: What was happening to the English people under Queen Elizabeth I that caused her to be more tolerant of religious diversity than former English monarchs had been? In the later middle ages, dozens of working-class rebellions testified to people's clamoring for a better life. Why were these lower classes aroused so often in this period? Why could so small a band of American colonists who wanted independence from Great Britain so greatly affect the majority among their fellow citizens who were either indifferent to them or loyal to the old crown at the time of the American Revolution? Such questions require us to find ways of looking at mass culture, the life of people, often scarcely literate, who left little writing behind. Because it is difficult to resurrect the life of the masses, answering the *why* questions of history becomes a complex and uncertain problem. Its difficulties do not remove from historians the obligation to consider the problem.

Third, be cautious in your judgments. Do not seek easy and simple causes for complex and difficult problems. Part of that caution is related to what I have said about single causes in history. Do not argue that the Roman Empire fell only because Romans drank water from lead pipes, that the South lost the Civil War only because Lee was defeated at Gettysburg, that the Reformation came only because Martin Luther protested against papal policy in Germany, or that the American civil-rights movement was all the work of the Rev. Martin Luther King, Jr. All these events were caused by many complex influences. We become foolish when we try to put too much responsibility on to one dramatic event.

Extend this caution also to your judgments about motivation in history. We know that Roman Emperor Constantine legalized Christian worship in the Roman Empire after about A.D. 313. Was he a sincere Christian or not? Or did he see that the Christians were numerous and so strongly organized that they might help hold his decaying empire together? Was he devout? Or was he cynical? Some have said that he was entirely cynical; a more recent school holds that he was sincere in his profession, although his understanding of Christianity was warped and vague. Each brings evidence to support its conclusions. We cannot know for certain what motivated Constantine. Even if we have a pretty good idea one way or another, we should not present our conclusions so vehemently or so intolerantly as to make it seem that our view is the only possible one to be taken from the evidence, especially when we know that much can be said for the other side—or for several other sides.

Questions of motivation arise in every branch of historical study. Why did Franklin Roosevelt not open the gates of America to Jews persecuted by the Nazis in the 1930s under Hitler? Why did Thomas More die? Why did Richard Nixon try to cover up the Watergate burglaries? Why did Ernest Hemingway write so often about bravery and courage? Why did city people in the late Roman Empire accept Christianity while most country people stayed with the old gods?

Some *why* questions may appear to have been answered. Agreement on these is almost complete. Yet an inquiring historian may look on the evidence again and find another answer. Of such stuff is revisionism in history made. Why did the South suffer so much poverty in the years after the Civil War? An earlier answer was "Reconstruction," the supposedly merciless exploitation of the South by carpetbaggers from the North. Now the prevailing opinion is that white southerners themselves, with their one-crop economy, their resolve to suppress black citizenship, and their unwillingness to support public education were responsible for many of their own difficulties. The *why* questions in history may appear closed, but careful study may open them again.

When and Where?

When and *where* questions often illuminate tricky puzzles in history. Sometimes we know exactly when and where something happened. We know the moment at which the first Japanese bombs fell on Pearl Harbor, the moment at which Franklin Roosevelt died, exactly where the Confederate charge reached its high-water mark on the third day in the battle at Gettysburg. But asking when something happened in relation to something else can provide a fascinating topic for research. We don't know when Richard Nixon first learned that members of his White House staff were involved in the Watergate burglary on June 17, 1972.

When did Israel leave Egypt in the Exodus that is described in the Bible? Several dates have been argued. Different dates mean different chronologies for Israel's relations with other nations in the region and for the development of Israel's own history. When did volcanic eruptions destroy Minoan civilization on Crete? The question is related to the rise in power of the Greek mainland under states such as Athens and Sparta. When did Woodrow Wilson first express himself in opposition to American black aspirations. Was it an attitude thrust upon him by others when he became president, or had he opposed black progress before he entered politics?

Questions about *where* things happened can often be absorbing. No one knows exactly where the Rubicon River was that Caesar crossed with his army, violating a Roman Republic law forbidding the army to approach too near the capital. We know that the Rubicon was in North Italy, that it formed the border between the Roman province known as Cisalpine Gaul and the Roman Republic itself, but we do not know which Italian river was then called the Rubicon. Deciding where the Rubicon was might help us understand how much warning the Roman Senate had when Caesar started with his troops toward the capital.

Where questions involve geography, which often makes *where* questions overlap with *why* questions. Where are the rivers in the Netherlands? The rivers in France? The rivers in Germany? Various historians have argued that the rivers in France and the Netherlands provided a natural unity to those countries, whereas the German rivers flow in such a way as to cause Germany to remain disunited. Where did the Greeks live? Studying patterns of Greek settlement may reveal many things about Greek culture in the classical age. Where did ethnic groups settle when they came to America? Where has most fundamentalist literature been produced? Where did the working classes live in eighteenth-century London? Where were most of the factories that produced iron and steel in the United States at the outbreak of the Civil War? Where were the first railroads built?

All these questions have profound meanings for history, and they may provide topics for original research. Any good historian will examine the geographic context of any study. Geography may yield nothing special for your study, but if you ask the questions, you may discover a door opening in your mind on a hitherto unimagined landscape of events and explanation. The *Annales* school of history in France has made geography one of its fundamental principles, asking such questions as how long it took to travel from one place to another in Europe, what the major trade routes were, where different crops were grown, which cities had the closest relations to one another, and so on.

Bernard DeVoto, an American who wrote several popular and scholarly books on the settlement of the American West, used to collect maps, and loved to spread them out on the floor to demonstrate some of his major theses about the western migration. For all historians, a good topographic map showing the roads, the rivers, the mountains, the passes, the coasts, and the towns remains an indispensable resource. How long did it take news to travel from place to place in Europe during the middle ages or the renaissance? That question requires us to know the location of the roads and their condition. Look at a contour map showing mountains and valleys, and you can understand many reasons for the outbreak of World War I in 1914 and the subsequent German invasion of France through then-neutral Belgium. The same sort of map will provide some reasons for continued African disunity. Geography will not explain *everything*. It will often help you understand some things.

Using Inference

In discussing the journalistic questions we have assumed a mental activity that we call *inference*. We infer many things daily without thinking much about what we are doing. We waken in the morning and see dark clouds blowing across the sky. When we leave the house, we take along an umbrella. Why? Because the clouds make us infer that it may rain today. We have seen such clouds before, and they have often brought rain.

To *infer*, we bring some experience or knowledge to a present situation to try to make sense of this experience. We cannot always be certain that what we infer is true. All of us have had the experience of looking out in the morning at black clouds that threaten rain, but of having the wind blow them away quickly, leaving the skies clear and ourselves lugging around an umbrella or a raincoat that we will not use. We have made an incorrect inference.

All historians use inference. We infer some of the answers to all the journalistic questions. When we do so in our study, we are striving to make sense of our source; when we infer some answers to questions we raise in our writing, we show that we are thinking about the material, trying to put it all together in coherent form—striving, in short, to make sense of it.

Here is a letter written by General Robert E. Lee, leader of the Confederate Army of Northern Virginia during the American Civil War. The letter was written to his wife, an invalid, on April 5, 1863, a scant three months before Lee's army was defeated in the battle of Gettysburg. Lee has been sick, and in the letter he describes his illness to his wife:

> Genl Stuart brought me this morning your letter of yesterday dear Mary. I am much better I think, in fact when the weather becomes so that I can ride out, I shall get quite well again. I am suffering with a bad cold as I told you, & was threatened the doctors thought with some malady which must be dreadful if it resembles its name, but which I have forgotten. So they bundled me up on Monday last & brought me over to Mr. Yuby's where I have a comfortable room with Perry to attend to me. I have not been so very sick, though have suffered a good deal of pain in my chest, back, & arms. It came on in paroxysms, was quite sharp & seemed to be a mixture of your's & Agnes' diseases, from which I infer they are catching & that I fell a victim while in R[ichmond]. But they have passed off I hope, some fever remains, & I am enjoying the sensation of a complete saturation of my system with quinine. The doctors are very attentive & kind & have examined my lungs, my heart, circulation, &c. I believe they pronounce me tolerable sound. They have been tapping me all over like an old steam boiler before con-

demning it. I am about a mile from my camp & my handsome aids ride over with the papers after breakfast which I labour through by 3 p.m., when Mrs. Neal sends me some good soup or something else which is more to my taste than the doctors pills. I am in need of nothing. . . .[1]

What illness did Lee have? Knowing how limited was medical knowledge in his day, we can only infer. Was he describing a heart attack? Or was it, suggests Edwin B. Coddington, a historian of the Gettysburg battle, "pericarditis," an inflammation of the chest cavity where the heart is located?[2] Lee died in 1870, apparently from a heart attack. Were the symptoms manifest earlier? Historian Kent Masterson-Brown, describing Lee at Gettysburg, says, "Lee had been troubled with angina pectoris, and during the campaign he contracted a severe case of diarrhea."[3] Diarrhea can be a symptom of heart trouble. Angina pectoris is pain in or around the heart, but in itself does not diagnose Lee's ills. Harry W. Pfanz dismisses Lee's ailment before Gettysburg as pericarditis brought on by a sore throat.[4] Did illness affect his conduct of the battle? The consensus seems to be in the negative. We cannot know for sure. Such questions show some of the frustrations brought on by inference: at times we cannot know whether the answers we give to questions are right or wrong; we can know only that which seems plausible or believable.

We can infer some qualities about General Lee. He shows here a delightful sense of humor, an appreciation of people around him, and seemingly a wish that his wife not worry about him. Did he really forget the name of the disease that the doctors supposed he might have? Or was he seeking to minimize the entire experience? It is difficult to know, but we may infer throughout the letter a wish to put his wife's mind at ease.

[1]Robert E. Lee, *The Wartime Papers of R. E. Lee,* New York, Bramhall House, 1961, pp. 427–428.

[2]Edwin B. Coddington, *The Gettysburg Campaign: A Study in Command,* New York, Charles Scribner's Sons, 1984, p. 628, note 10.

[3]Kent Masterson-Brown, "Lee at Gettysburg: The Man, the Myth, the Recriminations," *Virginia Country's Civil War,* vol. 1, Middleburg, Va., Country Publishers, 1983, p. 35.

[4]Harry W. Pfanz, *Gettysburg: The Second Day,* Chapel Hill, University of North Carolina Press, 1988, p. 4.

Examples of inference abound in history written on any subject. French medievalist Jacques Le Goff classified the standing of various jobs in the Middle Ages by listing jobs that the church refused to allow priests to hold. If a priest could not hold the job, Le Goff reasoned, it must be work generally scorned. He mentioned innkeepers, owners of bath houses, and jugglers, among others. Many scholars have used wills as points of inference. Wills bequeathing possessions of course show what the maker of the will possessed, and that information may in turn show some things about the life that person lived, but wills can show other things as well. In England, we may get some indication of orthodox Catholic sentiment in the sixteenth century by looking at the religious formulas expressed in wills. If we have formulas mentioning the Virgin Mary and the saints, we may infer strong Catholic sentiment. If we have formulas that mention only God and Christ, we may have some form of Protestantism. Any interpretation of a document involves us in inference. What principles underlie the words a writer uses and the statements the writer makes?

Laws of all sorts offer ample field for inference. We may infer that laws were made to respond to needs or feelings held by many in the society. Laws are responses, and we can usually infer the issues for which the laws were designed. Here are paragraphs describing sanitation in medieval London that rely heavily on inferences made from laws, regulations, and trials.

> No very fastidious standards could be expected in this environment, yet conditions may on the whole have been better than in later centuries when the city was more crowded and its cemetery problem was a serious matter. The larger medieval houses were properly equipped with cesspits having exit pipes, which should have rendered the sewage innocuous. In the smaller houses next-door neighbors shared the use of a privy, and there were street privies for the poor. Liquid refuse of all kinds, it is true, was emptied from buckets and kitchen gutters into open channels in the streets and into the streams that drained the city area; and in the early fourteenth century pigs were able to root about in garbage piles. Later the public scavenging service became more efficient, superseding the pigs, and it was supplemented by private enterprise in shipping stable refuse off in dung boats, to be used as fertilizer on the citizens' fields and gardens up and down the river.

Well-to-do households did not lack facilities for washing. All inventories included metal basins and ewers and often the more elaborate *lavatoria,* hanging basins with drainpipes that could empty into gutters. Sir John Pultney had six of these of silver and three of copper and dozens of basins, ewers, pots, and tubs. John Malewayn had five *lavatoria* of silver, four other basins, and three tubs. Richard Lyons had a tent to put up around his bathtub. . . . How often bathtubs were in use is uncertain. During the first century or so of recurrent plague medical opinion was doubtful of the wisdom of bathing in the winter months or of opening the pores with hot water at any time when an epidemic was in progress, but in spring and summer frequent herb baths were normally prescribed, especially for elderly people with pain in their limbs. The doctors may have been more cautious than the urban public, for in all large medieval cities the bathhouse was a popular institution. In early fifteenth-century London there were at least three respectable ones for women and two for men. It is probable that these were of service chiefly to the people of moderate means, the larger households making their own arrangements. The apothecaries' shops sold castile soap and sponges, and every garden grew some of the herbs that doctors recommended. In between baths there was piecemeal washing. A merchant's widow bequeathed a friend "a bolle basen . . . to wash his fete in."

The heavy furred woolen clothing that was worn must have grown extremely dirty. Servants and professional laundresses, however, washed everything that could be washed—table linen, bed linen, women's headdresses, and other linen clothing. Apprentices had to be given clean clothes and clean bedding. Part of a charge of neglect and ill-treatment of an apprentice that sent a tailor to prison dwelt on his having forced the boy to sleep in a bed "foule shirtyd & full of vermin."[5]

I have omitted the notes from this passage, but I shall summarize them and show how author Sylvia Thrupp inferred from her evidence. She found the details about cesspits in legal records. Some cesspits were built with thin walls too close to cellars. The sewerage flowed into these cellars; the owners complained; the cases went to court. Cities made regulations for such cesspits, and

[5]Sylvia Thrupp, *The Merchant Class of Medieval London,* Ann Arbor, University of Michigan Press (Ann Arbor Paperbacks), 1962, pp. 137–139.

Thrupp inferred that the regulations meant that the cesspits were common.

The information about the pigs and their replacement by public "scavenging" or garbage collection comes also from legal records. Cases involving the keeping of pigs in the city began to appear in the court records. At that moment keeping pigs, except by the very poor, was a violation of the law.

Especially interesting are Thrupp's cautious inferences about bathing. Because inventories and wills often listed vessels used for bathing, she assumes that people bathed. But how often did they bathe? Thrupp recognizes that this is an unanswerable question. She was able to consult fourteenth-century medical books to see what doctors recommended about bathing. Did Londoners follow this medical advice? She is inclined to doubt it, knowing how popular were the bathhouses that she finds in other records.

She infers that wool garments must have become very dirty. No means of cleaning heavy wool without ruining it were discovered until the method we call dry cleaning was invented in the nineteenth century. Linen, a common cloth, could be washed, and Thrupp infers that it was washed frequently because the city records give citizens' occupations, and laundresses' names abound in them. These people had to have something to do. Thrupp infers that they exercised their trade, that therefore linen clothing was washed. The court case about the tailor sent to jail partly because he let his apprentice sleep in filthy bedclothes that were full of vermin shows that cleanliness was a common standard and that violating the standard brought punishment under the law.

Thrupp gives us here a network of inferences, telling a story about sanitation in London. The story she tells contradicts a perception, common at the time she wrote, that people in the middle ages were always filthy. She has woven together a story about the private lives of the common people—always the most difficult people for the historian to reach.

Inference is one of the historian's most serviceable tools. Recognize inference when you see it in your sources, and use it circumspectly yourself. Do not infer wildly. Infer according to a deduction from the evidence that seems plausible to you.

Statistics

Statistical information has been applied increasingly as a source for writing history. Statistics require interpretation. By themselves, they tell us little; inferences we make from them may tell us a great deal, but if we infer wrongly, we can run into gross errors.

To some students of history, studying statistics seems tedious; for others it is exciting and original, a truly new departure in understanding the past. The historian's statistical interest has come about partly because the statistics are available, partly because computers have made using statistics much easier, and partly because of a change in philosophy among historians themselves. Many historians no longer believe that their most valuable subjects are the great leaders: the heroes, the villains, the writers and speakers, the famous and the notorious who have long been the staple of historical inquiry. Many historians have become much more interested in the common people, the masses who have left us few direct records and whose names and personalities are mostly lost to history.

These people have not vanished without trace. By applying statistical reasoning to such records as we have, we can sometimes understand who these people were, what they were thinking, which questions most agitated them, how they lived, and how they received new ideas in their times.

What influences prepared the way for the Protestant Reformation in the sixteenth century? Statistical information offers clues. We have a fairly good idea about which books were most popular among literate people in sixteenth- and seventeenth-century England by seeing the titles that were most frequently published. (The titles of all surviving English books published in that time have been catalogued.) We can study at second hand peoples' emotions by looking at the illustrations popular pamphleteers thought were most appealing or exciting, and these can be classified and counted. We can often infer what people were reading by counting such things as the number of copies a book sold or the number of books about a subject. We infer that a great many early sixteenth-century English readers wanted to read stories about saints because in modern catalogues listing books published in that period, titles involving the saints turn up with great frequency. A few years later they were nearly all gone.

We have the records kept by many great European banking companies for this time, and we can chart the ebb and flow of economic forces that may have contributed to the Reformation. In his Ninety-Five Theses of 1517, which brought him to wide public notice, Luther protested about the flow of gold from Germany into Italy on account of papal exactions. By examining accounts of banking houses operating in Germany and Italy, we can gain some insight into the truth or falsehood of this claim.

We can have some idea about relative prosperity in different regions, and we can roughly estimate populations. In late medieval times both businesses and the Catholic Church kept extensive records, which are now open to historians. Governments taxed their people and kept records of who paid. By patient hard work and with great care, we can translate much of this information into statistics, and from these statistics we can infer something about the lives of the people who have left few or no individual records. Historian David Herlihy of Brown University is compiling lists of late medieval and renaissance Italian names and correlating them with the names of saints. The saints venerated by medieval Catholics had special attributes and were called upon for help in special times. St. Sebastian and St. Roche were called upon for help in time of plague. By studying the rise and fall in popularity of names, Herlihy hopes to understand an aspect of late medieval sensibility.

Our Puritan forebears in New England named their children after characters in the Bible. What does it say about the acceptance of biblical religion when New Englanders began using other names? What can we tell about religious sensibilities in a nineteenth-century community by walking through its graveyard and enumerating the kinds of inscriptions on the tombstones? How many of them are specifically religious? How many of them are secular? What if anything does it mean about a community if we find three inscriptions that say, "Asleep in Jesus" and twenty-five from the same period that say, "Gone but not Forgotten"? This may sound like an elementary inquiry, but in fact it is the kind of question that may be translated into statistics and interpreted.

The worship of statistics by modern bureaucratic societies

makes the historian's task both easier and harder as we move from renaissance to present. The task is easier because statistical information nowadays is often recorded in precise, accessible, and usable form. We can know the predominant ethnic and economic composition of voting precincts in the United States, and we can know how those precincts voted in elections. We can analyze the difference in voting patterns between, say, an Italian Catholic precinct and a conservative Jewish precinct in a large American city such as New York or Boston. We may then try to infer the issues that accounted for the differences or similarities we may discover. We might assume that both such precincts would be influenced by issues related to the family. We might be wrong, or we might discover that other issues mattered more than family. Analyzing the voting patterns in such precincts—an analysis made familiar by the media—helps us understand why one candidate won and the other lost or why one may win and the other may lose.

Analyzing statistics to understand voting patterns only scratches the surface of possible uses to which historians may put statistical information. The data gathered by the United States Bureau of the Census and by myriad government agencies allows us to infer many things about populations—whether they go to church or not, whether they practice birth control, whether they send their children to school, whether they go to college, how many times they move, how much family income they have, and so on. Private polls by agencies such as the Gallup organization and many others tell us changes in taste: What television programs were most popular in the 1950s? How did public opinion develop on United States entry into World War II?

Statistical information can be put to use whenever we can reduce evidence to numbers. Numbers measure things, but what do we measure? That is always the question. We can choose to measure some things that tell us a great deal, others that tell us nothing significant. One of the more controversial books based on statistics in recent years is *Time on the Cross: The Economics of American Negro Slavery* by Robert William Fogel and Stanley L. Engerman. As the title indicates, the authors set out to see the face of slavery by looking at statistics left over from slave days before the American Civil War. Historian Oscar Handlin in reviewing the book discussed the authors' contention that the average age of slave mothers when they gave birth to their first child was 22.5 years. Handlin pointed out that Fogel and Engerman drew their data from wills probated in "fifty-four counties in eight Southern States between 1775 and 1865 which enumerated 80,000 slaves."[6]

Eighty thousand is a considerable figure. One might assume that statistical data drawn from such a sampling would have much validity. But what about the significance the authors read into their finding about slave mothers' average age? The authors argued that slave mothers were mature women at the birth of their first child and that therefore they must have been married. This fairly late age for the first birth would indicate stable family life. Yet that is not clear, though Fogel and Engerman used this evidence to infer that sexual promiscuity among slaves was limited and that family life was close and enduring. Handlin argues that such an elaborate conclusion cannot be drawn from this evidence.[7]

Handlin's thoughts about the work by Fogel and Engerman are worth pondering, for difficulties abound in using statistics. Sometimes the quantity of statistical information available may seem daunting. Anyone is likely to feel overwhelmed by a project that may involve seemingly endless tables of numbers, charts, and graphs. Interpreting statistics requires much skill. Statistics itself is a substantial academic discipline involving a rigorous introduction to the methods for getting statistics to make sense. Even with such instruction, misinterpretations of statistics are common. Numbers may provide a comforting appearance of exactitude to some students, but the appearance may not match the reality. Statistics can lie and lead astray.

Statistics cannot measure intensity of beliefs. In political campaigns, polls show the percentage in a sampling of voters who favor this or that candidate. But do those supporters feel strongly enough about their favorites to vote for them? The candidate who can get out supporters may have a great advantage over the candidate who may be supported lukewarmly by many more citizens. With what intensity did citizens in the American Revolution sup-

---

[6]Oscar Handlin, *Truth in History,* Cambridge, Harvard University Press, 1981, p. 211.

[7]Handlin, pp. 210–226. This is only part of the lengthy criticism Handlin directs against use of statistics in *Time on the Cross*.

port American independence or continued union with Great Britain? Questions like these often take us beyond the power of statistics to measure.

Many who criticize the quantitative method of writing history protest that its practitioners often claim to know more than they really do about the past. Nothing takes the place, say the critics, of understanding history by reading the lively words written by those who participated in it; to these more humanistically inclined historians, statistics are skeletons without muscle and breath. The quantitative historians reply that the humanistic historians go on and on arguing over the same old things, and that if statistics are often inexact they are nonetheless more reliable than impressionistic work by thinkers who are historians writing about other thinkers who made history. In particular, the statistical historians point out that the humanists are likely to take expressions by people who write as typical of the entire community. In fact, writers in every age are special people, and they may not adequately represent the tastes, the beliefs, the prejudices, the yearnings held by the masses who do not write. Interpreting statistics helps us go where other sources will not allow us entry.

The debate will continue. The quantitative historians will flourish on just because of the many records that can be analyzed by statistical methods, and computers now make such analysis both possible and exciting.

If you do a quantitative paper in one of your courses, be sure that you do have enough data, and learn enough about interpreting statistics to avoid obvious errors. Be cautious.

You may examine the voting records precinct by precinct for the two referenda the state of Tennessee took on secession from the Union in 1861. The first referendum, taken before the firing on Fort Sumter, showed a majority for staying in the Union. The second showed a majority for secession, and Tennessee duly joined the Confederacy—the last of the Confederate states to do so. In both referenda, the upper counties in East Tennessee voted solidly to remain in the Union.

Having looked at those statistics, you would be most unwise to conclude that the vote for the Union was a vote for enlightened treatment of blacks as equal to whites in the South. Other statistics would show that relative to the rest of the South, Tennessee had fewer slaves, and the slavery issue was not so important. Therefore, Tennesseans saw little value in a secession movement intended to protect slavery. East Tennessee was one of the few industrial areas in the South, and its rail connections and markets tied it to the Northeast. After the war, the Ku Klux Klan was begun in Pulaski, Tennessee. One of the Klan's major aims was to keep blacks from voting. Much evidence shows, then, that opposition to secession by many Tennesseans had little to do with humanitarian feelings for black Americans.

Statistics can be used to great effect. Here is part of a celebrated essay by English historian Peter Laslett. Laslett examines the casual statement by Juliet's father in Shakespeare's *Romeo and Juliet* that Juliet was not yet fourteen years old when she and Romeo fell into their tragic romance. We will start at the beginning of Laslett's essay, where he quotes from Shakespeare's play:

> My child is yet a stranger in the world
> She hath not seen the change of fourteen years
> Let two more summers wither in their pride
> Ere we may think her ripe to be a bride

Capulet says this in the second scene of *Romeo and Juliet*. But whatever he said and whatever he felt, his child Juliet did take Romeo to husband at about her fourteenth birthday. Juliet's mother left her in no doubt of her opinion.

> Well, think of marriage now; younger than you,
> Here in Verona, ladies of esteem,
> Are made already mothers. By my count
> I was your mother much upon these years
> That you are now a maid.

So she had been married at twelve, or early thirteen, and all those other ladies of Verona also. Miranda was married in her fifteenth year in *The Tempest*. It all seems clear and consistent enough. The women in Shakespeare's plays, and so presumably the English-women of Shakespeare's day, might marry in their early teens, or even before, and very often did.

Yet this is not true. We have examined every record we can find to test it and they all declare that, in Elizabethan and Jacobean England, marriage was rare at these early ages and not as common in the late teens as it is now. At twelve, marriage as we understand it was virtually unknown.

Some of the evidence for these blank statements will have to be presented here, and we shall have to discuss what constituted marriage, leaving *espousals* to a later chapter. An espousal was a promise which became marriage as we understand it if sexual intercourse took place. People could marry by licence as well as by banns in England then, just as they still can in the Church of England today. They had to apply for the licence to the bishop of the diocese they lived in, and very often they were required to give their ages; the reason was that no one under 21 could be married by the Church without his parents' permission: it was a grave sin to do so at an older age without good reason. We have examined a thousand licences containing the ages of the applicants, issued by the diocese of Canterbury between 1619 and 1660, to people marrying for the first time. One woman gave her age as 13, four as 15, twelve as 16: all the rest were 17 and over, and 966 of the women got married for the first time after the age of 19, that is, nearly 85 percent. The commonest age of first marriage for women in this sample was 22, and the median age—the age below which as many got married as got married above it—was about 22¾: the average, mean age was about 24. Bridegrooms were something like three years older than brides, though some of the unions recorded show an extraordinary discrepancy in age. Only ten men married below the age of 20, two of them at 18, and the most common age was 24; the median age was something like 25½ and the mean age over 26¾.

Put in the familiar form we use in conversation, the average age of these Elizabethan and Jacobean brides was something like 24 and the average of bridegrooms was nearly 28. Surely these figures by themselves ought to be sufficient to dispel belief that our ancestors married much younger than we do.[8]

Notice that Laslett has some materials necessary to anyone who wants to use statistics in a paper. He has a data base—applications for marriage licenses preserved by the English Church in the diocese of Canterbury. He counts out his statistics carefully. He measures something that gives plausible evidence for his thesis.

He distinguishes between the median and the average in his statistics. (The *median* is a number at the middle of a group of numbered items; as many examples are below the median as above it. The *average* is obtained by simply dividing the number of instances

[8]Peter Laslett, *The World We Have Lost,* 2nd ed., New York, Charles Scribner's Sons, 1973, pp. 84–85.

by another number betokening some other quantity. In a group of ten people whose ages were 18, 19, 20, 32, 16, 28, 13, 25, 40, and 90, the average age would be 30.1—an average derived from the total of the various ages, 301, divided by 10, the number of people who interest us. The median age would, however, be 22.5, a figure midway between the middle figures 20 and 25 in this series. The median tells us that just as many items are below it as above it.)

He infers that the records for these marriages in these years are typical of marriages in the rest of England. It is not absolute proof for his argument, but it is persuasive. We believe Laslett unless someone can come up with persuasive evidence stating why we should not. So it is often with inferences from statistics and indeed from any sort of inference; the argument is persuasive unless someone can produce evidence to show us why it should not be accepted.

Statistical information is often not complete—one more reason for caution. Modern polls are an instructive illustration of the limitations in statistical sampling. Pollsters may draw their predictions about an election from a base of 1,000 or 1,500 random interviews out of a whole population; rarely are their predictions exact. Yet they are close enough to be taken seriously. Political pundits use them as the beginning of speculation about elections. If you have a large data base for a historical subject, as Laslett did when he compiled his figures on marriages in England, you may usually infer with confidence that your figures represent a typical situation. But as Handlin pointed out in his comments about *Time on the Cross,* you must also be sure to ask the right questions about the statistics at your command, and be careful to measure the right things. Even a large data base cannot help you if you seek to read more into those statistics than you should.

CONCLUSION

Studying history requires you to ask questions not only about the sources you read but about the papers you write. The journalistic questions are a means for scanning both your sources and your own work. When you think about inference, you should be able to recognize good and bad inferences from the material you read—

including your own work. The same is true of statistical information, which always requires interpretation before it can be useful to the historian. You must draw inferences from the statistics you have; how you draw them determines whether your conclusions are valid or not.

3

Modes of
Historical Writing

Like other writers, historians use the four common modes of expression—description, narration, exposition, and argument. These modes correspond in some ways to the journalistic questions. Just as we may ask those questions in dozens of versions about our reading or writing, we may apply all the modes in one paper. Although they often overlap, the varieties are distinct, and one will usually predominate in each book or essay. Having a clear idea about which mode is best suited to your purpose in the paper will make the task easier for you and your readers.

DESCRIPTION

With description we present an account of sensory experience—telling how things look, feel, taste, sound, and smell. Popular history includes vivid descriptions. Nonspecialist readers can identify with sense experience, for no matter how learned or unlearned we are in the limitless facts recorded about a historical period, we have all had sensations similar to those felt by people in the past. Our senses are the fundamental common denominator in human life.

Perhaps because we rely on sense experience, we like to find concrete details about physical reality in books and articles about history. Details reassure us that the world in the past was enough like our own to let us imagine it, place ourselves within it for at least a moment, and find it familiar and partly understandable. You may tell how a building or a landscape looks. You can describe the condition that brings to life people in a sculpture, a photograph, or a painting—how they dressed, their facial expressions, whether they were tired, happy, wet, dry, miserable, in anguish. You may describe the appearance peculiar to an object—a tool, a weapon, a piece of furniture, a landscape, a building, a portrait. You can describe geography—the mountains in Greece, the situation in which a battlefield lay, the African rivers.

You can write about how the wind sounded on the American Great Plains as innumerable pioneers (keeping innumerable journals) went overland toward their new homes. You can tell, as Barbara Tuchman does in her *Guns of August,* how troops in World War I stank so that the towns they occupied reeked with sweat-soaked clothing. You can write of the summer heat in Washington, D.C., when Franklin Roosevelt was building his New Deal in a world that had no air conditioning but in which public figures were expected to conduct their business in wool suits and carefully knotted neckties; you can tell how food given to the American slave tasted in the years before the Civil War.

Few historical papers are devoted to description alone, though an account of the geography surrounding the Battle of Thermopylae might give a detailed description of the Malliac Gulf and the narrow ledge or pass between it and Mount Callidromion. There, in August 480 B.C., three hundred Spartans stood off thousands of Persians until the Spartans died to the last man. Since then the hot sulphur springs in Thermopylae (the Greek word means "hot gates") have continued to flow, perhaps helping silt up the gulf and driving back the sea so that working out the exact geography of the battle is difficult. A paper on the subject might be carefully descriptive, providing the writer's reconstruction of those events. But that descriptive paper would surely include elements of narrative as the writer told how the stages in the battle followed in this landscape.

Description provides details that suggest a scene without telling everything about it; no writer can give every detail. If you try to do so, you kill the paper. Tell enough to inspire readers' imaginations to make them relive episodes in their experience that allow them to respond to the facts you tell them.

In his *Sacco and Vanzetti: The Case Resolved,* part history, part autobiography, Francis Russell tells us how he changed his mind about the celebrated 1921 trial and execution in 1927 of Nicola Sacco and Bartolemeo Vanzetti. The two were accused of murder in a payroll robbery in South Braintree, Massachusetts, on April 15, 1920. They were tried in Dedham, Massachusetts. More than twenty years ago, Russell began his interest in the case by believing that they were innocent. After long and detailed study, he concluded that Sacco was guilty of murder and that Vanzetti could be described in legal terminology as an accessory after the fact. This descriptive passage sets a tone for the carefully reflective book:

> Someday, I promised myself, I was going to sit down and study the Sacco-Vanzetti trial transcript. But with the coming of the war, my interest lapsed. If I had not been called for a month's jury duty in the Dedham courthouse in the spring of 1953, I doubt that I should ever have concerned myself with the case again. I was then living in Wellesley, eight miles away, and when the weather was good I used to walk along the back roads to Dedham. By starting at quarter to eight I could get to the courthouse just before ten o'clock, when the morning session began.
>
> I liked those brisk bright mornings, the earth smelling of spring, the maples in misty shades of mauve and red. From Wellesley the road dipped past the country club, curving down to Needham, a semi-suburb of repetitive three-bedroom houses, commonplace enough, yet—as I was later to discover—singularly interwoven with the Sacco-Vanzetti case.
>
> Spring was late that year. Not until my second week, as I crossed the bridge over the Charles River the other side of Needham, did I hear the creaky notes of the redwings among last year's cattails. A few mornings later I saw a couple of painted turtles still torpid from hibernation. From the bridge I headed up the winding road to Dedham, past much empty land, orchards, stone walls, and the driveways of discreetly hidden river estates. Then, from Common Street on Dedham's outskirts, I swung into High Street, ahead of me above the still-bare elms the courthouse dome, mosquelike in the early light, crowned by an ornate metal grille and a flagpole. On those placid mornings the flag hung limp.

1500
Ken C.

It was almost a third of a century since Sacco and Vanzetti had been tried, yet the ghost of their trial still seemed to haunt the courthouse. Scarcely a day passed while I was on jury duty but some reference to it came up. It shadowed us all. We served in the same paneled room with the marble-faced clock where Sacco and Vanzetti had been tried and sentenced. There was the same enclosure for the prisoners that Sacco-Vanzetti partisans referred to as a "cage"—as if the two defendants had been exhibited like animals in a zoo. Actually, it was a waist-high metal lattice, slightly higher in the back, with nothing formidable or forbidding about it. Our white-haired sheriff, Samuel Capen, in his blue-serge cutaway, its gleaming brass buttons embossed with the state seal, and his white staff of office that he wielded like a benevolent shepherd, had been sheriff at the time of the great trial. In the overlong lunch hours he would sometimes talk about it, telling of the day Sacco and Vanzetti were sentenced, how Vanzetti made his famous speech, and how Judge Thayer sat with his head bent and never looked at him. I don't suppose any doubts had ever crossed the sheriff's mind as to the guilt of the two Italians or the rectitude of Massachusetts justice.[1]

There are several forms of description here. The passage begins with a direct appeal to the senses, as when Russell tells us of colors ("misty shades of mauve and red"); objects ("the marble-faced clock"); sounds ("the creaky notes of the redwings"); and smells ("the earth smelling of spring"). All these descriptions of physical reality depend on our having had some experience with them. When he tells us that the Dedham courthouse dome looked "mosquelike in the early light," he assumes that we have at least seen pictures of mosques so that we have a rough idea of what he saw. We may not have had all the experiences: some readers may not have heard redwing blackbirds' "creaky notes." Still, they follow Russell's account because his own concrete description conveys authority: he has been there; he knows what he is talking about; he is able to describe what he has experienced in language that suggests reality. These qualities help readers believe the writer.

Another kind of description here is more impressionistic. He tells us that the enclosure where prisoners sat in the courtroom had

---

[1]Francis Russell, *Sacco and Vanzetti: The Case Resolved,* New York, Harper and Row, 1986, pp. 34–36.

"nothing formidable or forbidding about it." The sheriff carried an official staff "that he wielded like a benevolent shepherd." These are the writer's impressions. Someone else might have seen the "waist-high metal lattice, slightly higher in the back" as formidable and forbidding; someone else might have supposed that Sheriff Capen wielded his official staff like a warrior's club. Subtly, Russell has prepared us to believe his impressions because earlier he provided vivid and believable details about things he had observed. These observations give us an "implied author." They make us think we know the kind of person this author is: dispassionate, warmhearted, sharply observant. His care in the more concrete descriptions of his walk gives him authority, and we believe him readily when he passes to more subjective, impressionistic observations: the nonthreatening quality of the prisoner's "cage," the benevolence in the sheriff's flourishing his staff of office.

Description often combines these two elements—the concrete and the impressionistic. Here is a passage from Evan S. Connell's *Son of the Morning Star,* a much-admired account of the life and death of General George Armstrong Custer, who came to a bad end with his Seventh Cavalry in 1876, when he attacked a Sioux Indian encampment on the Little Big Horn River in land that is now Montana. Connell describes General Phil Sheridan and Custer:

> Like Napoleon, Sheridan was uncommonly short: five feet, five inches. He is said to have had such a lumpy skull that his hats did not fit, an allegation which cannot be verified from photos. With black almond eyes and a dangling mustache he resembles those ancient portraits of Mongol emperors, although one staff officer called him "thick-set & common Irish-looking"—adding that Sheridan combed his hair "in the Bowery soap-lock style." Historian Stephen Ambrose characterized him as an obstinate little man, "given to intense rages, mad with battle lust during an engagement, quick to censure and slow to forgive, bursting with energy, forever demanding the impossible of his men."
>
> Custer stood half-a-head taller, women found him exciting, and unlike Sheridan he seldom cherished a grudge; otherwise they must have been much alike. Custer might erupt at any instant; he loved to fight and was quick to blame. He could be sarcastic and impossibly demanding. They understood each other, these two. Sheridan perceived in the audacious young cavalryman a sympathetic spirit,

one who was not reluctant to discipline troops and who thought the best way to handle dangerous redskins was to crush them.[2]

This impressionistic account includes concrete details. Connell subtly lets us know how fallible descriptions of historical personages may be: he gives us slightly contradictory impressions from people who knew and wrote about the men he describes. He has gone to his primary sources, and though he has found that they do not provide perfect consistency, he has managed to reconcile them into coherent portraits.

Never make facts up when you describe anything. Always be sure you have evidence for anything you say in a description. Some historians get carried away by a novelistic impulse that may smack of dishonesty. Though some readers may be entertained by such flights of fancy, serious historians find them dismaying. Here are two paragraphs written by Paul Murray Kendall in his biography of Richard III, king of England between 1483 and 1485. He describes the battle of Barnet, in which Richard, then Duke of Gloucester, fought on the side of his older brother, Edward IV, against an effort by the Earl of Warwick to overthrow Edward.

> Suddenly, there was a swirl in the mist to the left of and behind the enemy's position. A shiver ran down the Lancastrian line. Exeter's men began to give way, stubbornly at first, then faster. Warwick's center must be crumbling. Richard signaled his trumpeters. The call to advance banners rang out. The weary young commander and his weary men surged forward. The hedge of steel before them began to fall apart. Then the enemy were in full flight, casting away their weapons as they ran.
>
> Out of the mist loomed the great sun banner of the House of York. A giant figure strode forward. Pushing his visor up, Richard saw that the King was smiling at him in brotherly pride. The right wing, driving westward across the Lancastrian rear, had linked up with Edward's center to bring the battle to an end. It was seven o'clock in the morning; the struggle had lasted almost three hours.[3]

[2]Evan S. Connell, *Son of the Morning Star,* San Francisco, North Point Press, 1984, p. 180.

[3]Paul Murray Kendall, *Richard the Third,* New York, Doubleday Anchor Books, 1965, p. 97.

Kendall's description evokes a vivid image of battle, perhaps true in spirit to the events. But his scene is almost entirely made up. Our sources for the battle of Barnet are skimpy, lacking entirely the descriptive details that Kendall gives us. Historian Charles Ross, remarking on Kendall's account of Barnet, comments drily, "The incautious reader might be forgiven for thinking that the author himself was present at the battle."[4] Kendall's book illustrates some of the most difficult problems in "popular" history. He writes well, and thousands of people have read his work. But his incautious exaggeration ruined much of his credit among historians who took seriously the limitations in their sources. Don't sacrifice accuracy in the name of vividness, or you may sacrifice your reputation, too.

Don't describe too much, even when you have the sources. No words can convey a scene exactly. We have all had the experience of reading a description about a place or a scene or a person—perhaps with accompanying photographs—and then of discovering on our personal encounter with the events described that it is not quite what we imagined it to be. Sometimes, although we realize that the description is completely accurate, we are startled at the difference between the scene we imagined and the one we see.

Descriptions create a mood. But when we extend them with too many details, we expect more from them than they can produce. That is why readers tire of long descriptions. They realize that so many details do not help them see the scene or the person any more clearly, and they want to get on with the story. Descriptions are best when they tell just enough to help readers understand something significant and then move on. They are worst when they bog readers down.

What quantity is "just enough"? No one can give an easy answer to this question. Go back again to Francis Russell's description of his walk to the Dedham courthouse and his observation of the courtroom and the sheriff. Think of all the other things Russell could have described. He might have given us much more detail about the three-bedroom houses in Needham, or the mansions he

---

[4]Charles Ross, *Richard III,* Berkeley and Los Angeles, University of California Press, 1983, p. 21.

passed later on; he could have told us how the courtroom interior was painted and the pictures if any that hung on the walls and how the windows looked and whether a view was visible beyond them. He did not indulge himself in those details because they did not fit his purpose. He tells us enough to let us imagine much of the scene for ourselves, and then he goes on. Later we see that these descriptive passages help us understand many things he tells us about the Sacco-Vanzetti case: poor Italian immigrants tried for murder, the trial held in a quiet courtroom in a middle-class Yankee town a world away from the crowded, poor, and noisy Italian Boston slums. Those and other contrasts fueled the intense international debate about whether Sacco and Vanzetti received a fair trial. In most history papers, description should serve narrative, exposition, or argument, as it does in Russell's work.

Russell's use of description is more personal than much of the descriptive material that historians include. In an earlier book, *Tragedy in Dedham,* he had carefully set down the evidence for Sacco's guilt and Vanzetti's "guilty knowledge" of the murder. For this book, Russell was vehemently attacked by Sacco-and-Vanzetti partisans. Finding that yet more evidence for their guilt turned up, Russell decided to publish it in the book I have quoted. Because of the furious attacks on his work, he felt moved to make this second book an autobiographical account of his experience with the case, certifying himself as he did so as a dispassionate and objective observer.

In John Keegan's *Face of Battle,* he describes the "Physical Circumstances of Battle" at Waterloo in 1815, when the English and the Prussians defeated Napoleon in his last great battle. Here, in a more traditional history, descriptive elements are useful:

> Besides being hungry and travel-worn the combatants at Waterloo were clearly rain-sodden. The regiments that had spent the night marching lay down to sleep in wet clothes and probably woke up to fight the battle still very damp. Those which passed the night in the fields, though they slept worse, or had no sleep at all, generally found means to dry out after sunrise. A young officer of the 32nd, who had woken wet through, managed to get into a shed where there was a fire, and the men made large fires outside. The light company men of the 3rd Foot Guards, who had spent the night

"cramped sitting on the side of a wet ditch" south of Hougoumont, got a fire going "which served to dry our clothing and accoutrements," and Leeke, of the 52nd, found a fire large and hot enough to get some sleep by. Wood, of the 10th Hussars, an officer whose Waterloo letter breathes the authentic cavalry spirit, "got into a small cottage close to our bivouac . . . most of us naked, and getting our things dry at the fire. . . . Old Quentin burned his boots and could not get them on." Other cavalrymen, too, found their clothes spoiled by the wet. The Greys' scarlet jackets had run into their white belts overnight, and Sergeant Coglan of the 18th Hussars attempted to dry his clothes by hanging them on the branches of trees. The Assembly was sounded before he had succeeded, and he dressed in the saddle, "crying out to those I had charge of to mount also." Waterloo day was overcast, rather than sunny, so those who, like Coglan, failed to get near a fire at the beginning presumably stayed damp until well after midday. Houssaye's "kaleidoscope of vivid hues and metallic flashes," his "bright green jackets . . . imperial blue collars . . . white breeches . . . breastplates of gold . . . blue coats faced with scarlet . . . red kurkas and blue plastrons . . . green dolmans embroidered with yellow braid, red pelisses edged with fur" must have covered many limp stocks, sticky shirts, and clammy socks.[5]

We can see here the common denominator that carries sense experience. We know what it is to have to go about in wet clothes; we recognize colors; we know how hard it is to dry things in the open on an overcast day. Or at least we know enough about wetness on an overcast day to imagine that we know these things. I can imagine a soldier pulling wet clothes onto his body in great haste because once in a great while I have had to put on wet clothes, and I recall the miserable experience.

Keegan shows in the passage quoted above that description can not only give a sense of immediacy but can make us understand the events better. His thesis throughout the book is to answer this question: "How do men act in battle?" His description of the men's condition in the British and the French armies on the day of Waterloo, as it fits into the rest of his book, helps us understand his thesis.

[5]John Keegan, *The Face of Battle,* New York, Penguin Books, 1984, p. 137.

NARRATIVE

Narratives tell stories, and narratives are the bedrock of history. Without narratives, history would die as a discipline. Narratives answer the question we have posed as an analytical tool in studying history: What happened? The most popular history has always been narrative history, the story of what happened. What happened when your college was founded? What happened when the United States recognized the State of Israel in 1948? What happened during the Boston Police Strike in 1919?

Narrative history can look easy to write because it is relatively easy to read. In fact, storytelling is a complicated art. As in description, part of the art lies in knowing what to include and what to exclude, what to believe and what to reject. Narrative must also take into account contradictions that lie in the evidence and either resolve them or admit frankly that they cannot be resolved.

Who fired the first shot on the morning of April 19, 1775, when British regular soldiers clashed with the Minutemen on Lexington Green in Massachusetts in the battle that began the American Revolution? The incident makes a nice subject for narrative history—but it is not an easy narrative to write. Sylvanus Wood, one of the Minutemen, dictated his account of the battle more than fifty years afterward. Here is part of what he said:

> Parker led those of us who were equipped to the north end of Lexington Common, near the Bedford Road, and formed us in single file. I was stationed about in the centre of the company. While we were standing, I left my place and went from one end of the company to the other and counted every man who was paraded, and the whole number was thirty-eight, and no more. . . .
>
> The British troops approached us rapidly in platoons with a general officer on horseback at their head. The officer came up to within about two rods of the centre of the company, where I stood, the first platoon being about three rods distant. They were halted. The officer then swung his sword, and said, "Lay down your arms, you damned rebels, or you are all dead men. Fire!" Some guns were fired by the British at us from the first platoon, but no person was killed or hurt, being probably charged only with powder.
>
> Just at this time, Captain Parker ordered every man to take care

of himself. The company immediately dispersed; and while the company was dispersing and leaping over the wall, the second platoon of the British fired and killed some of our men. There was not a gun fired by any of Captain Parker's company, within my knowledge. . . .[6]

Lieutenant John Barker of the British army was also at Lexington, fighting with the regiment called the King's Own. Here is part of the account of the battle he wrote only a few days afterward:

> About 5 miles on this side of a town called Lexington, which lay in our road, we heard there were some hundreds of people collected together intending to oppose us and stop our going on. At 5 o'clock we arrived there and saw a number of people, I believe between 2 and 300, formed in a common in the middle of the town. We still continued advancing, keeping prepared against an attack tho' without intending to attack them; but on our coming near them they fired one or two shots, upon which our men without any orders rushed in upon them, fired and put 'em to flight. Several of them were killed, we could not tell how many because they were got behind walls and into the woods. We had a man of the 10th Light Infantry wounded, nobody else hurt.[7]

Who told the truth? Perhaps we will never know; the writer of a historical narrative must deal with the contradiction. You cannot pretend that it does not exist. Often you must use analysis in your text, some thinking about the text that will allow you to make sense of it. Here is an acceptable version of the story that remains true to the sources:

> Exactly what happened at Lexington is buried in the confusions of the morning. Sylvanus Wood, one of the Patriot soldiers, claimed that Parker threw a thin line of armed minutemen across the green to face the British regulars marching down what is now Massachu–

[6] *The Spirit of 'Seventy-Six,* edited by Henry Steele Commager and Richard B. Morris, New York, Harper and Row, 1975, pp. 82–83.
[7] *The Spirit of 'Seventy-Six,* pp. 70–71.

setts Avenue. Wood claims he counted the minutemen and that they numbered only thirty—eight, but Wood set down his account fifty years after the event, and his memory may have played tricks on him. British Lieutenant John Barker, marching with the King's Own regiment, said there were two or three hundred, but he may have been counting curious spectators who turned out to see the show. It was early in the morning, and Barker was angry and perhaps frightened—not emotions that might have made him count objectively.

In any case the minutemen were heavily outnumbered, and Parker knew it. He ordered his men to fall back. Someone fired a shot. Barker said the shot came from the minutemen; Wood said the British fired first. We can never know who did fire the first shot, and in the confusion the British and the Patriots on the scene probably did not know, either. Shooting did break out. Several minutemen were killed. The fighting of the American Revolution had begun.

Sometimes you may write the best narrative you can put together and mention the contradictions in your footnotes, perhaps explaining why you have rejected some sources and accepted others. However you do the job, you must let readers know about significant contradictions if you find them in the sources.

Narratives usually follow chronological order. Starting at the beginning of the events you are reporting, you write on to the end, telling about the first events first and the last last. Sometimes good storytellers and good historians begin with an important event and then go back to explain why it happened or why it was significant. James MacGregor Burns begins the second volume of his three-volume narrative history of the United States with this story:

> Belching clouds of steam and hazy blue smoke, the stubby little locomotive chugged along the iron rails that wove through the low Allegheny Mountains. While the fireman heaved chunks of walnut and cherry into the roaring firebox, the engineer looked out through his narrow window past the small boiler, the polished brass fittings, the stovepipe-shaped smokestack, watching for the village stations along the way: Relay House, Lutherville, Timonium. . . . In a rear coach sat Abraham Lincoln, regaling cronies with droll stories and listening imperturbably to politicians who climbed aboard to exhort and complain, while a little party of diplomats silently watched this loose-framed man who, with his seamed face, deep-sunk eyes, and rough cut of a beard, appeared in mourning even as he told his small-town anecdotes.[8]

Burns is about to tell the story about Abraham Lincoln's delivery of the Gettysburg Address at the dedication of the Gettysburg National Cemetery on November 19, 1863, four months after the great battle that had turned back Robert E. Lee's invasion of the North. Burns had done thorough research on all these details—he knew the kind of locomotive that pulled Lincoln's train and even the kind of wood that locomotives burned in that part of America and the color of the smoke that cherry and walnut gave off in combustion. In an endnote, he gives us the evidence for each of these details; he does not make things up as Paul Murray Kendall did.

His method of narration is to tell an anecdote and then to develop its significance by going back to the larger story of which the anecdote is a part. After the story about the dedication of the cemetery, he goes back to tell briefly about the American Civil War and its significance in American history. In the book itself he develops themes introduced in this early chapter.

In a narrative an author begins by setting some sort of problem or conflict that later development of the narrative should solve. In the story that James MacGregor Burns tells, we have to ask, "Why did Lincoln go to Gettysburg?" As Burns gets into his story, we are forced to ask, "What did the Gettysburg Address signify and what did the Civil War mean for the history of the United States immediately afterward?" These questions set up the narrative

---

[8]James MacGregor Burns, *The Workshop of Democracy*, New York, Alfred A. Knopf, 1985, p. 3.

problem, and the narrative is written to solve it. You cannot proceed far into a narrative without showing your readers that you are setting up a story that must come to a resolution. You cannot hold readers' attention merely by telling them one interesting detail after another. You must tell them that there is a point to what you are telling them, and they must understand that your narrative will make that point clear. You must set up some tension, not a melodramatic tension but some conflict, however mild, that must be resolved in your story.

Let us return to thoughts about history expressed in the introduction to this book. Children's stories demonstrate the qualities that apply to any good narrative. We read, "Once upon a time a little girl named Cinderella lived in a house with her wicked stepmother and her two wicked stepsisters. Now the prince of the country gave a great ball, and he invited Cinderella's sisters, but poor Cinderella had to stay home and sweep out the ashes while her sisters went off and had a good time." We immediately know that Cinderella has troubles and that somehow the story involves the sisters, the stepmother, the prince, and the ball. The story tells us why all these details are introduced at the beginning. A good narrative in history has the same qualities: it introduces elements that later in the story the author shows belong together. These elements have some destiny in the story. A corollary is not to introduce large elements into your narrative at the beginning if you do not intend to do something with them later on.

A narrative paper should have a climax that embodies the meaning the writer wants readers to take from the story. At the climax everything comes together—the bill is passed, the battle is over, the candidate is elected, the leader is assassinated, the speech is made. Because it gathers all the threads and joins them to make the writer's point, the climax usually comes fairly close to the end of the paper. When you arrive at the climax, you are ready to wrap up your narrative, and readers should feel that you have kept a promise you made them at the beginning. If you cannot think of a climax for the paper, reexamine your topic. A good narrative has a place where everything the writer has been setting down comes to a head. If you cannot find a climactic point, you need to reorganize the story.

A historian of the battles in Lexington and Concord might

choose to assign the climax to the moment in Lexington when the first shots were exchanged between the Patriots and the British. That moment is significant in that it marked the beginning of combat in the Revolutionary War. Or one might make the climax the hot skirmish that took place by the wooden bridge later that day outside Concord. The significance here is that this fight forced the British to retreat and gave the Patriots anticipation of victory and the British anticipation of defeat. Or the climax might be the bloody retreat into Boston by the British troops, under fire from every stone wall and every woods as they fell back. The significance might be the human drama of men who had walked about forty-five miles, encountered opposition greater than they dreamed possible, and barely escaped with their lives as others of their number were killed.

How you decide to end a narrative depends on what you deem significant in the story you are telling. Place the story's climax at any number of places. Your choice should make an organizing principle for the entire paper. Readers should realize when they get to the climax that this has been your goal all along, that they have read all these other things to get here.

Let us review some of the ideas about narrative that we have covered, now reaching back for the journalistic questions that I suggest as analytical tools in both exploring the sources and writing about them.

In writing a narrative you must answer these questions. You don't have to write them down, though sometimes writing helps you think about them better. At least ponder them and be sure you have some answers.

1. Why am I telling this story?
2. Where do I want to begin?
3. What happened?
4. When did it happen?
5. Who or what caused those things to happen?
6. Which were the most important events that happened and which were the less important?
7. Who were the major characters in the drama?
8. What is the climax of the story, where everything in the

story comes to a head and where both my readers and I realize that the story is now ready to end?
9. Where do I want to end?
10. What does the story mean?
11. Which details help me tell the story more effectively?
12. Which details, though interesting, get in the way of my story and slow my readers down, perhaps hiding from them the real story I want to tell?

EXPOSITION

Expositions explain—philosophical ideas, causes of events, significance of actions, participants' motives, an organization's working, a political party's ideology. An exposition may show that one event mattered more than another in a historical situation. Expositions may define significant words; they may make comparisons.

Because exposition is a mode of writing, it may coexist with other modes in an essay. The narrator who tells *what* happened usually devotes some paragraphs to telling *why* it happened; answers to the question *why* lead to exposition, to explanation. Some historical essays may be balanced between narrative and exposition, telling what happened and why.

Some essays will be primarily expositions. You might write a paper explaining an idea or a complex of ideas. What did the founding fathers mean when they wrote the Second Amendment to the United States Constitution: "A well-regulated militia, being necessary to the security of a free State, the right of the people to keep and bear arms, shall not be infringed." You might compare books or thinkers or leaders or events. You might follow an idea through the years as thinkers wrestle with and redefine it. How did the communism of Plato, Marx, and the Brook Farm community in New England differ? What has laissez faire meant to different thinkers?

How one thinker influenced another or one set of ideas affected a historical event can make a good expository paper. You might even expound the significance of some technological invention. Here are a few expository subjects that may be appropriate in history courses:

> The view of human nature expressed in *The Federalist Papers*.
>
> A comparison between Thomas More's *Utopia* and Niccolò Machiavelli's *The Prince*.
>
> Luther's understanding of justification by faith alone.
>
> The meaning of Woodrow Wilson's attitude toward blacks.
>
> The concept of chivalry in nineteenth-century southern literature in the United States.
>
> The influence of Sir Walter Scott's novels in the American South during the nineteenth century.
>
> Sir Walter Scott's influence on Leopold von Ranke.
>
> A comparison between the constitutions of the United States and the Confederate States of America.
>
> Significance of the John Deere plow.
>
> Was World War I inevitable?
>
> The changing scholarly attitude toward Arthur Schlesinger Jr.'s *The Age of Jackson*.

All these subjects require us to analyze texts or events. You must explain things, relate some things to other things, infer things, perhaps ask some questions that no one can answer.

Here is an excerpt from one of the most famous books of the renaissance, Baldassare Castiglione's *Book of the Courtier:*

> There are also other exercises which, although not immediately dependent upon arms, still have much in common therewith and demand much manly vigor; and chief among these is the hunt, it seems to me, because it has a certain resemblance to war. It is a true pasttime for great lords, it befits a Courtier, and one understands why it was so much practiced among the ancients. He should also know how to swim, jump, run, throw stones; for, besides their usefulness in war, it is frequently necessary to show one's prowess in such things, whereby a good name is to be won, especially with the crowd (with whom one must reckon after all). Another noble exercise and most suitable for a man at court is the game of tennis which shows off the disposition of body, the quickness and litheness of every member, and all the qualities that are brought out by almost

every other exercise. Nor do I deem vaulting on horseback to be less worthy, which, though it is tiring and difficult, serves more than anything else to make a man agile and dextrous; and besides its usefulness, if such agility is accompanied by grace, in my opinion it makes a finer show than any other.

If, then, our Courtier is more than fairly expert in such exercises, I think he ought to put aside all others, such as vaulting on the ground, rope-walking, and the like, which smack of the juggler's trade and little befit a gentleman.[9]

Here is an exposition using this passage in a general treatment of the renaissance. The exposition explains the passage for general readers today. Insofar as possible, the expositor puts Castiglione's thoughts in other words, which may be more familiar and hence more understandable for readers today.

Baldassare Castiglione's The Book of the Courtier, the most frequently translated and printed book of the sixteenth century other than the Bible, presents it-self as a dialogue on the qualities that make a good courtier. Courtiers, as the name implies, were members of a prince's court or entourage, helping him in various ways to rule his domain. In the sixteenth century, when Italy was divided among multitudes of city states, princes needed talented men to help conduct finances, war, diplomacy, and other affairs so that they might retain power over a fickle and often rebellious populace. Courtiers rose on their talents but also on their ability to get along with other people and to impress their princes. Castiglione's dialogue became not only an entertainment but also a sort of

[9]Baldassare Castiglione, *The Book of the Courtier,* trans. Charles S. Singleton, Garden City, N.Y., Doubleday (Anchor Paperback), 1959, pp. 38–39.

handbook. Aspiring courtiers read it to learn how to conduct themselves as gentlemen and how to rise. It was the great manners book of its day, popular alike with Spanish kings and English Puritans.

Castiglione throughout writes on two levels. On one level the courtiers in his dialogue discuss ways of becoming more useful, better men. It is good to hunt, for hunting calls on many of the skills required in war. Evidently he referred to life in the open air, to riding on horseback in the chase, and to marksman- ship—all helpful training for soldiers. Swimming, jumping, running, and throwing stones offer what we would call physical conditioning and provide a sort of basic training for war.

On another level Castiglione's characters are al- ways eager not only to better their skills but to make a good impression. By performing feats of physical strength and agility, one wins a good name with the crowd, "with whom one must reckon after all." Tennis, with its leaping and quickness, displays the body. Jumping on horseback both helps a man become "agile and dextrous" and "makes a finer show than any other."

Some things make a bad show and are to be avoided no matter how useful they may be as bodily exercises. For some reason Castiglione cites "vaulting on the ground" as an act to be avoided, perhaps because that sort of leaping was a game for peasants who could not afford jumping horses. "Rope-walking," balancing one- self on a tightrope, is also scorned because it is one

of the tricks familiar to "jugglers," the traveling
entertainers who put on shows for city crowds much as
their spiritual descendants do today. Such entertainers were considered to be of the lower class and even
slightly dishonorable. They were often magicians and
practiced sleight of hand, and the trickery in their
acts smacked of deceit. The laws of the church forbade
priests to be "jugglers," and Castiglione obviously
felt that would-be courtiers lowered themselves by
learning such skills.

Throughout his big book, these two qualities come
to the fore again and again—skill and reputation. In
Castiglione's mind, the good courtier possessed both.
Thousands of readers pored over his pages to learn not
only what they should be but what they should seem to
be.

In this exposition the writer tries to make sense of a text from
the past, so that we can understand the ideas though the world has
greatly changed from the one that produced them; Castiglione's
thoughts are put into different words. The writer explains some of
the main purposes in the text and defines words. Castiglione used
the common word "juggler," which we might interpret as someone
who tosses several balls in the air at once without dropping any of
them. The older meaning in both Castiglione's Italian and in English was a street entertainer, usually some sort of magician. By
explaining this broader use, the writer makes the text he is ex-
pounding clearer. Always define the essential words in your exposition.

The exposition includes some inferences. The writer infers
that juggling is forbidden to the courtier because it seems like deceit, and courtiers are supposed to be honest. The writer infers that

jumping or "vaulting" on the ground is forbidden because that sort of athletic activity is common to peasants who cannot afford horses. One cannot prove an inference, but inferences provide plausible explanations that may help fill out the meaning in a text.

ARGUMENT

Historians use the mode named argument to take a position on a controversial subject. It can be said that every paper includes an argument, in that every paper has a main theme presented as the truth by the writer. In telling what happened at the Democratic National Convention in 1896, where William Jennings Bryan made his famous "Cross of Gold" speech, I argue in effect that my version of these events should be believed. In defining the word "mercantilism" as it was used by seventeenth-century economic thinkers, I argue that my definition is correct. Specialists in rhetoric often speak of "argument" as a synonym for "thesis," the point that the writer wishes to establish in an article or a book.

Yet in common usage, an argument is part of a debate, a dialogue between opposing views. Arguments include exposition, for they have to explain or expound the writer's point of view. In an argumentative essay the writer also seeks to prove that other points of view are wrong. Arguments are most interesting when the issues are large and important, the evidence is fairly used on both sides, and the writers are skilled and quick. The questions that create good arguments arise naturally as historians do their research, weigh evidence, and make judgments. Was Christianity, as Edward Gibbon held in the eighteenth century, a major cause for the decline and fall of the Roman Empire? Was Alger Hiss guilty of perjury, a crime for which a court convicted him in 1950 when he denied he had been a spy for the Soviet Union? Was Martin Luther anti-Semitic? Did Al Smith lose the presidential election in 1928 to Herbert Hoover because Smith was a Catholic? Was slavery the main cause behind the American Civil War? Did the peace movement in the United States shorten or prolong the Vietnam War?

The writing of history abounds with major arguments about what happened and why things happened in the past. These arguments go on because the evidence can be interpreted in different and often contradictory ways. Sometimes arguments go on until a consensus is gradually achieved. Some southern historians argued for years that Reconstruction was an economic and social calamity for the South after the Civil War; the consensus now is that Reconstruction was superficial and ineffective and that it hardly changed the social and economic conditions of the old Confederacy. Sometimes arguments rage for years, die down, smolder awhile, and flame up again. Was Socrates a threat to Athenian society, as claimed in the trial in which he was condemned to death? Consensus seemed to be reached that he was not; but in a recent book, journalist I. F. Stone has raised the issue once again, and his book has been attacked by modern defenders of Socrates.

If you read carefully in your sources, you will find places where authorities disagree. To find disagreements among historians fairly easily, you can look up reviews of their books. Historians often write articles about books or points of view. Jacob Burckhardt's *The Civilization of the Renaissance in Italy,* published in 1860, has provoked a library of response, books and articles arguing that he was right or wrong in his interpretation of the renaissance—or arguing that he was partly right and partly wrong. So too has Frederick Jackson Turner's frontier thesis.

The usual experience that the student of history undergoes is to study a great deal and to become convinced that someone else's argument is wrong. Francis Russell's books on the Sacco and Vanzetti case represent this sort of discovery. The consensus has been that Sacco and Vanzetti were innocent Italian immigrants hounded to their death by a vicious Yankee society for murders they did not commit. In 1955 Russell wrote an article supporting this point of view, an article published first in the *Antioch Review* and reprinted three years later with photographs in *American Heritage.* Slowly he changed his mind, and his publication of the books *Tragedy in Dedham* and *Sacco and Vanzetti: The Case Resolved* make a formidable attack on the previous consensus.

Stay tuned to your own intellectual impulses when you read sources. Where do others' arguments seem weak? How can the evidence be plausibly shown to add up to a conclusion other than that given in your sources? Often good argument is simply a matter of common sense: Can we believe that something might have happened in the way a writer tells us it happened? Many haters of President Franklin Roosevelt argued that Roosevelt knew about the Japanese attack on Pearl Harbor in 1941 before it happened but kept it secret because he wanted the United States to go to war. Such a conspiracy would have involved dozens, even hundreds of people—those who had broken the Japanese secret code for sending messages to their military and their diplomats, those who monitored Japanese broadcasts, those who translated them and took them to the State Department and to the White House, the officials to whom they reported. Is it plausible to believe that such a vast conspiracy could have taken place without anyone who was part of it ever stepping forward to tell about it? Our experience with human beings and their apparently immortal yearning to tell secrets seems to indicate that the answer to such a question would be no.

When you feel uneasy with someone else's argument about how things happened or why they happened or who was involved, take time to check the reason behind your uneasiness. Study the evidence over and over. See where your study leads you. Don't take anything for granted.

RULES FOR ARGUMENT IN HISTORICAL WRITING

Here are a few rules that will help you make convincing arguments. Study them carefully, and keep them in mind when you are reading others' arguments.

1. Always state your own argument quickly and concisely as early as possible in your paper.

> In recent years, Thomas More's Utopia of 1516 has been savagely attacked as a repressive police state akin to modern totalitarian states. Max Beerbohm, famed British wit, is supposed to have said, "Utopia? Oh, pardon me. I thought it was hell." And the late Richard S. Sylvester, first executive editor of the Yale Edition of More's complete works, so disliked the vision of the Utopian commonwealth that he argued in a

well-known article that More never intended his myth-
ical island's society to be taken as an ideal. These
are the views of moderns who have had experiences and
developed a culture that More never dreamed of, and
they are off the mark. We do not know just how literally More intended readers of his time to take every
detail of Utopian life, but we can know that he intended for them to take the work seriously and that
behind the details lies a glittering ideal that he
proposed as a reforming impulse for his society.

In this opening paragraph, the argument for the paper is set
within the context, a scholarly debate that is here summarized. Like
most formal papers in history, this one is directed toward an audience that already knows something about the subject. The writer
does not have to identify Thomas More. He assumes his readers
know that More was an English statesman, author of a work published in 1516 and called *Utopia*. The writer assumes, too, that readers will know that the book *Utopia* is an account of an island society
off the coast of the New World, where a European traveler has
found people living according to their idea of reason. Assuming
that his readers have this background knowledge, the writer can
move quickly to the substance of his argument, that the more traditional interpretation of *Utopia* is true and that more recent at-
tempts to revise this view are mistaken. Within one paragraph,
readers know which position the writer will take in this argument.

2. When you make an assertion, provide examples as evidence.

Assertion	Luther grew more and more conservative af-
Examples	ter the 1525 peasants' rebellion. He had de-
Examples support- ing the generaliza- tion made in the first sentence.	clared that Christians had no need for the law but only for the grace of God. This had been Luther's "gospel" of faith instead of works.

> Now he declared to people sitting with him at
> table that one should preach the gospel to the
> good and the law to the evil masses. The evil
> masses included the peasants. "One should not
> preach the gospel to peasants," he said.

Assertions alone cannot carry an argument, no matter how sincere you are about them or how true you think they may be. Readers must always have some reason for believing you.

3. Always give the fairest possible treatment to people against whom you may be arguing.

Never distort work done by someone who disagrees with your position. Such distortions are cowardly and unfair, and if you are found out in such conduct, readers will reject your work, the good part along with the bad. Treat your adversaries as erring friends, not as foes to be slain, and you will always be more convincing to most readers, who want writers to be fair and benign in argument.

> William L. Shirer, one of the most popular commen-
> tators on the history of Nazi Germany, thought that
> Martin Luther started a current in Germany that led to
> Adolf Hitler. Shirer quoted Luther's fierce pro-
> nouncements against the Jews as proof of his case, and
> it is doubtless true that Luther's hostility to the
> Jews makes him sound like a precursor to the Nazis.
> But far more differences than similarities separated
> Luther from the Nazis, and although Mr. Shirer's vivid
> account of the rise and fall of Nazi Germany has the
> vitality peculiar to an author who was eyewitness to
> the events he describes, in likening Luther to Hitler,
> he was wrong.

4. Always admit weaknesses in your argument.

> As Robert Caro amply points out, Lyndon Johnson
> was an ambitious and ruthless man. No one can doubt
> that he drove relentlessly toward the top and that he
> was not always scrupulous with the truth. He lied when
> lying suited him. But even if one admits to Lyndon
> Johnson's dark side, one is still left with Johnson's
> impressive legislative leadership in relieving the
> humiliations and hardships suffered by many who had
> been the outcasts of American society. Johnson may not
> have been a good man, but he did much good for his
> country.

If you deny obvious truths about the subject you are arguing,
knowledgeable readers will see what you are doing, and they will
lose confidence in your objectivity. If you admit the weaknesses or
the counterarguments, you will appear more authoritative and
more honest, and readers will be more inclined to agree with your
arguments.

5. Stay on the subject throughout your essay so that your
argument is not submerged in meaningless detail.

Writers may be tempted to put everything they know into a
paper. They have worked hard to gather the information; they find
it interesting; they want readers to see how much work they have
done and how much they know; they therefore pad papers with
much information not relevant to the subject. If you argue that
Lyndon Johnson's leadership helped blacks and the poor and other
groups in America, do not clutter your paper with needless biographical information. Limit yourself to the evidence that supports
your case, to the arguments that might be brought against your
case, and to building your own conclusion. You do not need to
give us details about Johnson's school days, the election campaigns
that he waged, or matters about his private life. Such details,

though interesting to a biographer, would only clutter your paper and perhaps keep readers from following the theme of your argument throughout.

6. Avoid common fallacies.

"Fallacies" are illogical arguments that pose as logical statements. We have mentioned one without defining it—the "straw man." People set up straw men when they argue against positions that their opponents have not taken or attribute without evidence bad motives to opponents. A historian might argue that the sixteenth century was marked by much skepticism in matters of religion; an opponent might unjustly argue in response that the sixteenth century could not have experienced religious skepticism because the scientific world view held by Galileo and Newton was unknown—as if religious skepticism depended on a scientific world view. Worse, opponents might argue that the historian who was not religious wanted to find skepticism in the sixteenth century. Neither of these issues has anything to do with the original argument; they are straw men, arguments that may be easily defeated and so give the appearance of victory—except that they are beside the point. They have nothing to do with the evidence the writer has brought forward to establish that religious skepticism lived in the sixteenth century.

Don't assume that merely because something happened after something else, the first happening caused the second. Forms of this fallacy abound in historical writing. (The common Latin expression often used to describe this fallacy is *post hoc ergo propter hoc,* "Because this happened after that, it happened because of that.") Some religious people have argued that because art recovered from the ruins of Pompeii shows vivid portrayals of homosexual and heterosexual intercourse, the Roman Empire fell on account of sexual promiscuity. Pompeii was destroyed by a volcanic eruption of Mt. Vesuvius in A.D. 79. The last Roman emperor in the West was deposed in A.D. 476. It would seem a bit extreme to say that because of sexual license in the first century, Rome fell in the sixth century. Historical causation is much more complicated than that.

A subtler problem with this fallacy arises with events that are closely related though one does not necessarily cause the other. The stock market in New York crashed in October 1929; the Great

Depression followed. The crash contributed to the lack of confidence that made the Great Depression a terrible event, but it would be a distortion to say that the crash caused the Depression. Both seemed to have been caused by the same economic forces. In this sort of relation it becomes most necessary to think out the various strands leading to causation and to avoid making things seem too simple.

By all means avoid the bandwagon fallacy, the easy assumption that because a great number of historians agree on an issue, their position must be the right one. Consensus by experts is not to be scorned, but experts can also be prone to prejudices. Francis Russell tells about the rush of hostility directed against him when he attacked the previous consensus about the Sacco-Vanzetti case. Great historical work has been done by people who doggedly pursued the evidence against the influence set up by the consensus.

CONCLUDING REMARKS ABOUT MODES

Thinking about modes of writing will help you define more precisely the reason for your paper in history. Too frequently in history courses, students start writing with no idea about why they are writing or the point they finally want to make about a topic. Forcing yourself to think about the modes will make you face this issue, and that approach will make your writing easier. It will also help your readers understand your purposes quickly and follow your prose as you develop your thoughts.

Knowing the modes is not in itself a solution to the problems that come up in writing. You don't sit down at your desk and say, "Well, I'll throw in a few narrative paragraphs here, and then I'll give some exposition." Thinking about the modes will guide you in editing your work. A paper that you conceive as primarily an exposition can fall into a long narrative that does not really explain much of anything. You can spot that narrative sprawl when you reread your paper and edit to return to your major purpose. The idea is not to force yourself into unnatural manipulation of your paper but simply to let you keep in mind some of the broader possibilities in any writing task.

Gathering Information and Writing Drafts

Writing is hard work, but multitudes of people do it successfully. It is not miraculous or magical. To write well you must cultivate the ability to see clearly and to record accurately what you observe and read and think about. You can write well if you are willing to work patiently at it. The frustrations are immense; every writer suffers them. Yet the rewards of good writing make the labor worthwhile.

To start, you may need to rid yourself of some common superstitions about writing. One is that writers are somehow inspired, that real writers sit down at the desk and turn out articles and books with the greatest of ease. Another is that if you have to write several drafts of an essay or even a book, you are a not a good writer. Still another is that if you labor to get what you want to say on paper, you are not going to improve it very much if you write a second or even a third draft.

A few writers manage to write without revising—but only a few. The almost unanimous testimony by good writers in all disciplines is that writing is always difficult and that they must write several drafts before they are satisfied with an essay or a book. A rule of thumb holds that the easier a piece of writing is to read, the harder it was to write.

Good writers work through to clear understanding of their own thoughts. All writers sometimes begin an essay without a clear idea about what they think or what they want to say. The work of writing and rewriting clarifies their own minds and strengthens their hold on their own ideas. Once they have worked out an essay, they have thoughts that cannot be blown away by the first person who comes along with a firm opinion. Writing has a confirming quality, valuable for all those who want to know their own mind. When we have measured out our words on the page, tested them all to see if each is the word we want in that place and for that purpose, questioned our arguments and answered those questions, and arranged the whole in a readable essay, we can have confidence in the fruit of our own mind. Confidence does not mean that we will never change our opinions. Far from it; it does mean that we have challenged our opinions, disciplined them, and made them fit to be put abroad in the company of educated men and women.

Good writing influences others. The most influential historians have usually written well. A well-written book or article can profoundly influence both other historians and ordinary people who happen to be interested in history. Well-written books are those most likely to become subjects of public discourse. Barbara Tuchman's *Guns of August,* about the opening days of World War I in 1914 and *Proud Tower,* her study of European culture at the turn of the century, have often been quoted by public officials. It is said that President John F. Kennedy was reading *Guns of August* during the Cuban Missile Crisis in 1962 and consequently did his best to avoid any escalation of the crisis that might lead to a horrible war.

Even historians who lack the dramatic popular success won by Barbara Tuchman can be influential. A solid monograph on a difficult subject may make other historians rethink their positions, and that in turn may influence the young historians whom they teach. Ideas once committed to writing remain alive to be picked up years later. American historian Frederick Jackson Turner wrote little throughout his long life, but a paper he wrote in 1893, "The Significance of the Frontier in American History," continues to be debated, attacked, defended, and modified almost a century afterward.

All writers use some sort of process—a series of steps that lead them from discovering a subject to writing the final draft of the paper. Different writers write according to different rituals. Eventually you will find your own way of doing things. In this chapter we will walk you through some steps followed by many writers as they work. Read them carefully; some of the suggestions may help you. At least they will illuminate your own writing procedure and perhaps help you understand it better and make it more efficient.

I. FIND A TOPIC

History papers, like all other papers in college, begin with an assignment:

> One requirement in this course will be a research paper. Choose a topic. Let me approve it. Make the paper ten to fifteen pages long. Don't make it longer than fifteen pages. The paper will be due two weeks before the end of the term.

> I want you to write a ten-page paper defending the British side in the dispute between Great Britain and the American colonies that led to the American Revolution.

> Do a book review of William J. Bouwsma's *John Calvin*.

> You must do a book review for this course.

The more specific assignments come with a built-in advantage: you know what you are going to write about before you start. Nowadays most assignments in history courses are probably more like the first in this list. You are told how long the paper should be. The paper must be on a topic related to the course you are taking. If it is a research paper, you assume that it will involve work in the library, and you must document your sources with footnotes or endnotes and bibliography. What will you write about? That is up to you.

For many students, finding the topic is one of the hardest parts of writing. Professional historians discover the same difficulty. What can I write about that will interest others? What topic offers me the chance to write something original? How can I define an issue in such a way that I can find an absorbing problem in it, one that I can comment upon intelligently? The ability to find your own topic in part reflects how much you know about the material and in part tests your ability to think about it. Defining your own subjects for papers is good discipline. A liberal-arts education—including education in history—should teach you to ask questions. Writers ask themselves interesting questions and then try to answer them.

Start with your own interests; few of us do well with topics that do not interest us. You must have some interest in the material, or you would not have taken the course. You must be curious about people, events, documents, or problems considered in the course. This curiosity will make you pose some questions, even when the material you are studying seems fairly straightforward. Why did Machiavelli say that it is better to be feared than loved? Was Samuel Gompers conservative or progressive? Why did the Grant administration have all those scandals? How historical is Gore Vidal's novel *Julian,* or his novel *Lincoln*? What in American culture in 1936 made the novel *Gone With the Wind* so popular? How has capital punishment evolved in America? These questions give you a start toward a paper.

Sometimes you may be interested in a well-worn topic. Why did the Confederate Army under General Lee lose at Gettysburg? What qualities in Christianity made it attractive to people in the Roman Empire during the first three centuries after Christ? What was humanism in the renaissance? Don't be afraid to tackle these problems. Yes, at first glance you may think that everything has been said that can be said. Usually your own study of the sources will show you that yet other questions lie within these topics to be asked and answered. If nothing else, you can survey the literature about these problems and write about the different conclusions other historians have arrived at in their studies. Such interpretive papers on work by other historians are extremely common and very valuable.

Yours should be an *informed* interest. You have to know something before you can write anything about history. Don't write an opinionated article off the top of your head. Good historians read, ask questions about their reading, read again, and try to get things right. It is typical of a historian to write with a pile of notes or a collection of notebooks beside the paper or the keyboard.

Write Down Your Early Thoughts about the Material

Pianists do finger exercises before they play, and baseball players take batting practice before a game. These activities help them limber up for the real thing, getting their bodies into the rhythms of a relaxed situation, rhythms that continue even under the greater tensions in the game.

You can do similar exercises as you prepare to write. You can think about what you have heard in lecture or in discussion sections and about what you have read, and you can jot down as many questions as you can make up about the material. It's a good idea to keep a notebook for every paper you do, perhaps one of the hard-bound blank books you can easily carry around and use when thoughts pop into your head. You can write on 3 × 5 cards, on yellow pads, or even on a computer. I find notebooks easier to carry around and easier to write in on the spur of the moment.

The main point is to start jotting down ideas about several possible topics unless some idea has already struck with such force that you know you will write about it. When you make a preliminary scan of secondary sources, ask as many questions as you can. Write these questions down. Set down your thoughts about the topic. As you go on in this random, almost playful writing, several things may happen.

You may become more aware of your own interests.

You will define and then refine your topic.

You will start assembling evidence for your paper.

You will start shaping the argument that you will make in the paper.

It's usually good to start writing down your ideas as soon as you can. Don't make this preliminary writing a rough draft. Simply set down your thoughts, perhaps in disconnected paragraphs that allow you to work out some of your ideas. You may even write sentences without trying to work them into paragraphs. You may just ramble about aspects of your subject.

Inexperienced writers often assume that a writer does all the research first and then writes. The writing process falls then into neat blocks: one learns; one writes. On the contrary, most experienced writers find that no matter how much they know about a subject at the start, the act of writing itself stimulates them to ask new questions, to pursue new leads, and even to come to conclusions different from those they earlier assumed to be the fruits of their research. For the experienced writer, the writing proceeds by leaping forward and then leaping back, which we may diagram like this:

Preliminary investigation
> Writing some preliminary notes, including thoughts and questions

More investigation
> Writing more notes, perhaps a rough outline of the paper the writer intends to write

More investigation
> A first draft that reveals to the writer the shape of his or her thoughts, new questions to ask, gaps or fuzziness in facts the writer knows

More investigation
> A second draft that begins to look fairly near completion, though it may even now reveal more questions

More investigation
> A final draft

Of course different writers proceed in different ways. The procedure outlined here is typical, but it is not the only one. Now and then everyone is able to grasp a topic so thoroughly after careful research and note-taking that the only task remaining is to set the notes out on the table and write the paper. That is a relatively rare proceeding.

To postpone writing until one has done all possible research on the subject can be disastrous. Many historians have frustrated themselves and those who had great expectations for them by assuming that they had to read one more book or gather one more bit of information before they could start writing. That was Frederick Jackson Turner's fate: after propounding his "frontier thesis" of American history, he was expected to write a great deal on the subject. He signed several contracts with publishers without ever being able to produce the books. Historian Richard Hofstadter wrote these sad words about Turner; they should be stamped on the skin of every historian tempted to put off writing.

> He became haunted by the suspicion, so clear to his biographer, that he was temperamentally "incapable of the sustained effort necessary to complete a major scholarly volume." "I hate to write," he blurted out to a student in later years, "it is almost impossible for me to do so." But it was a self-description arrived at after long and hard experience. In 1901 when he was forty, Turner had signed contracts for nine books, not one of which was ever to be written and only a few of which were even attempted, and his life was punctuated by an endless correspondence with disappointed publishers. For an academic family, the Turners lived expensively and entertained generously, and the income from any of the textbooks he promised to write would have been welcome, but the carrot of income was no more effective than the stick of duty and ambition. Turner's teaching load at Wisconsin was for a time cut down, in the hope that it would clear the way for his productive powers, but what it produced was only a misunderstanding with university trustees. Turner's reluctance to address himself to substantive history was so overwhelming that A. B. Hart, a martinet of an editor who presided with ruthless energy over the authors of the American Nation series, extracted *Rise of the New West* out of him only by dint of an extraordinary series of nagging letters and bullying telegrams. Hart in the end counted this his supreme editorial achievement. "It ought to be carved on my tombstone that I was the only man in the world that secured what might be called an adequate volume from Turner," he wrote to Max Farrand; and Farrand, one of Turner's closest friends, who watched his agonized efforts to produce his last unfinished volume in the splendid setting provided by the Huntington Library, sadly concluded that he would not have finished it had he lived forever.
>
> Over the years Turner had built up a staggering variety of psychological and mechanical devices, familiar to all observers of academia, to stand between himself and the finished task. There was, for example, a kind of perfectionism, which sent him off looking for one more curious fact or decisive bit of evidence, and impelled the elaborate rewriting of drafts that had already been rewritten. There were the hopelessly optimistic plans for what he would do in the next two or twelve or eighteen months, whose inevitable nonfulfillment brought new lapses into paralyzing despair. There was an

undisciplined curiosity, an insatiable, restless interest in *everything,* without a correspondingly lively determination to consummate anything; a flitting from one subject to another, a yielding to the momentary pleasures of research as a way of getting further from the discipline of writing. ("I have a lot of fun exploring, getting lost and getting back, and telling my companions about it," he said, but "telling" here did not mean writing.) There was overresearch and overpreparation with the consequent inability to sort out the important from the trivial—a small mountain of notes, for example, gathered for a trifling projected children's book of 25,000 words on George Rogers Clark. There were, for all the unwritten books, thirty-four large file drawers bulging with notes on every aspect of American history. There were elaborate maps, drawn to correlate certain forces at work in American politics. There were scrapbooks, and hours spent filling them in. . . . There were, of course, long letters of explanation to publishers, and other letters setting forth new plans for books. There was indeed an entire set of letters to Henry Holt and Company, examining various possible titles for the last unfinishable volume—letters that the exasperated publishers finally cut off by suggesting that the matter might well wait until the book itself became a reality.[1]

Most writers discover a remarkable stimulus to the mind in writing. Ideas begin to flow as the hand grips the pen or taps on the keyboard. It may have something to do with hand–brain coordination. Whatever it is, writers often find that their minds start acting so rapidly as they write that they can scarcely write down everything they think about a subject. You may think you do not have a lot to say on a subject. As you write down random questions and thoughts, you may discover that you have more to say than you thought. That in turn will give you confidence to continue. All writers face these nagging questions: Do I really have anything to say? Is this hard work worth the effort? Will anyone ever be interested in this project? By starting to put down your ideas early, you learn to answer these questions in the affirmative. Hardly anything is more beneficial to your writing.

[1]Richard Hofstadter, *The Progressive Historians,* New York, Alfred A. Knopf, 1968, pp. 115–117.

Here are some questions that someone wanting to write a paper on Woodrow Wilson might write after preliminary reading and perhaps after hearing lectures about Wilson in class:

What did people who knew him think of Woodrow Wilson?

Who supported him, and who opposed him?

How did diplomats at the Paris Peace Conference in 1919 regard Wilson? What did they say about him in their memoirs?

What were Wilson's relations with his Secretary of State William Jennings Bryan?

What was Wilson's attitude toward blacks?

Who were the people closest to him?

Why did Wilson feel compelled to be the leader at the Peace Conference in 1919?

Why did people vote for him?

Where in the country did Wilson have his greatest support? Where the least?

When did his popularity begin to wane?

When was his popularity at its height?

You can pursue your questions until you find one especially interesting to you. These preliminary questions may overlap; don't worry about that. The questions make you think, and in time you will find one that especially interests you. You can then narrow your research to try to answer it. You cannot learn everything there is to know about Wilson in one semester, and you certainly cannot write everything there is to write about Wilson in one paper. A good list of questions will eventually turn up one that will give you a direction for further inquiry.

II. LIMIT YOUR TOPIC

Our last paragraph brings us to essential wisdom that every writer must learn: You can't write about everything. Keep these two points in mind:

1. Your topic must be defined narrowly enough to allow you to write an interesting, informative essay within the limits imposed by your assignment.
2. Your topic must be defined according to the sources available.

On the first point, be sure your topic is narrow enough to let you say something interesting and original about it. Most papers in history courses run from about eight to about twenty-five pages, depending on the instructor's requirements. Within those limitations you cannot write an interesting and original paper entitled "Martin Luther" or "Abraham Lincoln" or "Woodrow Wilson" or "Susan B. Anthony." You can only do a summary about the person's life—suitable, perhaps, for an encyclopedia article but not for a thoughtful essay in which you try to make a special point. Pick an issue that you can study in depth and write about within the space you have. People will believe you only if you give them some reason to believe you—some evidence. Dealing with evidence takes time—or space on the pages of a manuscript. By the time you have dealt with significant evidence, you will find yourself straining to keep within the limits of the assignment.

You can interpret an influential doctrine propounded by Martin Luther: what power did he think ministers should have over lay people in the church? You can consider an issue in Abraham Lincoln's administration; what did Abraham Lincoln think of the American Indians? You can consider how a policy such as racial segregation evolved in the federal bureaucracy during the Woodrow Wilson administration. For any of these subjects you can collect a number of primary and secondary sources, study them thoroughly, and use them to support the case you want to make for your interpretation of the material.

Be sure you have access to sources for material you want to write. Students usually underestimate the sources available to them. A good prowl through the library as you are looking for a subject may reveal more than you dreamed was there. It's worth repeating again and again that reference librarians are underused helpers in most schools. Smart students and smart professors interested in writing quickly learn to talk to reference librarians about material that is available and where sources can be found. Interlibrary loans can bring in books from all over the country, usually for a nominal fee and sometimes for nothing.

Even so, you may come up with a paper topic for which adequate sources are not available in the time you have to work. If you should try to write about Woodrow Wilson's attitude toward blacks, you would be hard pressed to do so if you cannot study the Princeton edition of Wilson's works. If you want to write about the early development of printing, you will have a hard time if your library does not have some examples, at least on microfilm, of early printing. When you cannot find adequate sources, you cannot write an adequate paper. You may be able to change your topic to fit the sources you have; if your library does not have the Princeton edition of Wilson's papers, it may have enough biographical studies to allow you to write a good paper on the different opinions about Wilson that various writers have put forth.

III. DO RESEARCH

When you do research you do several things:

You consult sources.

You formulate a thesis that helps you interpret those sources.

You weigh the sources to decide which are most important to your purpose. That is to say, you look at the sources critically to see any evidence they may hold for and against your thesis.

You organize the evidence you draw from sources to tell the story you want to tell.

You put a design on the information so that it makes an essay.

You cite the sources to let readers know where you have gotten your information.

Remember my earlier advice. Because of the linear way in which I have described the steps in research, you may think that historians invariably follow these steps neatly one after the other. Not so! In practice things seldom run so smoothly. Historians may begin with one topic, discover another when they do their research, and change their minds at least slightly again when they start writing. As they write, they may go back and redefine their topic profoundly, and as they redefine the topic they must do more research. Writing often reveals gaps in our knowledge that drive us back to do more research.

A. Start in the Reference Room

Start your research in the reference room of your library. A good first step is to read several encyclopedia articles related to the subject you think might provide a good paper. Consult the most recent edition of several encyclopedias, though older editions may be enlightening about scholarly opinions current when they were published. If you look up the same subject in a multitude of reference works, many essential facts about your topic will be stamped in your memory. If in an American history course you decide that you might like to do a paper on President Woodrow Wilson, read five or six encyclopedia articles about him. Read some written for old editions of encyclopedias published during his life and more recent editions published after his death. You will have different perspectives on his career as well as background knowledge about many events in his life.

Your reference room will have the standard general encyclopedias—the multivolume sets such as *Britannica, Americana,* and *Collier's,* and the single-volume encyclopedias such as *New Columbia Encyclopedia* and *Random House Encyclopedia.*

Look also into the reference works that may be specifically addressed to your field of inquiry. You might choose a topic related to religion. *The New Catholic Encyclopedia* in fifteen volumes is a treasury of modern scholarship on religious figures and religious movements of all sorts. (*The Catholic Encyclopedia,* which *The New Catholic Encyclopedia* replaced, will probably be in the stacks of your library; it is still extremely useful, though the writing is not so sprightly as that in the newer version.) *The New Standard Jewish Encyclopedia* is a similar source gathering the history of the Jewish people and Judaism. It is enlightening to read the articles on, say, Martin Luther, in these works. All these articles will have brief bibliographies at the end listing some of the standard works, in which you can find more information on the subject.

The *International Encyclopedia of the Social Sciences* in nineteen volumes provides much information on issues interesting to historians. The *Social Science Encyclopedia* published in one thick volume in 1985 and edited by Adam Kuper and Jessica Kuper, is a mine of recent scholarship on social studies. The *Funk and Wagnalls Standard Dictionary of Folklore, Mythology and Legend* in two volumes will give you information about beliefs prevalent in many societies.

The *Encyclopedia of World Art* in fifteen volumes is filled with information about artists, works of art, museums, patrons, and the subjects of art. *The New Grove Dictionary of Music* in twenty volumes does much the same thing with music, so that if you want to know something about how Luther figured in art you can look him up in one, and to learn about his musical contributions you can look him up in the other.

There are also special reference books for historians. The American Historical Association's *Guide to Historical Literature,* last published in 1961, is out of date now, but it is a good account of works in history published before that date. The multivolume *Cambridge Ancient History,* the *Cambridge Mediaeval History,* and the *New Cambridge Modern History* are filled with authoritative articles, sometimes written with little verve, but still worthwhile. The *Harvard Guide to American History* in two volumes is useful. The *Dictionary of National Biography* is indispensable for any work on British history. The *Dictionary of American Biography* is much inferior, but one can find there interesting information about important Americans who may be subjects of historical research.

Don't hesitate to use current works in foreign languages in your reference room. Even if you do not know the language, you may discover illustrations or other useful materials. With a year or two of study in the language, you may discover that you can read the materials far better than you suspected, and that discovery may draw you into further use of it—an advantage to the student of history, for which knowledge of foreign languages is essential to advanced work in nearly all the historical fields.

REFERENCE LIBRARIANS

Use your reference librarians at this stage in your research. Reference librarians help people find information. Perhaps because of vanity, inexperienced writers hesitate to ask questions; they do not want to appear ignorant. Experienced writers ask questions all the time. They know they do not know everything; they know they have not read all the books. Reference librarians are there to be helpful, and experienced writers seek their help.

BIBLIOGRAPHIES

Always compile a bibliography while you are doing research. Start early, and you will save yourself much grief. You can jot down titles in a notebook or on 3 × 5 cards. If you begin in the reference room of your library, record the full bibliographic references both to the articles you read and to the recommendations for further reading that you will find in the bibliographies appended to those articles. Look up your subject and related subjects in the library card catalogue. Consult books and articles in which bibliographies and notes appear. In all the places where other scholars have done research on your subject or on subjects related to yours, you will find titles. Be sure you study the journals in your field. Now let's consider these steps one at a time.

B. Use Primary Sources: Editions of Complete and Selected Works

Be on the lookout for editions of written works by the people who may enter your paper. Using works by the people you write about will help satisfy the general requirement that good history papers be written from primary sources. When you use any edition of collected or selected works, check the dates of publication. Sometimes several editions of the same works have been published; usually, but not always, the best editions are the latest.

These editions of works may be of different sorts. The most valuable are editions of the complete works in which every surviving text is collected, sometimes with other materials. The papers of all the American presidents are slowly making their way into print. Some of these, such as the papers of Woodrow Wilson and those of Andrew Johnson, are nearly complete. Others are only beginning. The most valuable source for a paper on Woodrow Wilson is the great Princeton edition of his complete papers, edited by Arthur Link and others.

Use the indexes in such editions. If you become interested in

Wilson's attitudes toward black Americans, look in the index to see both where blacks are mentioned in general and to see which black leaders are mentioned. (In the Princeton edition of Wilson's works, entries for black Americans are found under the heading "Negroes.")

The papers of many presidential confidants and government servants are published. The papers of Edward Mandell House, long a confidant of President Wilson, have been published. Political papers of many sorts in other countries may be published, and you should examine the library card catalogue to see if any of these editions are available to you in considering your chosen topic. Lloyd George, prime minister of Great Britain at the end of World War I, published a large autobiography in which he spoke frequently—and critically—about Wilson. If you write on the attitude toward Wilson among heads of state with whom he worked, consult Lloyd George's work. As your knowledge about people around Wilson enlarges, you can consult the library or bibliographies in encyclopedia articles about them to see what books they wrote.

Complete editions of works by people with extremely varied careers are also widely available. The works of Benjamin Franklin, James Boswell, and Thomas More have been rolling off the presses at Yale University for several decades now. Almost every large university press is involved in publishing somebody's complete works. Often these editions have long and informative introductory essays and extended commentaries. In *The Yale Edition of the Complete Works of St. Thomas More,* every quotation More gives from the works of another writer, ancient or otherwise, has been either located or else reported as unfound. Nearly all have been found. Indexes to each volume make finding various topics and names easy. The Toronto edition of Erasmus' works in English translation offers a similar wealth of information in its notes, as does the Latin edition of Erasmus' works (he wrote only in Latin), which is a joint Dutch-English publishing venture. An excellent way of writing a paper for almost any course is to find an edition of works by someone studied in the course, to read in that edition for a time, and to discover a subject that makes you curious.

Sometimes editions of selected works are available. The danger in selected works is obvious; the selection depends on judgments by editors working at a specific time and place, and anything important to them may mean less to later generations.

Editions of correspondence are common. Most of us love to read letters because, like photographs, they give us a sense of intimacy with bygone times and people we have not known. Like photographs, letters are quickly datable. One quickly sees that they belong to a time and place, and so in the eternal flux of things, they seem to make time stand still for a moment. Collections of correspondence provide intimate insights to historians for the very reasons we all enjoy them. They give us figures in relatively unguarded prose, commenting on the daily life, often without the caution that limits more public utterances. The letter writer's private *persona* or personality is often different and more winning than the public image displayed in speeches or writings intended for a large audience. Or it may be less so. Cicero's speeches and his writings on subjects such as old age reveal an attractive man, removed from self-seeking and pettiness. His letters often give an opposite view. But then that is the way with letters. They may reveal contradictions between the writers' private thoughts and public utterances—and they become grain for the historian to grind and to bake into bread. Letters also provide factual information that allows us to know where people mentioned—including the writers—were and what they were doing at specific times.

Published diaries are often available, and unpublished diaries—usually in the original form in which they were written—abound in many library collections. Keeping diaries has been common for centuries. Like letters, they are often popular enough to cause someone to publish them after the writers have died. Ralph Waldo Emerson kept an extensive journal throughout the nineteenth century, and in it we see anxieties that do not appear in the serene prose of his published essays and lectures. In our century Harold Nicolson, English writer and diplomat; Virginia Woolf, English writer; Harold Ickes, New Deal politician; and dozens of other outstanding figures or witnesses of important events have kept journals that have been published. They provide a mine of information and impressions. Whether the information is accurate or the impressions widespread will always be a problem for historians. People do not like to write bad things about themselves, even in their private diaries, and so diaries are not necessarily altogether accurate merely because they are personal. But they are still fascinating and valuable as historical sources.

Bibliographies will also include major works written by the person you are studying. Many people write autobiographies, among the most untrustworthy of historical sources because of the writers' natural desire to put themselves in the best possible light for posterity. Still they are there, and all carry some truth—though some are more truthful than others. Autobiographies are not, of course, the only works you will consult if you are interested in a historical personage. The other works that person has published will also furnish information that may be useful for your paper.

Thus far we have spoken of editions relating to the individual's writing and career. Often editions of sources relating to a general topic are also collected and published. One of the most monumental of these collections is *The War of the Rebellion: A Compilation of the Official Records of the Union and Confederate Armies,* published in seventy volumes and incorporating, it seems, a record of almost every scrap of paper exchanged within the armies on both sides in the Civil War. The *Calendar of State Papers, Spanish* includes English translations of all the letters exchanged between the Spanish ambassadors in London and their sovereigns at home during much of the sixteenth century and so is an edition of many sorts of documents, not all by the same author. Generations of historians have used *Documents Illustrative of English Church History,* edited by Henry Gee and William John Hardy, in one large volume published in 1921. These and many other collections may help in your research. Whatever the topic, check to see, for you might well find a collection of published documents related to your paper.

More recent editions are usually better than the older ones. The discipline of scholarly editing is difficult, its techniques demanding, and its technology constantly changing and improving. The scholarly editor's aim is first to publish a text as near to the original as possible and as faithful to the author's intentions as those can be known.

Faulty editions sow confusion and misinformation in historical studies. Patrick Henry's speeches were probably never given in the form they had when once memorized by American school children; we know these speeches from an unreliable edition put together—and probably much of it composed—years after the originals were delivered. Some older editors of selected or complete works changed the incorrect grammar and spelling in documents that came into their hands. Sometimes they even changed the wording in an effort to clarify meanings, often departing drastically from the author's intention. Far too frequently editors eliminated profanity, obscenity, and other comments they thought likely to reflect poorly on the writer.

Sometimes writers change their own minds and amend their works. The most authoritative handwritten copy of Abraham Lincoln's Gettysburg Address differs in several ways from the published version that Lincoln edited before it was printed. Indeed, Lincoln made several handwritten copies, and no two of them are exactly alike. Sometimes these variations in documents are insignificant, but they can be meaningful. Political figures change their minds, and one can trace the zigzagging ideas in their works. President Harry Truman was at first unwilling to make an American commitment to defend South Korea after World War II, but he changed his mind before the fact of invasion of South Korea by the North Koreans supported by Joseph Stalin of Russia in 1950. Letters and memos from the Truman administration give evidence for this change of heart—and for some vagueness in expressing it to the North Koreans and to the Russians.

The *Calendar of State Papers, Spanish,* mentioned above, calls to mind the English practice—sometimes duplicated elsewhere—of publishing calendars that may be chronological lists of documents held in an archive. The *Calendar of State Papers, Spanish* includes full or partial translations of huge numbers of letters sent to and from Spanish diplomats in London during the sixteenth century. Other calendars may give only short summaries of the documents in the English archives. Often these summaries are sufficient to the historian's purposes. Sometimes researchers must look at the documents themselves because they discover that the summary does not make sense or is otherwise inaccurate. Even with all the headaches associated with their use, such calendars are essential for some research. You can use them to trace an issue as it develops or to see the rise and fall of a man in royal service. Often they provide helpful background information for a subject you are exploring. They give powerful immediacy to your sense of the period you may be studying, and you will probably find them exciting to read.

C. Secondary Sources

The bibliographies in the articles you read in reference works will give you a start toward the primary sources for your study. They will also start you toward the secondary sources.

BOOKS

The secondary sources will be of two general types—books and articles. A few bibliographies are annotated. That is, the compiler of the bibliography tells you something about the books and articles listed there.

> Contamine, Philippe, *War in the Middle Ages,* trans. Michael Jones, New York, Basil Blackwell, 1986. A lively account of how wars were fought from the barbarian age to the renaissance. Includes not only an analysis of tactics and strategy but also discusses theological and ethical attitudes toward war. Illustrated with both photographs and diagrams.

An annotated bibliography may be unreliable; the writer may judge some books too harshly, some too generously. Most of the time such a bibliography will give you worthwhile information about the content of books and articles.

You can usually locate books about your subject more quickly than you can find articles. The reason is simple: the titles of books show up in the card catalogue of your library. To find article titles, you must do a bit of detective work.

The card catalogue in your library lists books under subject headings and by author. Under "Wilson, Woodrow," you will find biographies of Wilson and other books that have Wilson as a major subject as well as books Wilson wrote himself. The alphabetical listing of books by their authors will perhaps help you locate several titles by the same scholar. Because many historians specialize, several books by the same author may be related to your inquiry. Another excellent way of locating books is to go into the library stacks and look at the volumes classified in one section. Many books about Woodrow Wilson will be on the same shelf. Books with footnotes or endnotes can help by referring you to other books and to articles about your subject.

In looking for books about Woodrow Wilson, you would not limit yourself to those written primarily about him. You might consult books about World War I, books about the progressive era that he represented, books about people close to Wilson, and books about issues in which he was involved.

ARTICLES

Hundreds of periodicals deal with history. Some of them publish articles on facets of history—the middle ages, military history, history of science, art history, and so on. Some of them have a scope as wide as the discipline of history itself. An afternoon spent consulting the annual indexes of bound periodicals in your field of special interest can open your eyes to great numbers of issues involved in your general subject. New interpretations and information about history usually get into print first in articles. To stay on top of a field, you must consult the periodical literature. Academic titles usually are fairly straightforward—often a catchy phrase followed by a colon and an explanatory subtitle. When you consult an index, you can usually find articles of interest quickly.

Your library will have an index for all the periodicals it takes, usually keeping it in the periodical room. Here are a few historical journals you might wish to consult. The list is by no means complete. I include it only to provide a start in your own efforts. Looking at these journals will help you see how vast periodical literature can be and how historians write about their subjects. Because the essays you write in a history course are more like journal articles than books, you will get some idea about how historians write and think.

Your reference room almost certainly has the *American Historical Review,* a recent issue of which includes the article "Cotton Mill People: Work, Community, and Protest in the Textile South, 1880–1940," by Jacquelyn Dowd Hall, Robert Korstad, and James Leloudis. Another issue has this article: "The Politics of Divorce in France of the Belle Époque: The Case of Joseph and Henriette Caillaux." Don't be misled by the title of the periodical; it is not limited to topics about American history. The *AHR,* as the title is usually abbreviated, carries articles about all aspects of history in all the world's regions.

The journal *Past and Present* carries many diverse articles. In a recent article, Isser Woloch treated "Napoleonic Conscription: State Power and Civil Society." Other articles have treated civic ceremony in the English town of Bristol and the sixteenth-century image of Martin Luther.

The English Historical Review includes articles from the entire range of history, and one is likely to see an essay on early modern China not far from another on nineteenth-century America. *The Historical Journal,* also published in England, strives for similar breadth.

The Journal of Modern History will carry no articles about the period before 1500, and most of its authors consider topics from the eighteenth century to the present. In a recent article, Raymond Grew and Patrick J. Harrigan treated "The Catholic Contribution to Universal Schooling in France, 1850–1906."

The Journal of the West is much more specialized, carrying articles dealing with the history of the part of the United States that lies west of the Mississippi River. A typical recent article is entitled, "National Management Takes to the Woods: Frederick Weyerhaeuser and the Northwest Wood Products Industry," by Roland L. DeLorme. Another regional publication is *Journal of Southern History,* which treats the southeastern United States, the region of the old Confederacy. A recent article was "The Persistence of the Past: Memphis in the Great Depression," by Roger Biles. *The Tennessee Historical Quarterly* narrows the field even further, treating topics dealing with the state of Tennessee. Every state in the United States has a similar journal, and some have more than one. *The Journal of American Culture* is specialized in a different way; there you are likely to read about popular culture, and you may see articles on television commercials and on the history of comic books. The journal *Church History* is specialized in still another way, featuring scholarly articles about the history of Christianity. A typical recent article is "Papalist Reaction to the Council of Constance: Juan de Torquemada to the Present," by Thomas M. Izbicki. It may also include articles about early Christianity or about early twentieth-century Christian social reformers. *The Catholic Historical Review* includes articles about the same field, and despite its title often carries essays about Protestants and Protestant theology.

D. How to Find the Relevant Articles

These titles are only a few of the journals published in history. In this mass of publication, how do you find the articles that may pertain to your subject?

I have counseled looking for sources in the notes and bibliographies of books about your topic. Outstanding articles get read and quoted and often appraised by other scholars. Most of us learn our area within history by paying close attention to the scholarly notes made by our predecessors and our peers. Concentrate on footnotes or endnotes wherein a writer mentions the literature related to the subject.

Searching the annual indexes in historical periodicals is another method. While searching for articles on Luther's ideas about justification by faith in *Journal of Modern History* indexes, you may run across Jean Wirth's 1985 review article in which he surveys the major works on Luther published to commemorate the five-hundredth anniversary of the German reformer's birth in 1483. Wirth's wisdom, wit, and comprehensiveness will give you an insight into modern Luther scholarship that you might not have seen otherwise.

Book reviews in historical journals are another valuable source of bibliographic information. Most journals publish reviews, usually at the back of the issue, written by specialists. Journals may classify the books reviewed by historical period; the commonest means of sectioning is general, ancient, medieval, early modern, and modern. You can easily locate the books published about the period that interests you most. Reviews vary widely in value; some are impressionistic, some bad tempered and malicious, some far too gentle or laudatory, some mere cursory summaries. But some provide excellent appraisals of the book's strengths and weaknesses. Very often a good reviewer will mention another book or article relating to the theme of the book being reviewed. By reading reviews you can pick up information about the field itself that you might miss, and you can find bibliographic references that will help you find books and articles relevant to your topic. Read seven or eight reviews of a book, and you will get a pretty good idea about how specialists in the field regard it.

Of great value are the indexes to periodical literature to be found in all good libraries. The most familiar of these and the best known is *Reader's Guide to Periodical Literature,* which has been regularly published since 1900. Updates appear throughout the year, and at the end of each year a large, comprehensive edition is published. The *Reader's Guide* surveys only magazines intended for a general audience, but don't scorn this purpose, for you may find interesting, well-written articles by outstanding specialists by consulting the *Reader's Guide.* You will not find there articles published in the specialized journals and intended for professional historians, articles most likely to provide the information and the interpretations you need in a paper intended for a history class.

Fortunately the computer has come to the rescue. *The Permuterm Subject Index* and *Citation Index* for the arts and humanities and for the social sciences are now essential tools for every working historian. The indexes are issued annually. Here one may find the name of every author who has published an article in the many specialized journals surveyed by the editors. One may find a listing of every significant word that has appeared in every title of the articles surveyed; these words are arranged so that one may rapidly locate articles related to one's field of inquiry. If you were looking up material on Woodrow Wilson, these indexes would include the title of every article that included the words "Woodrow Wilson." If you were looking up material on the Great Depression in the 1930s, these indexes would cover every title that included the word "depression."

Full bibliographic information is given for each article, and every source mentioned in the footnotes or endnotes of the article is also listed. The result is a splendidly usable guide that will allow you to find quickly and easily the latest scholarly articles on the subject you are pursuing. Complete, clear instructions for using the Permuterm indexes are at the front of each volume. If you have trouble getting the hang of it, the reference librarian can help you.

Almost as spectacular is the computer index called *American History and Life,* published annually in three volumes, one with article abstracts and citations, one an index to book reviews in American history, and the third an American-history bibliography. Abstracts are valuable wherever you find them; they summarize the argument in an article, leaving you the option of seeking the article out and reading it yourself.

These computer-index publications do not include articles published before computer indexing began in the early 1980s. But compilation of computer-indexed bibliographies in many fields has become an academic industry, changing and growing constantly. Firms are putting older material on computer software now with as much zeal as publishing businesses in the 1950s and 1960s put old records on microfilm. Your reference librarian can help you locate firms that will provide a computer-generated bibliography for almost any subject. Prices and quality vary, but the technology is improving all the time, and this sort of bibliographic aid will soon be a common and indispensable tool for historical researchers.

E. Unpublished Materials

Most history papers are written from printed sources. But do not dismiss the possibility of using other kinds of information. Many libraries include archives that house immensely rich and varied collections of unpublished papers. Why was a specific building constructed on your campus? Why was your college founded? Why did the founders locate it where they did? How did a nineteenth-century college president at your institution construe the job? Answers to these and a multitude of other questions may be found in letters, journals, memos, and other materials if you take the trouble to find them in the archives. Ask the librarian if your school has archives open to students.

Many libraries now include oral-history collections, tapes and records of people both well known and obscure, discussing the past and their participation in events then. You can learn something by the tone of voice people use in describing past events. A comparison between someone's oral recollections of an event and written accounts might be an interesting topic for a paper.

Interviews are valuable for studies of recent or fairly recent history. If you are writing about some aspects of World War II, you can find many veterans who can tell you of their experiences, giving you a first-hand view of history. The same is true of the civil-rights movement, the Vietnam War, the Great Depression, and other events in the past fifty or so years. The precise definition of your topic will help you decide whether such interviews are helpful or not. People who participated in great events are often eager to talk about them. Don't be afraid to call people up to ask for an interview.

The pleasures in all these methods of inquiry are immense. Historians who have worked in the archives, or who have heard the actual voices of people who have made history, or who have talked with people in on the making, experience a pleasure that can hardly be described. Reading one of Henry David Thoreau's essays, looking at his handwriting, holding the paper that he held when he wrote it, are all special delights to the person writing about Thoreau. To some it is even more moving to hold the letters or other papers written by people much more obscure, people forgotten except for some striking personal imprint of themselves left in writing. Both Yale University and the Huntington Library in California have large collections of diaries kept by people who went across the western plains in covered wagons or on foot in the mid-nineteenth century. Sometimes a reader can see on the paper the stains left by a rain that fell more than a century ago, and one can often tell something about the difficulty of the journey from changes in the handwriting. At some time, every student of history, whether amateur or professional, should have the pleasure of looking at such a source.

F. Taking Notes

Both gathering titles and later reading of these books and articles will require you to take notes. Take scratch notes as you do your preliminary reading. Ask yourself questions, jot down significant phrases, perhaps listing places where historians disagree on the general subject you are pursuing. Record facts that interest one historian and do not matter to another. One writer may write much about Luther's hatred for the Jews; one may write little or nothing. Jot these different opinions down.

Jot down your own opinions, too. Even in the early stages of your research, important ideas may pop into your head. Write them down. Test them with further study. You will discover that further research will prove some of your first impressions to be gems.

People take notes in different ways. Some use 3 × 5 cards, putting a different thought on every card. A friend of mine carries a bundle of 3 × 5 cards bound with a rubber band tucked in his shirt pocket. When he has a thought, he jots it down on the card. I have always preferred to carry a bound notebook, a blank book available in all office-supply stores and in many bookstores as well. The pages don't get lost, and I have a complete record of my notes in a convenient and easily portable form. I can slip the notebook into the shoulder bag that I use as a briefcase and carry it with me anywhere. Yes, the notebook is more disorderly than 3 × 5 cards, but I find that I can leaf through the notebook quickly and find a note without much trouble. For a paper fifteen or twenty pages long, we do not need an elaborate filing system.

Computers add facility to note taking. If you copy your notes into a computer file, you can locate key words by using the search function on your word-processing program. Most programs will allow you to shift your notes to the file holding your essay when you start your writing.

Review your notes at the end of each day. Many students take notes and then do not go back over them later on. Our short-term memory is flighty. You can read something, be intensely engaged in it, take notes about it, but forget it quickly if you do not do something to renew the experience. Reviewing the notes fixes them in your mind and makes you remember them better so that you find them easily among your thoughts when you start to write. Reviewing the scratch notes will help you hold on to ideas that will then be nurtured by your subconscious powers of incubation, the mind's almost miraculous ability to work while thinking of other things or even sleeping. Reading the notes over again will stir up thoughts that will contribute much to the final conception of your paper, and such reading will clarify the method you use to approach that goal.

FORMS FOR NOTES

Always include bibliographic references in your notes. For books, write down name of author, title of book, place of publication, usually the publisher, and date of publication. For articles, include name of author, title of article, journal in which the article appears, and year in which the article appears, together with page numbers of the article in the issue of the journal. In your notes on content, you may abbreviate the bibliographic references. If you plan to use Irwin T. Hyatt, Jr.'s book on missionaries to China in the nineteenth century, you will take the bibliographic reference down on a card or in your notebook like this:

```
Hyatt, Irwin T., Our Ordered Lives Confess, Cambridge,
Harvard University Press, 1976.
```

Later on, you can refer in your notes simply to "Hyatt, p. 27" to locate your source of information. If you cite several books or articles by the same author, you may give the author and an abbreviated form of the title for your notes. Instead of listing full bibliographic information for Woodrow Wilson's *History of the American People,* you can say, "Wilson, *History,* 4 [to indicate the fourth volume in the set], p. 160."

You can, of course, use other systems. The main principle is this: *Be sure you know where you got your information.* You must be able to refer accurately to your sources when you write the paper. Save yourself much grief by keeping track of them carefully while doing your research.

In addition to your bibliographic notes, you will take three kinds of notes as you read. The first is *direct quotation.* Always place direct quotations within quotation marks in your notes, and copy the quotation accurately. Make an accurate reference to the page number or numbers of the book in which the quotation is found. You may want to put a heading on the note to help you remember why you set it down, and, if you use a computer, to help you find the note by means of the search function in the word-processing program. Here is an example:

```
Civil War Nursing; role of women; Kate Cumming:
"Nothing that I had ever heard of or read had
given me the faintest idea of the horrors witnessed
here. . . . I sat up all night, bathing the men's
wounds, and giving them water. . . . The men are lying
```

```
all over the house, on their blankets, just as they

were brought in from the battlefield. . . . The foul

air from this mass of human beings at first made me

giddy and sick, but I soon got over it. We have to

walk, and when we give the men anything kneel, in

blood and water, but we think nothing of it."
```

```
Selections from Kate Cumming's diary, telling of her

work with wounded Confederate soldiers. Quoted from

James M. McPherson, Battle Cry of Freedom: The Civil

War Era, New York, Oxford University Press, 1988, p.

479.
```

A search through your computer file of notes would pick up "Civil War Nursing," "women," "Kate Cumming," and of course it would also pick up any of the words in the quoted section.

Always review the quotation once you have written it down to see that you have it correct. The eye and the hand can slip while you are looking first at the source and then at your notebook or card. When you type, fingers can go astray, typing one word when you meant another. It may help to put a little check mark by the quotation to tell yourself that you have reviewed the quotation for accuracy once you have written it down.

Here is another sample note showing direct quotation:

```
Wilson mocks blacks' fear of the Klan/KKK
```

```
"It threw the negroes into a very ecstasy of panic to

see these sheeted 'ku klux' move near them in the

shrouded night; and their comic fear stimulated the

lads who excited it to many an extravagant prank and

mummery. No one knew or could discover who the masked

players were; no one could say whether they meant se-
```

```
rious or only innocent mischief; and the zest of the
business lay in keeping the secret close."
```

```
Wilson, History, 5, pp. 59–60.
```

If this note were on your computer and you wished to retrieve it as an example of Wilson's attitude toward the Ku Klux Klan, you could search for it on the computer by using "Klan" or "KKK" in your heading. The note would also be easy to retrieve if you wrote it in a notebook.

Avoid copying too much as direct quotation. Writing down the quotation takes time, and you can easily make errors in transcribing the quotation from source to note. You can save time and help your own mental processes by summarizing or paraphrasing material rather than quoting it directly. Paraphrasing is especially valuable if your source is in a foreign language or in a language with difficult syntax, such as early modern English. As you write, you may have Wilson's volumes at hand that you have checked out of the library. Looking through your notes and seeing your summary, you can go back to the original source if you want to quote it *verbatim*; that is, word for word. You may find that you do not have room in the paper to quote the passage directly, anyway. Then you may say something like this: "Wilson mocked the fear blacks had of the Klan," and you would put in a note the place where the mockery can be found. Here is an example of a summary note:

```
Wilson mocks black fears of Klan/KKK
```

```
Wilson seems to enjoy the fear of blacks before the Ku
Klux Klan and seems to regard the early Klansmen as
mere pranksters.
```

```
Wilson, History, 5, pp. 59–60.
```

The third kind of note is your own comment as you read. Try to comment often on what you read. As you write such comments, you force your mind to reflect on what you read. Commenting on your reading makes you an active rather than a passive reader.

Be sure to distinguish between the notes that are your own thoughts and notes that are direct quotations or summaries of your sources. I usually put an arrow before one of my thoughts in my notebook or when I am taking notes on a computer. The arrow lets me know that these are my thoughts, that I am not taking them down from someone else. Many notebook keepers write direct quotations on the right-hand page and keep their own comments on the left-hand page. Here is an example of how you would enter a note on a card about your own thoughts. You would enter the note in a computer without the indentation.

```
→Wilson's view of the Klan goes hand in hand with his
general view that blacks have no right to be free of
fear or to take part as citizens in the United States.
His mention of blacks' "comic" fear suggests uncon-
scious appropriation of the common stereotypes, that
blacks were either funny or dangerous. He never sug-
gests in the History that blacks are mistreated by
southerners——including the Klansmen. They are always
mistreated by northerners. Northerners always mistreat
them by asking them to assert themselves. Wilson sees
blacks as happiest when they are submissive. He seems
to have no sense that blacks might lose dignity by
being so regarded. History, 5, pp. 59—60.
```

Keeping your mind active during your reading and making notes like this, you may find that you have a design for your paper in your hand before you sit down to write. Sometimes that design comes only in the writing itself. But if you write many interpretive comments to yourself as you read, you will discover that the steps in making a design go much more smoothly.

IV. BRAINSTORM AND MAKE AN OUTLINE

"Brainstorming" is the name we give to making the mind work at a task by playfully, intensively forcing out our thoughts. We usually brainstorm in writing, jotting down ideas one after another as fast as we can think of them and knowing that we may reject most. Sometimes we brainstorm in groups by talking hard at each other, trying out ideas, tossing them to the group to see how they fare in open discussion. Brainstorming is an excellent way of arriving at a topic for a history paper.

By the time you have spent two or three afternoons refining your subject and gathering bibliography and doing spot reading, you will begin to feel more confident about your knowledge. Having left the somewhat flat and limited accounts in the encyclopedias and other reference books, you will have started looking at specialized books and articles. Your reading should have suggested several interesting topics. You should have asked questions along the way, writing those questions down in your notebook. You will have noticed patterns or repeated ideas in works by someone you are studying. Sometimes a pattern occurs as a consistent response to a subject. Woodrow Wilson constantly defended southern whites in writing and in speeches. Why did he do that, and what effect did this attitude have on American history?

You may have started by resolving to write a paper about Woodrow Wilson. If you were lucky, you thought of a limited topic you might cover in ten or fifteen pages, right away. Perhaps, however, even now you have not been able to limit your topic enough. List interesting topics or problems relating to Woodrow Wilson. Keep working at it until you arrive at something you can manage. These two notes illustrate this way of working to produce something both interesting and feasible.

```
"The Civil War in Woodrow Wilson's History of the
American People"
```

Too vague. Too many topics possible here.

"Wilson's Defense of the Ku Klux Klan in his <u>History</u>
of the <u>American People</u>"

Not bad. Wilson's defense of the Klan is surprising, because the popular conception of Wilson is that he was liberal for his time. But here the topic seems almost too narrow. Wilson defends the Klan over several pages in his book. He makes vague comments that might indicate disapproval of violence by the Klan. None of Wilson's *History* is very detailed. He makes general statements throughout, and the book serves much more to show what he felt and believed about the facts than what the facts were or might have been. The temptation might be to go from Wilson to general background information about the Klan itself. Then you have to ask questions like these: "Do I have primary sources for studying the Klan? Is that topic far too big for a paper in my course?"

Wilson's sympathetic words for the Klan provoke other ideas. What about Wilson's general attitude toward blacks in the South and in society at large? You consult the index to several volumes of the Wilson papers. Slowly you read Wilson's comments about blacks in various contexts. Here is much information, and you begin to see consistent patterns. Wilson has no sympathy for efforts by blacks to vote after the Civil War. He never writes as if blacks might some day fully share American society. He favors segregation in the federal Civil Service, especially the U.S. Post Office. He insults black leaders who come to visit him at the White House. The major pattern seems clear: Wherever Wilson speaks of race, he demonstrates negative attitudes toward blacks and aims at segregation. Now you feel a paper forming that can be done within the limits of the course. You adopt a provisional title: "Woodrow Wilson's Attitudes Toward Black Americans."

You can always change a provisional title. (You can change anything in a paper, and your changes may be sweeping.) While you use it, the provisional title will give some direction to your work. That sense of direction will help you work faster and more efficiently because it helps organize your thoughts, making you evaluate the information you have collected so that you can make proper use of it. You can't use everything you have gathered if you have done your research well. You must leave some information out that does not add to your argument or your thesis. You must organize the useful information so that you can put it together in an essay that makes sense. The provisional title will act as a filter in your mind, holding those things you should keep and letting go information that will not contribute to your argument.

The Outline

Once you arrive at a topic, you focus your reading. If you are going to write about Woodrow Wilson in relation to blacks in America, you can limit yourself to reading only the parts of the Wilson papers and of books about Wilson relating to that subject. You may become so interested in Wilson that you will continue to seek other information about him later on. While you are writing a paper, you must limit your reading as much as possible to things that will help in that task. For this paper you will not read about Wilson's views on Czechoslovakia after World War I, about his relationships with his first and second wives, or about his attitude toward the Prohibition amendment, which was ratified during his presidency. You limit yourself to sources that will help you understand his attitude toward black Americans.

At some time, you should write an outline to help organize your ideas. Notice a couple of things about this outline:

1. It is probably better to start with a list of points you want to cover than to begin with a detailed outline.
2. Be willing to change any outline or any part of it once you begin to write and ideas start to flow.

A list of points to be covered may be set down quickly, and you can arrange it easily. A more detailed outline sometimes gets in the way of spontaneity as you write. Most writers find that as they work they make discoveries and change their minds about some things. No matter what sort of outline you decide to use, be willing to change it when you feel that the changes will make you write better. Outlines should be guides, not dictators.

Here is an example of an outline listing topics you might want to cover.

The argument: Woodrow Wilson's attitudes toward blacks mixed paternalism with fear and contributed to the racial segregation introduced in the federal Civil Service early in his presidential administration.

1. William Monroe Trotter, an important black leader, had an angry interview with Woodrow Wilson in November 1914. Tell the story of that interview.

2. What larger meaning did the interview between Wilson and Trotter have? The Trotter episode exemplified Wilson's attitudes toward segregation in the federal Civil Service and toward blacks in general.

3. Why did Wilson accept racial segregation? Wilson's explanation for his attitude was always that segregation helped avoid "friction" that would necessarily arise if blacks and whites worked together.

4. Was another explanation possible? Yes, a deeper explanation lies in Wilson's lifelong attitudes toward blacks, feelings evident in many things he said and wrote long before he became president of the United States.

5. Some of these attitudes came about because of his feeling of being a southerner and his admiration for the old Confederacy. Tell of Wilson's southern roots and feelings.

6. These attitudes are especially sharp in his five-volume History of the American People.

7. These attitudes prepared him to accept without protest the racial policies of southerners in his cabinet and of southern politicians and editors

       eager to keep blacks politically and socially sub-
       jugated.

8. Although many did protest the policy of segregation
   inaugurated by the Wilson administration, probably
   most Americans went along with it.

9. Whatever Wilson's motives, the policy disastrously
   influenced race relations in America. Sanctioning
   of segregation by the president of the United
   States kept blacks from receiving their rights for
   decades.

A list outline such as this one avoids proliferating of Roman numerals and subheadings. You add subheadings if you want. This writer has posed several questions and has tried to answer them by statements that will mark major divisions in the paper. This series of sentences probably is sufficient to let him start writing and to carry the paper through successfully. The outline provides a shape for the paper, an orderly way of presenting the information the writer wants to present, and decides its mode; the writer will tell a story and explain some things about it. The paper will be an analytical narrative—a story with explanations built in, answering these questions: What happened? Who was responsible? Why?

When you have arrived at this stage, you are ready to write your first draft.

V. WRITE SEVERAL DRAFTS

Leave yourself time enough to do several drafts of the paper. All of us stay up through the night now and then to meet a deadline. Making this practice a habit, though, will leave you less good a writer than you can be if you allow more time. You may get by, but your work may leave you less than proud.

When you start writing, stick to it for at least a couple of hours. You may not go very fast, having to consult your notes continually. You may become discouraged about the shape of what you are writing. But keep going. The most important task in writing the first draft is to get it in being. Put a beginning, a middle, and an end down on paper or on the computer disk. Write more than you need to write at first. If your assignment is to write a fifteen-page paper, make your first draft twenty pages. Pack in information. Use quotations. Ruminate about the subject you are describing. Ask yourself the journalistic questions, and try to answer them about your paper.

Once you get that first draft in being, several things will happen. You will feel immense relief. An unwritten assignment hanging over your head is always much more formidable than one you have written—even in a rough draft. You have some idea now about what you can say in the space you have. You have some idea about the major questions you want to address. You know some parts that will need further research. You probably know which conclusions seem fairly certain and which feel shaky. You can now proceed to revise.

Revision nowadays proceeds in numerous ways. If you write with a computer and a word-processing program, you can bring your paper up on the screen and work back through it, inserting, deleting, and changing around the order of the ideas. (It's a good idea to make a back-up copy of that first draft so that if you cut something you decide to restore later on, you can do so without pain.) Many writers like to print out a draft and go over it with a red pen, making changes that they then type into the draft on the computer. Some research shows that the longer people work with computers, the more they do their revising directly from the screen without printing out the work. I have written with computers now for about six years, and I still find it valuable to print out and work from manuscript that the jargonist calls "hard copy." But there are no rules; the important thing is to read over and over all that you have written.

As you read your work, you must ask questions; here is my own list—add items of your own.

1. What point do I want to make in this paper? What is my major reason for writing it? What do I want to say?

2. Have I said clearly the thing I want most to say here?

3. What parts of this draft do not contribute directly to my main point? Should I cut them out?

4. How long must a reader read before knowing what my subject is and the point of view that I take toward it? Can I get into my subject more quickly than I do?

5. What evidence do I advance for what I want people to believe about this topic? How much of my paper is opinion unsupported by evidence?

6. How good is my evidence? Is it the best evidence I can get?

7. Where do I infer conclusions from the evidence? That is, where do I interpret the evidence?

8. Do I take contrary evidence into account? Have I been fair in presenting the evidence? Have I written in such a way that someone who knows the evidence as well as I do can compliment me for having done a careful job in putting everything together?

9. What is my tone in this paper? Do I sound emotional or preachy? Do I sound belligerent? Do I sound apologetic? Do I sound immature?

10. Does my conclusion end the paper gracefully? Is it the best conclusion I can write?

11. Do I need to add more information? Have I given enough facts to make my point clear and plausible?

12. Does my paper flow from idea to idea so that readers can follow without wondering how I got here or perhaps supposing that they have missed something?

13. Have I left any muddled sentences in this draft? Are my sentences clear enough to be understood at first reading? Can I make some of them simpler by eliminating cumbersome phrases or clauses?

14. Can I eliminate some sentences? Is every sentence I have written necessary to make the point I want to make?

15. Can I make some sentences more vivid by using the active rather than the passive voice?

16. Can I make some sentences more vivid by changing my word choice, using words that more precisely convey my meaning?

17. Can I simplify sentences by eliminating some words? Unnecessary adjectives, perhaps?

18. Can I eliminate sentences, phrases, or clauses that give information that everyone might be expected to know? Do I explain too much?

19. Do I repeat some words or phrases too often? Can I find other words and phrases to give variety to my prose? Are there echoes in my prose that I can change? That is, do I say things like, "The defendant defended himself," or "The writer wrote," or "Her description described," or "They considered all the considerations in the statement"?

20. Have I used clichés, those tired expressions which have been used again and again and again so that they have lost all power to be vivid? Have I talked about "the cold, hard facts" or a "bolt from the blue" or "dead as a doornail" or the "bottom line" or "stark reality"?

You can cultivate a good sense of revision by reading your own work again and again. Reading aloud helps. You can sometimes pick out rough places in your prose because they make you stumble in the reading. Reading aloud with inflection and expression will help you catch places where you may be misleading or confusing.

Professional writers often have others read their work and make suggestions about it. You can get help from your friends if you know what to ask them when they have read your work. Don't say to them, "What do you think of my paper?" They are most likely to say, "It's good. I like it." Ask them instead, "What do you think I am saying in this paper?" Make them tell you what they think they have read. You will sometimes be surprised by what comes out. If it is not what you want readers to get from your work, change it.

The drafting can go on and on, until you run up against the deadline, and you have to turn your paper in. You may be sure that the time spent on your drafts has made your work better than it would be if you had written the paper hurriedly and turned it in.

Drafting helps us see all parts of our work more clearly. It helps us see our thinking, our research, our factual knowledge, our expression, and the shape of our ideas. Very often as we write drafts we realize that our thought is flabby or that we suddenly can think of contrary arguments we had not thought of. We can then work to make our thought stronger and to react to those contrary arguments. Reading our work over and over again teaches us to track our own ideas so that we make them flow from one to another without leaving gaps that may hinder readers from making the connections we want them to make.

5

A Sample Research Paper in History

A sample history paper written for a course in American history using the procedure outlined in Chapter 4 appears on the following pages. Study the paper and the annotations that explain what the writer is doing. The papers you write will of course be your own, but they should have many of the general qualities mentioned in the notes that explain this one.

Woodrow Wilson's Attitude Toward Black Americans

Dick Curry

American History 101

Mr. Norman

10:30 section

April 7, 1989

Title of the paper: The title is a general, summary description, suitable for publication in a scholarly journal. A different kind of publication might require a different title.
The title is not set in quotation marks. It may be placed on
a separate title page that should also have the student's
name, the teacher's name, the time the class meets, and the
date of submission.

On November 12, 1914, black leader William Monroe Trotter and President Woodrow Wilson confronted each other in the White House. Trotter read the president an "Address" vigorously protesting against the policy of racial segregation recently introduced into the federal Civil Service, especially the United States Post Office. Afterward the two men entered into heated disagreement. At the end Wilson all but threw Trotter out of the Oval Office.

> An anecdote begins the paper. The anecdote seizes our attention. We want to know more about the story. An anecdotal beginning requires the writer to explain the significance of the anecdote.

The incident was one of the great setbacks in the struggle for racial equality in America, and it revealed Wilson's own attitudes toward black Americans. Perhaps more important, it revealed a general American attitude that was not to be substantially changed until the civil-rights movement of the 1950s and 1960s, culminating in the Civil Rights Act of 1964.

> The greater significance of the opening story is explained. We move from an anecdote, to the meaning of the story, to larger forces in American history.

Trotter was spokesman for the National Independent Equal Rights League, a rival to the then fledgling National Association for the Advancement of Colored People (NAACP). He was an M.A. graduate of Harvard, class of 1895, and the first Afro-American member of the Phi Beta Kappa honor society. In 1901 he became

editor of the <u>Guardian</u> in Boston and campaigned vigorously for black civil rights. He was more radical
than other black leaders, opposing the moderation
recommended by both Booker T. Washington and the
NAACP. By the turn of the century, the states of the
Old Confederacy had severely restricted black voting,
imposing poll taxes, literacy requirements, and ownership of property as qualifications for voting.
Booker T. Washington, founder of Tuskegee Institute,
believed that the franchise was not as important as
intellectual and economic betterment of blacks. He
looked forward to some distant future when blacks
might regain the franchise after they had made progress in other areas. Trotter believed that political
action by blacks was necessary before any other progress was possible. And political action required
blacks to have the vote.[1]

> Trotter is identified comprehensively. Whenever you intro-
> duce someone not already well known to your readers, tell
> who that person was. The identification tells them why
> you are bringing this person into your story, enabling them
> to follow the story much more easily. The issues that di-
> vided Trotter and Washington are briefly set forth. It is
> always helpful to show the sources of conflict within a
> historical situation. Without conflict, history would be un-
> interesting and perhaps impossible. State the reasons for
> conflict clearly.

It was an irreconcilable difference. Trotter attacked Washington furiously in the pages of the

---

[1]Stephen R. Fox, <u>The Guardian of Boston: William
Monroe Trotter</u>, New York, Atheneum, 1970, p. 36.

<u>Guardian</u>. In 1903 when Washington spoke in Boston, Trotter and his sister interrupted the speech and were arrested.[2] Trotter was eventually tried and briefly jailed for his part in the disruption.[3]

> The story continues. We see the extent of Trotter's opposition to Booker T. Washington. The story of his protest and his jail sentence illustrates how emotional Trotter felt. The story is far more effective than the bare statement that Trotter opposed Washington's views. Always be as specific as you can in writing history. Illustrate your generalizations with evidence to support them whenever possible.

In 1912, Trotter supported Wilson in the presidential election, which Wilson won only because the Republican Party was divided. Blacks had been Republican since the Civil War, when a Republican president, Abraham Lincoln, had issued the Emancipation Proclamation. They did not take kindly to Wilson, who was both a Democrat and a southerner. Arthur S. Link, Wilson's foremost biographer, points out that blacks had reason to be doubtful about Wilson. Josephus Daniels, one of Wilson's early supporters and friends, editor of the <u>Raleigh News and Observer</u>, wrote in an editorial on October 1, 1912, that the South voted solidly Democratic out of

> the realization that the subjection of the negro [<u>sic</u>], politically, and the separation of the negro, socially, are paramount to all other considerations in the South short of the preservation

---

[2]Fox, pp. 50–52.
[3]Fox, p. 57.

of the Republic itself. And we shall recognize no
emancipation, nor shall we proclaim any deliverer,
that falls short of these essentials to the peace
and welfare of our part of the country.[4]

Daniels wrote this editorial in the midst of the 1912
presidential campaign.

> The quotation is longer than five lines, and therefore is set off in a block indented five spaces from the left margin. Because it is set off in a block, it needs no quotation marks to introduce it. The block quotation is double-spaced, just like the body of the paper. The eye easily skips over block quotations; that is one reason they should be used sparingly. When you do use them, you make life easier for your reader by double-spacing them just as you do the body of your text. Publishers require block quotations to be double-spaced so that typesetters can follow them more easily; you may as well get into the habit of double-spacing them in the papers you do in college. The word *sic* in brackets indicates that the writer of the paper knows some readers may suspect him of copying his source incorrectly. Conventional English practice requires that the word "Negro" be begun with a capital letter. Daniels wrote the first letter of the word with a lower-case letter, which the writer of the paper indicated with the *sic* in brackets. If Daniels had misspelled a word, the writer might have reproduced the word as Daniels wrote it and indicated the correct copying of the misspelling with a [*sic*].
>
> We begin to get some background information here about Wilson and about his relations with black citizens of the United States. We see that he surrounded himself with people who were openly opposed to equality for blacks in American society. All this background information is not only interesting but also helps explain what is going to come in the paper.

---

[4]Arthur S. Link, <u>Wilson: The Road to the White House</u>, Princeton, Princeton University Press, 1947, p. 501.

Wilson appealed to blacks to support him, and many of them—including Trotter—did so. Trotter and Wilson met in July 1912 and apparently got on well. Wilson spoke feelingly to black groups about his willingness to deal with blacks "fairly and justly."[5] There was always something equivocal about these statements. What is "fair" or "just" to one person may seem unfair and unjust to another. Nevertheless, blacks had little choice, and many of them supported Wilson. Link points out that Wilson received more black votes than any previous president.[6]

> More background information. The writer is building a context to help us understand why the story of the confrontation that begins this paper is significant. When you begin a paper with a story, always tell readers precisely why that story is important.

Yet Wilson quickly disappointed his black supporters. When he took office, Trotter asked him not to appoint Albert Burleson, a Texan, to be Postmaster General. Wilson appointed him anyway, and on April 11, 1913, little more than a month after Wilson assumed office, Burleson told the Cabinet of his intention to segregate blacks and whites in the Post Office.[7]

> The background story continues. We have further details about previous relations between Trotter and Wilson, and

---

[5]Link, The Road to the White House, p. 502.
[6]Arthur S. Link, Wilson: The New Freedom, Princeton, Princeton University Press, 1956, pp. 243–244.
[7]Fox, pp. 169–170.

now we learn how Albert Burleson moved toward segregation in the U.S. Post Office.

Trotter had personal reasons to care about racial discrimination in the Post Office. His father James worked at the post office in Boston. He resigned in 1882 because a white man was promoted over him.[8] In 1914 Trotter was plainly furious over the act he felt was Wilson's betrayal. In November 1913 he led a delegation to the White House, bringing with him a petition signed by about 20,000 people protesting against segregation. As he would do in the following year, Trotter read an "Address," telling Wilson that "Segregation such as barring from the public lavatories and toilets and requiring the use of separate ones must have a reason. The reason can only be that the segregated are considered unclean, diseased or indecent as to their persons, or inferior beings of a lower order, or that other employees have a class prejudice which is to be catered to, or indulged."[9]

> We have more background information here. The information that Trotter's own father had been a victim of racial discrimination in the Boston post office adds drama to the story. The further development of the story about relations between Trotter and Wilson provides background that makes the paper more dramatic and more understandable.

Trotter pointed out that no other racial grouping of Americans was segregated and that any of them would

---

[8]Fox, p. 19.
[9]*The Wilson Papers*, November 6, 1913, vol. 28, p. 491.

regard such segregation as an insult. "If separate
toilets are provided for Latin, Teutonic, Celtic,
Slavic, Semitic and Celtic Americans, then and then
only would African Americans be assigned to separation
without insult and indignity."[10] Federal employees had
worked together without segregation in the two Cleveland administrations, Trotter said. And he recalled
that when an effort was made to segregate federal employees on racial grounds, Cleveland stopped it.[11]

> We have a summary of Trotter's statements to Wilson in
> the 1913 meeting at the White House, an earlier encounter
> than the one that begins this paper. The writer quotes only
> one sentence from Trotter and summarizes the rest of Trot-
> ter's remarks. This selective sort of quotation is usually
> much more effective than a long block quotation that
> might give Trotter's words exactly as he gave them. Long
> block quotations may be valuable, but more often they in-
> terrupt the flow of a paper. Readers are inclined to skip
> over long block quotations. It is almost always better to
> summarize a long text that you wish to write about. Here
> and there where you have a particularly meaty sentence—
> one that, like the sentence from Trotter quoted here, gives
> special flavor to the story—you may safely quote that sen-
> tence or a few important words from it. But in general
> avoid block quotations.

On this occasion Wilson's response was concilia-
tory. He claimed ignorance and promised to investigate. He assured Trotter that things would be worked
out.[12] John Lorance, a writer for the <u>Boston Daily</u>

---

[10]<u>The Wilson Papers</u>, November 6, 1913, vol. 28,
p. 492.
[11]<u>The Wilson Papers</u>, November 6, 1913, vol. 28,
p. 493.
[12]<u>The Wilson Papers</u>, November 6, 1913, vol. 28,
p. 496.

Advertiser, reported on December 9 that in consequence of the meeting with Trotter, Wilson was rolling segregation back. Lorance's article expressed a sense of triumph that Wilson had championed the cause of equality. Other northern papers reflected the same sentiments.[13]

> The background information continues. The writer is developing a chronological framework that provides a context for the paper he is writing about Wilson's attitudes. You must be careful not to give so much background that you bury your thesis. This writer is giving enough to provide drama and information that will be valuable later on without providing so much information that we are smothered by it. We can see the purpose in the information.

In fact, segregation continued. Josephus Daniels was now Secretary of the Navy. William Gibbs McAdoo of Georgia by way of Tennessee was Secretary of the Treasury. Albert Sidney Burleson was Postmaster General. All these men were especially close to Wilson; all were uncompromising segregationists.[14]

> This short paragraph is an important transition in the paper. Wilson made a promise and apparently broke it. The breaking of the promise reveals an immediate cause that

---

[13]Excerpts from these papers, including a long quotation from Lorance's article, appear in the notes to The Wilson Papers, vol. 28, pp. 498–500.

[14]In his article in the Boston Daily Advertiser, Lorance wrote, "The most active segregation has been found under Sec. McAdoo of the Treasury Department, under Postmaster General Burleson of the Post Office Department, and under Sec. Daniels of the Navy Department." See The Wilson Papers, November 6, 1913, vol. 28, p. 499.

helps us understand why Trotter came to Wilson in the angry way that we observed at the opening of this paper.

When Trotter returned with another "Address" and another delegation a year later, he was understandably angry. He felt betrayed, and his "Address" was an indictment. Though in it he maintained an icy sort of courtesy, the fire of outrage burned beneath the surface. He expressed his disappointment in Wilson's record on race. Wilson had promised to help "Afro-Americans," Trotter said. Instead, segregation was advancing steadily, and Wilson was doing nothing about it. Trotter recalled the national petition protesting against segregation and presented to the president by black Americans a year before. Such segregation existed in "working positions, eating tables, dressing rooms, rest rooms, lockers, and especially public toilets."[15]

> The writer summarizes Trotter's "Address" here. Again notice that the summary is far more effective than a long block quotation from the address itself would be. We tend to skip over block quotations. Their style naturally differs from that in the body of the essay. And because we expect the essay's writer to explain the information in the block quotation, readers almost unconsciously accept the writer's explanation and let the quotation go.

Wilson had promised to investigate. Trotter pointed out that segregation had gone on and that in fact it had increased. He reeled off a long list of

---

[15]*The Wilson Papers*, November 12, 1914, vol. 31, p. 300.

government departments and structures in which segregation was enforced. Trotter said that American "citizens of color" realized "that if they can be segregated and thus humiliated by the national government
at the national capital the beginning is made for the
spread of that persecution and prosecution which makes
property and life itself insecure in the South." He
pointed out that blacks who had voted for Wilson were
now regretting what they had done. "Only two years ago
you were heralded as perhaps the second Lincoln, and
now the Afro-American leaders who supported you are
hounded as false leaders and traitors to their race.
What a change segregation has wrought!" The indignity
of segregation robbed blacks of their rights of citizenship, Trotter said. "Fellow citizenship means congregation. Segregation destroys fellowship and citizenship. Consider that any passerby on the streets of
the national capital, whether he be black or white,
can enter and use the public lavatories in government
buildings, while citizens of color who do the work of
the government are excluded." Trotter and his delegation were there to ask Wilson to "issue an executive
order against any and all segregation of government
employees because of race and color and to ask whether
you will do so."[16]

> Again notice that we have a mixture of summary and quo-
> tation. We do not have a long block quotation.

---

[16]The Wilson Papers, November 12, 1914, vol. 31,
p. 300.

Having presented his "Address," Trotter entered
into a dialogue with Wilson. If he expected the president to grant his desire, he was quickly disappointed. The American people rejoiced in the "really
extraordinary advances" that blacks had made, Wilson
said. "But we are all practical men," the president
said. Being "practical" meant that everyone had to
recognize that the races could not mix. Segregation
was installed to eliminate "the possibility of friction." And Wilson was sure friction would result if
blacks and whites mixed. People should be "comfortable," he thought.

> Wilson's reply to Trotter is summarized, spiced here and
> there with quotations of phrases from Wilson that give the
> flavor of his remarks. The writer of the paper interprets
> these remarks, helping readers to follow. The interpreta-
> tion is an inference—a leap from the words of the text to
> the writer's judgment about their significance.

Segregationists within the government "did not
want any white man made uncomfortable by anything that
any colored man did, or a colored man made uncomfortable by anything that a white man did in the offices
of the government." He was assured, Wilson said, that
conditions for blacks and whites were separate but
equal. "I haven't had time to look at the conditions
myself, but I have again and again said that the thing
that would distress me most would be that they should
select the colored people of the departments to be
given bad light or bad ventilation yet worse than the
others, and inferior positions, physically consid-

ered." Solving the problems between the races was
going to take generations, Wilson said. Blacks and
whites were equal in that they both had souls, he
said. But there was the matter of economic equality—
"whether the Negro can do the same things with equal
efficiency. Now, I think they are proving that they
can. After they have proved it, a lot of things are
going to solve themselves."[17]

Trotter asked a question. What did the president
think about the humiliation black federal employees
had suffered? Wilson claimed not to know about some of
the incidents that Trotter mentioned. He suggested
that humiliation was all in the mind. "If you take it
as a humiliation, which it is not intended as, and sow
the seed of that impression all over the country, why
the consequences will be very serious. But if you
should take it in the spirit in which I have presented
it to you, it wouldn't have serious consequences."[18]

> The summary of the confrontation goes on. The writer of
> the paper is thus able to condense to a few paragraphs ma-
> terial that in the edition of the Wilson papers takes up sev-
> eral pages.

Another member of the black delegation, whom the
stenographer was unable to identify, protested that
whites and blacks had been working together as clerks

---

[17]*The Wilson Papers*, November 12, 1914, vol. 31,
pp. 300—303.
[18]*The Wilson Papers*, November 12, 1914, vol. 31,
p. 303.

for fifty years "without distinction and separation based on their race." It was untenable, this person said, to claim that there was any reason to make the separation now.

Trotter broke in. Segregation was inevitably a humiliation, he said.

> It creates in the minds of others that there is something the matter with us—that we are not their equals, that we are not their brothers, that we are so different that we cannot work at a desk beside them, that we cannot eat at a table beside them, that we cannot go into the dressing room where they go, that we cannot use a locker beside them, that we cannot even go into a public toilet with them.

There was no friction in going to a public toilet, he said. Black government workers had been going to public toilets for fifty years. But when the Wilson administration came in, Trotter said, "a drastic segregation was put into effect at once." This segregation was not caused by friction; it was caused by prejudice on the part of the official who put it into operation.[19]

> The writer has judged that here Trotter's words are so powerful they deserve to be quoted in full, even if it means using them in a block quotation. He could have placed a

---

[19]*The Wilson Papers*, November 12, 1914, vol. 31, pp. 304–305.

footnote at the end of the block. But because he finishes the paragraph with a summary of other things Trotter said in the same speech and with another quotation, he decided to combine both references in footnote 19.

Wilson broke in here, obviously angry. He condemned Trotter's tone. No one had ever spoken to him like that in the White House before, he said. If this organization wished to speak to him again, it had to have another spokesman. "You have, spoiled the whole cause for which you came," he told Trotter.[20]

> The writer's use of the phrase "obviously angry" is an inference. Wilson did not say he was angry. But the transcript indicates anger. The writer infers that anyone who used these words would have been angry.

Trotter insisted that he was telling the truth about what blacks in America believed about Wilson and segregation. But Wilson gave not an inch. When Trotter implied that blacks would not vote for Wilson again, Wilson dismissed the threat as "blackmail" and concluded, "You can vote as you please provided I am perfectly sure that I am doing the right thing at the right time." With that Wilson broke off the meeting.[21]

> The summary narrative of the meeting between Wilson and Trotter is now complete. We are prepared for the writer to go on developing some ideas about this meeting and how it relates to Woodrow Wilson's attitudes toward black Americans.

---

[20]*The Wilson Papers*, November 12, 1914, vol. 31, p. 306.

[21]*The Wilson Papers*, November 12, 1914, vol. 31, p. 308.

And so the conversation ended in failure. The New York Times, in a story headlined, "President Resents Negro's Criticism," reported the next day that Wilson would continue the segregation begun during his administration. Trotter expressed his disappointment in the meeting and announced a mass meeting to be held on the following Sunday.[22] A number of newspaper editorials in the North condemned Wilson's policies. Oswald Garrison Villard, editor of the New York Evening Post, wrote, "The Wilson Administration went out of its way to create the issue it now deplores, and cannot see its way clear to admitting its mistake and reverting to the only defensible position of absolute equality in Government Service."[23]

> Some account is given here of public reaction to the meeting between Trotter and Wilson. This paragraph provides details not entirely necessary to the paper. But they are interesting, and they help flesh out the story.

Wilson held his ground and apparently never reconsidered his position. Had Trotter and others investigated Wilson's past utterances on the subject of race, they might never have entertained the expectations that were now so keenly disappointed.

---

[22]The Wilson Papers, November 12, 1914, vol. 31, p. 309.
   [23]The summaries of these newspaper stories are presented as footnotes to The Wilson Papers, November 12, 1914, vol. 31, pp. 308–309. Editorial of November 17, 1914; quoted in a note to The Wilson Papers, vol. 31, p. 328.

Another important transition. The writer now takes us to Wilson's life and works and will show that Wilson had a long history of lacking sympathy with blacks and their aspirations to achieve equality with white Americans.

Wilson was a southerner, born in Staunton, Virginia, in 1856. His father, Joseph Ruggles Wilson, was a Presbyterian minister. Less than a year after young Woodrow (christened Thomas Woodrow Wilson, he was called Tommy in those days) was born, the Wilsons moved to Augusta, Georgia, and it was there that he passed the Civil War. Link says this about Wilson's sense of being southern:

In later life Wilson developed a romantic and extravagant love for the South of legend and song. His letters and addresses are full of expressions of deep feeling for the region. He was one historian, for example, who was not apologetic about the South's history. On one occasion he declared that there was "nothing to apologize for in the history of the South—absolutely nothing to apologize for."[24]

The quotation from Link is an argument from authority. Link, best known of the Wilson biographers, has great stature among historians. The writer of this paper, by quoting Link, indicates both careful study of the issue treated here and a rhetorical sense of facts that will persuade readers. The paper's author is developing many negative ideas about Wilson. If the writer can quote from a historian known to love Wilson's memory, his argument in the paper will be all the more compelling.

---

[24]Link, The Road to the White House, p. 2.

That history, of course, included slavery. And
Link says, "He was characteristically a Southerner in
his attitude toward the Negro. Like most Southerners
of the upper class, his tolerance of and kindliness to
the Negro were motivated by a strong paternalistic
feeling."[25]

Paternalism and kindliness meant that though Wilson did not believe in violence toward blacks, he
thought they should be kept in inferior status until
some unspecified time when they might have earned some
rights to general advancement. Link's ''paternalism''
scarcely expresses the extent of Wilson's sense that
blacks did not know what was good for them and had to
be regulated by discreet and wise white men.

> Now the writer of the paper has moved from Link's words
> to the writer's own interpretation of what Wilson's general
> attitudes meant to his view of American blacks. We move
> from factual information to the sort of interpretation that
> shows the writer has thought deeply about the texts used
> as evidence.

Wilson saw blacks in the South as politically incompetent. In an article he tried and failed twice to
publish in 1881, Wilson explained the solidity of the
old Confederacy behind the Democratic Party. It was
all caused by the enfranchisement of blacks. Black
voting had been solidly Republican. Southern whites
were thus presented with two choices—"to be ruled by
an ignorant and an inferior race, or to band them-

---

[25]Link, <u>Road to the White House</u>, p. 3.

selves in a political union not to be broken till the danger had passed."[26]

> The writer proceeds with summary and interpretation. He is showing why he has inferred what he has about Wilson. He is not giving naked opinion as a basis for interpretation; he is carefully spelling out the evidence.

Were blacks born inferior, or were they made inferior by their environment? Wilson is unclear on the point. He quotes with favor the sentiments of the Virginian A. H. H. Stuart, who had recently written that southerners opposed "ignorant suffrage entirely irrespective of race or color. . . . We object to their votes because their <u>minds</u> are dark--because they are ignorant, uneducated, and incompetent to form an enlightened opinion on any of the public questions which they may be called on to decide at the polls."[27] There were, he said in conclusion, some blacks who had become "extensive land holders and industrious farmers of their own lands," and these people appeared the start of "an exceedingly valuable, because steady and hardy, peasantry."[28]

> The writer of the paper here asks a significant question: Did Wilson believe that blacks were born inferior to whites, or that they happened to be inferior because of their condition? The writer admits that he is unable to tell precisely what Wilson's point was on this question, though his extensive quotations from Wilson's work show clearly

---

[26]*The Wilson Papers*, vol. 2, pp. 51–52.
[27]*The Wilson Papers*, vol. 2, p. 51.
[28]*The Wilson Papers*, vol. 2, p. 54.

enough Wilson's negativism toward blacks. Never be afraid to admit that you do not know the answer to an important question that you pose in your paper. The questions are worth posing even if you cannot answer them precisely.

The South was striving, he thought, to lift blacks "from degradation."[29] If the Republican Party would accept the situation in the South, the fears of southern whites would be mollified. It is difficult to know if these sentiments represented genuine conviction that blacks could be uplifted until most of them might have the vote. His mention of a "steady and hardy peasantry" may be an almost subconscious statement of how far Wilson expected blacks to advance—to a position of recognizable worth but just as recognizable inferiority. He gives no indication anywhere that he expected blacks to rise in business or the professions. Certain it is that he expected blacks to improve themselves first and only then to be allowed to vote. He expected this progress to require a very long time. Because progress was under way (he thought) but nowhere near complete, his energies went to restricting black participation in political life.

Here the writer is again interpreting—thinking about his evidence and trying to puzzle out its meaning. A good history paper nearly always has some interpretation by the writer. No good historian merely compiles the facts. The good historian is also a *thinker*, always fitting the evidence together as coherently as possible, and trying to answer im-

---

[29]*The Wilson Papers*, vol. 2, p. 54.

portant questions about it. If the questions cannot be answered, the historian must say so.

These sentiments of the young Wilson did not change. In his mature work, <u>A History of the American People</u>, published in five volumes in 1901 and 1902, he discussed the origins of the Ku Klux Klan just after the Civil War. The Fifteenth Amendment, giving the freed slaves the right to vote, ensured that "The dominance of the negroes [<u>sic</u>] in the South was to be made a principle of the very constitution of the Union." It was a "radical Amendment," said Wilson, and it caused "the temporary disintegration of southern society and the utter, apparently the irretrievable, alienation of the South" from the Republican Party.[30]

> The writer moves to additional evidence. After citing Wilson's earlier work on the black's place in the civic life of the South, he passes on to Wilson's influential later work, written when Wilson was fully mature.

He says not a word to support the notion that blacks required the right to vote if they were to make good their freedom.

> This one-sentence paragraph is set off for emphasis. The writer wants to make its statement stand out. There is no set length for paragraphs. Often a paragraph will have four or five sentences. But sometimes, as in this instance, a writer will make an entire paragraph of one sentence.

---

[30]Woodrow Wilson, <u>A History of the American People</u>, New York, Harper & Brothers, 1901–1902, vol. 5, p. 58.

The Klan grew up, he says, around Pulaski, Tennessee, when young men "finding time hang heavy on their hands . . . formed a secret club for the mere pleasure of association."[31] He describes how these young men rode around at night under the moon, wearing white masks and with horses sheeted up like ghosts. The aim of the Klansmen was to frighten blacks. And they succeeded, much to Wilson's evident pleasure.

> It was the delightful discovery of the thrill of awesome fear, the woeful looking for of calamity that swept through the countrysides as they moved from place to place upon their silent visitations, coming no man could say whence, going upon no man knew what errand, that put thought of mischief into the minds of the frolicking comrades. It threw the negroes into a very ecstasy of panic to see these sheeted "Ku Klux" move near them in the shrouded night; and their comic fear stimulated the lads who excited it to many an extravagant prank and mummery.[32]

Here is another useful block quotation. The idea that a president of the United States might have taken such a lighthearted view toward the Ku Klux Klan may seem so startling to modern readers that the writer of the paper has decided to include a long quotation from Wilson as unmistakable evidence. He interprets Wilson's remarks by saying

---

[31]<u>History</u>, vol. 5, p. 59.
[32]<u>History</u>, vol. 5, p. 60.

that they show Wilson's "evident pleasure" at the Klan's activity.

Wilson admits that things went bad when "malicious fellows of the baser sort who did not feel the compulsions of honor and who had private grudges to satisfy" imitated the disguises of honorable Klansmen and did unspecified bad things.[33] It is clear from his account that he thinks things finally went too far, creating in some places in the South "a reign of terror."[34]

Yet it is also clear from his text that he sympathized with the Klansmen's original aims, even if he did not condone their later, more violent methods. He reports with obvious disapproval an 1871 act of Congress intended "to crush the Ku Klux Klan and all lawless bands acting after its fashion." Most startling is Wilson's acquiescence in the breaking of the law by white southerners. It was not their law; therefore, he seems to say, they were not bound by it. White leaders in the South were shut off from the ballot, he says. And so they had to act in other ways:

Those who loved mastery and adventure directed the work of the Ku Klux. Those whose tastes and principles made such means unpalatable brought their influence to bear along every line of counsel or of management that promised to thrust the

---

[33]*History*, vol. 5, p. 62.
[34]*History*, Vol. 5, p. 64.

carpet bagger out of office and discourage the negro in the use of his vote. Congress saw where
they meant to regain their mastery, at the polls,
and by what means, the intimidation and control of
the negroes without regard to law,—the law thrust
upon them, not their own; and hastened to set up a
new barrier of statute against them.[35]

> Another acceptable block quotation, intended to show Wil-
> son's lack of condemnation for the Klan and his sense that
> white Southerners had a right to break the law when they
> disapproved of it. Should the writer have summarized this
> information?

Throughout his discussion of Reconstruction, Wilson takes the view that by his time was the canonical
southern attitude: Reconstruction was an unmitigated
evil thrust upon the South by the victorious North,
and the heart of the evil was the franchise extended
to the former slaves. He never asks questions that
might have helped him and his readers understand why
Reconstruction came about. The southern states had
been in rebellion against the authority of the central
government. In other societies, the leaders of a van-
quished rebellion had usually been shot or hanged and
sometimes publicly tortured to demonstrate the futil-
ity of rebellion. The defeated southerners were not
treated so cruelly, but the victorious Washington
government did have some reason to put the former
secessionist states on probation. Depriving former

---

[35]*History*, vol. 5, pp. 72–74.

rebels of the vote was better than depriving them of
their lives. But to Wilson the historian, the Republican Party in charge of Reconstruction was dastardly
to the core and its measures wicked just because they
attempted to make full citizens of blacks who had so
long been in bondage. Because the Reconstruction measures were imposed on the South by force, southerners
had no moral obligation to obey them.

> A paragraph of interpretation. The writer of the paper
> summarizes Wilson's view of reconstruction and attacks
> Wilson for holding it. But there is more than mere attack
> here. The writer explains Wilson's views, trying to see
> them as Wilson himself did.

Though Wilson never quite praises or condones the
violence done by Klansmen and others, he does explain
it and excuse it. Clearly, in his view of things, violence was a lesser evil than black suffrage. He is
particularly indignant with Charles Sumner, the Senator from Massachusetts, who before the war had been an
abolitionist and after the war an advocate of federal
support for black rights in the South. Sumner, says
Wilson, insisted that blacks have "social rights" as
well as political rights.[36]

What were these "social" rights? They were incorporated in the Act of Congress of February 1875, which
"gave the federal courts the authority, by appropriate
process and penalty, to enforce the right of negroes
to accommodation in public inns, theatres, railway

---

[36]History, vol. 5, p. 97.

carriages, and schools, and to service upon all jur-
ies, upon the same footing as white persons."[37]
Clearly for Wilson "social" rights included any public
association between blacks and whites on grounds of
apparent equality. In short, Wilson the historian was
advocating the segregation of the races that did not
legally end until the civil-rights legislation in the
1960s. The 1875 act, says Wilson, "For eight years
. . . was to fail utterly of accomplishing its object
and yet to work its work of irritation, to be set
aside at last by the Supreme Court (1883) as an invasion of the legal field of the States which no portion
of the constitution, new or old, could be made to
sustain."[38] The word "irritation" seems significant in
view of Wilson's later use of the word "friction" in
his discussions with William Monroe Trotter.

Wilson believed that any association between
blacks and whites in the workplace, in schools, or on
public transportation was bound to create problems.
This was the unexamined principle behind all his
pronouncements on relations between the races. Therefore, the states, and the federal bureaucracy, could
segregate the races. His interview with Trotter in
1914 shows unwillingness to consider that the humiliation experienced by blacks in such segregation had
anything to do with the matter. The humiliation was

---

[37]History, vol. 5, p. 98.
[38]History, vol. 5, p. 98.

not intended; Wilson's view was that blacks should
accept his own good intentions and make the best of
them. Southerners had been entitled to break the law
in their wish to enforce segregation; Wilson felt entitled to make rules to the same end.

> Further interpretation. The writer is summing up the
> meaning of Wilson's attitudes.

Most striking in Wilson's History of the American
People is how vague it all is. Wilson intended his
book for the broad general public. Today such a writer
would tell illustrative anecdotes about people. Wilson
almost never tells an anecdote. His statements remain
assertions that we are to believe on account of his
authority. He gives us little reason to accept that
authority. We learn that things were done, but we
never learn the mechanism by which they were done.
Only now and then does some specific detail break the
monotony built by tedious assertion. In describing
Grover Cleveland, Wilson says, "He was of the open and
downright sort that all men who love strength must
always relish."[39] He does not tell us that Cleveland
had sired a son out of wedlock, a fact well known to
the public, a story that might have added content to
the vague adjective "downright." In describing how
Oklahoma was settled, Wilson comes as close as he ever
does to a specific occurrence: "At noon on the 22d of

---

[39]History, vol. 5, p. 171.

April, 1889, at the sound of a bugle blown to mark the
hour set by the President's proclamation, the waiting
multitude surged madly in, and the Territory was peo-
pled in a single day."[40] The concreteness of that
lonely bugle is almost startling in Wilson's interminable catalogues of empty generalizations.

> Here the writer of the paper shifts ground. He changes
> from discussing Wilson's attitude toward blacks in history
> to a slightly different focus: to Wilson's view of history it-
> self. The attitude is critical; the writer suggests that Wilson
> did not know how to write history well or at least that he
> did not write good history when he wrote his *History of the
> American People.*

This quality of generality in his writing of history fitted the generalizations he could make about
blacks. If his mind had been turned toward the specific, he might have told stories about responsible,
intelligent blacks turned away from the polls by ignorant and violent southern whites. He might have told
stories about victims of the Ku Klux Klan that might
have inspired indignation and sympathy not only in
readers but in himself. Such stories, had he been interested in them, might have made him at least relax
some of the rigor in his views. If we know that a
specific man in a specific place has been cruelly denied the vote (no women, black or white, voted in
America at that time), and if we know all the details
about that denial and about the suffering of the

---

[40]*History*, vol. 5, p. 212.

would—be voter, we naturally spring to sympathy with his loss of rights. But Wilson protected his prejudices by throwing around them a wall of authoritative general statement that made these sound like virtues, not only to readers but to himself. Individual blacks did not appear in his pages. Indeed, individuals scarcely appeared at all except to have their names called if they were recognized leaders and to have something general said about them.

> The discussion of Wilson's way of writing history is now brought back to the thesis of the paper. An idea that might have appeared as a generalization is firmly attached to the argument of the essay.

His prejudices were not against blacks alone. Wilson's own ancestry was north European. When he taught at Bryn Mawr and at Princeton, he offered courses in English and French history. When he came to discuss immigration in the later nineteenth century, he wrote:

Throughout the century men of the sturdy stocks of the north of Europe had made up the main strain of foreign blood which was every year added to the vital working force of the country, or else men of the Latin—Gallic stocks of France and northern Italy; but now there came multitudes of men of the lowest class from the south of Italy and men of the meaner sort out of Hungary and Poland, men out of the ranks where there was neither skill nor energy nor any initiative of quick intelligence; and they came in numbers which increased from year to year, as if the countries of

the south of Europe were disburdening themselves
of the more sordid and hapless elements of their
population, the men whose standards of life and of
work were such as American workmen had never
dreamed of hitherto.[41]

> The long block quotation again serves the purpose of establishing that an American president did indeed express ideas that today would be shocking if they came from such a source. The block quotation calls forth the interpretation presented in the next paragraph. President Woodrow Wilson had a mind disposed to prejudice against people unlike himself. Is the block necessary, or should it have been condensed?

Wilson's ideas about democracy were built on the
assumption that only specific classes and people were
worthy of self-government. Arthur S. Link, devoted as
he is to Wilson, discusses this aspect of Wilson's
career with obvious pain. Wilson himself finally admitted to approving of segregation in government departments, claiming that it was "distinctly to the
advantage of the colored people themselves."[42] Support
for segregation from the president was bound to have a
powerful effect, and to Wilson belongs much of the
blame for the federal government's failure to support
the black struggle for equal rights until it was
forced to do so by the Supreme Court, the civil-rights
movement led by the Rev. Martin Luther King, Jr., and
many others, culminating in the Civil Rights Act of
1964.

---

[41]*History*, vol. 5, p. 213.
[42]Link, *The New Freedom*, p. 251.

> Arthur Link is again brought in as an authority for the
> writer's point of view, though Link does not condemn Wil-
> son as the writer of this paper does. The writer continues
> to interpret the sum of the evidence he has presented on his
> way to arriving at a conclusion.

Link points out that Wilson was not alone in his

prejudices. Many newspapers and leaders spoke out

against Wilson's segregationist policies. But, says

Link, speaking of Wilson's Cabinet, "If there were any

opponents of segregation in the Cabinet, they did not

then or afterward raise their voices."[43]

> Another transition now comes in the paper. The writer
> shifts from discussing Wilson to the larger American con-
> text that made Wilson's views unsurprising at the time. He
> does not want to place all the blame on Wilson, recognizing
> that Wilson's acts represented a large consensus among
> American whites. That fact does not excuse Wilson or the
> American people who agreed with him at the time. But it
> does help us understand why Wilson was able to establish
> a policy that today would be incomprehensible coming
> from an American president.

Despite the protests against segregation, a major-

ity of whites in America supported discrimination. In

the year after Wilson's last meeting with William

Monroe Trotter, D. W. Griffith brought out his Birth

of a Nation, glorifying the Ku Klux Klan and portray-

ing blacks as ignorant, malicious, arrogant, and

lusting after white women. The film-script writer

quoted Woodrow Wilson's History of the American People

to justify the Klan. It was shown in the White House,

though Link holds that Wilson did not thereby endorse

---

[43]Link, The New Freedom, p. 247.

the film. Even so, Wilson refused to condemn the film publicly. To do so, he said privately, would be to appear "to be trying to meet the agitation . . . stirred up by that unspeakable fellow Tucker."[44] "Tucker" was Trotter; Wilson got his name wrong. In April 1915, Trotter was charged with assault in Boston when he was refused in his request to buy a ticket for the film, which he may have intended to disrupt.[45] Wilson evidently had this incident in mind, and he could not bring himself to do anything that might seem to support Trotter's position.

> A short discussion of the film *Birth of a Nation* adds evidence to the point the writer has made about a generally racist climate in America at Wilson's time.

Others were bolder. In May 1915 former President Charles W. Eliot of Harvard spoke to a mass meeting on Boston Common about Birth of a Nation. He condemned the "dangerously false doctrine" taught by the film "that the Ku Klux Klan was on the whole a righteous and necessary society for the defence of Southern white men against black Legislatures led by Northern white men." Said Eliot, "Undoubtedly, grievous conditions existed in the South, but they did not justify the utter lawlessness and atrocities which marked the trail of the Ku-Klux. There can be no worse teaching,

---

[44]Link, The New Freedom, p. 253.
[45]Focus on "The Birth of a Nation," ed. Fred Silva, Englewood Cliffs, N.J., Prentice-Hall, 1971, pp. 72-73.

no more mischievous doctrine than this, that lawlessness is justified when necessary."[46]

> Mention of the exceptions to a general American pattern of
> discrimination help emphasize Wilson's position. Wilson
> cannot be excused with the claim that every white in
> America endorsed discriminatory policies against blacks.
> Eliot's willingness to speak out against discrimination
> shows that many Americans disliked the racist trend in
> their society.

The philosophy Eliot condemned happened to be the
express view of the president of the United States
about the Klan. Though Wilson did not formally endorse
the film, the quotation of his work in the film itself
was an endorsement of the film's fundamental message.
Nothing, not even violent lawlessness, seemed as bad
to Wilson as blacks in control, and surely they would
be in control in many southern states if they were
given equality with whites.

The popularity of the film was in part testimony
to Griffith's cinematic genius. But the record of the
country at large in civil rights shows that the popularity was also testimony to racial prejudice among
the American people that was to rule for decades.
Woodrow Wilson's influence on race relations was per-
nicious. His meeting with William Monroe Trotter in
November 1914 was a disaster for Wilson's long-term
reputation, but more important, it was a calamity for
blacks, now facing a president who thought he was
doing good. A sadder realization is that Wilson un-

---

[46]Focus on "The Birth of a Nation," p. 73.

doubtedly represented the views of most Americans in his day. Trotter received vigorous support from a few northern papers and liberal groups. None of these counted so much at the time as the conviction among most American whites that Woodrow Wilson's prejudices stood for truth.

> The final paragraph sums up the argument of the paper. It forms the climax of the writer's interpretations. Notice how many words and thoughts are repeated here from the first paragraph.

Bibliography

Focus on "The Birth of a Nation," ed. Fred Silva, Englewood Cliffs, N.J., Prentice–Hall, 1971.

Fox, Stephen R., *The Guardian of Boston: William Monroe Trotter*, New York, Atheneum, 1970.

Link, Arthur S., *Wilson: The New Freedom*, Princeton, Princeton University Press, 1956.

Link, Arthur S., *Wilson: The Road to the White House*, Princeton, Princeton University Press, 1947.

Wilson, Woodrow, *A History of the American People*, New York, Harper & Brothers, 1901–1902, vol. 5.

Wilson, Woodrow, *The Papers of Woodrow Wilson*, ed. Arthur S. Link and others, Princeton, Princeton University Press, vol. 2, 1967, vol. 28, 1978, vol. 31, 1979.

> Notice that the bibliography is listed in alphabetical order by the authors' last names. For further information on footnotes, endnotes, and bibliography, see Chapter 6.

SOME CONCLUDING NOTES
ABOUT THE PAPER

The author of this paper presents primary sources, secondary sources, and his own interpretations to arrive at a thesis: President Woodrow Wilson made federal-government policy according to his belief that black Americans were inferior to whites. The paper is far more than a mere sticking together of sources. The writer has thought about the material and has arrived at interpretations that help explain it. He has inferred much from his texts. Wilson does not say, "I heartily approve of the Ku Klux Klan." But he writes about the Klan in such a way that the writer feels justified in inferring that Wilson thought that the Klan was a better choice than giving black Americans the vote.

The author's own point of view is unmistakable: He laments the decisions Wilson made to enforce racial segregation in America. Yet the author does not spend time pouring invective on Wilson's head; he does not preach to us. A historian can make a judgment on whether actions in the past were good or bad; historians do that sort of thing all the time. It is not acceptable in the field of history to preach with vehement emotion either for or against a person or an act in the past. He realizes that it is sufficient to point out the things Wilson said and did without vehemently denouncing Wilson himself. Readers can then see that Wilson harmed the cause of equality in America, and they can make up their own mind about his character. We have a right to be angry with Wilson after studying the evidence. Yet anger does no good in writing history, and it can so irritate readers that they stop reading. The reader of this paper does not read it to see how angry the writer is; the reader reads to see what Wilson did and why.

The author moves the paper steadily throughout to develop its thesis. When new information is presented, we are told immediately how that information relates to the thesis of the paper; we are not left wondering. The paper is documented throughout so that we can look up the evidence if we want to know more about it. The emphasis on primary sources helps prevent the paper from being a collage of what others have said about Wilson. The author's thoughtfulness in dealing with his sources is so thorough that at the end we feel we have learned something worthwhile from someone who has taken pains to become an authority in this area of Wilson's life and thought.

It will help your own writing if you analyze your papers as this one is analyzed for you. Thinking through your work like this may be complicated at first. When you get a little practice, it becomes second nature, especially as you read your text again and again.

6

Documenting Your Sources

Throughout this book and other books you read about history, you become familiar with documentation—footnotes or endnotes, citations within the text, and bibliographic references. These citations are so common that you take them for granted. You saw them in the paper on Woodrow Wilson; you see them in nearly every book about history that you read.

You are aware that historians depend on primary and secondary sources to produce their stories about the past. Other historians want to be able to find that evidence. They can study the evidence for themselves and decide whether a piece of historical writing interprets the evidence correctly. They can also study the evidence for their own research, as you do when you use footnotes in articles and books to show the sources you use in writing a paper in history. Think of documentation as a generous act: it helps colleagues in the discipline.

Whenever you quote from a source or use information gathered from a source, let your readers know what you are doing. If you quote the exact words from a source, enclose those words with quotation marks and let readers know where you found the quotation. (If the quotation is more than about five lines long, you should usually set it off as an indented block and not use quotation marks. See pages 231–232.) If you express in your own words information gathered from a source, let readers know where you found that information. If you do not let readers know the source of your words or the place where you found the information, you may be guilty of plagiarism.

Here are some simple rules to help you avoid plagiarism and to know when to acknowledge that you have taken information from a source.

1. Use a footnote, an endnote, or a mention in your text whenever you quote directly from another person. A good rule of thumb is to give the attribution for any quotation of three or more successive words from a source. Always put such quotations within quotation marks in the body of your text.

Here is a text from a secondary source, Frederick A. Pottle's *James Boswell: The Earlier Years, 1740–1769.* Pottle speaks of Samuel Johnson, author of the first great English dictionary and sage of eighteenth-century England:

> Johnson was at this time in his fifty-fourth year, a huge, slovenly, near-sighted scholar, his face scarred by scrofula, his body distorted by compulsive tics, his speech interspersed with absent-minded clucks and mutterings.[1]

You might cite part of this text with a direct quotation followed by a footnote.

```
When Boswell met him, Johnson was fifty-four years
old, "a huge, slovenly, near-sighted scholar, his face
scarred by scrofula, his body distorted by compulsive
tics, his speech interspersed with absent-minded
clucks and mutterings."[2]
```

Or you can attribute your source in your own text like this:

```
Frederick A. Pottle says that when Boswell met him,
Johnson was fifty-four years old, "a huge, slovenly,
near-sighted scholar, his face scarred by scrofula,
```

[1]New York, McGraw-Hill, 1985, p. 113.
[2]New York, McGraw-Hill, 1985, p. 113.

```
his body distorted by compulsive tics, his speech in-
terspersed with absent-minded clucks and mutterings."³
```

In some kinds of publications—a newspaper story, for example—the format would not allow you to use footnotes or endnotes. Your teacher may ask you to do a short paper without footnotes or endnotes—a brief report, a position paper, a summary of your knowledge on a topic. Even without footnotes and endnotes, you can show in your text that you are quoting someone else's work.

2. Acknowledge any paraphrase or summary you make from a source. Here is a paragraph from the book by Philippe Ariès called *The Hour of Our Death,* a history of attitudes toward death in the Western world:

> Since death is not the end of the loved one, however bitter the grief of the survivor, death is neither ugly nor fearful. On the contrary, death is beautiful, as the dead body is beautiful. Presence at the deathbed in the nineteenth century is more than a customary participation in a social ritual; it is an opportunity to witness a spectacle that is both comforting and exalting. A visit to the house in which someone has died is a little like a visit to a museum. How beautiful he is! In the bedrooms of the most ordinary middle-class Western homes, death has come to coincide with beauty. This is the final stage in an evolution that began very quietly with the beautiful recumbent figures of the Renaissance and continued in the aestheticism of the baroque. But this apotheosis should not blind us to the contradiction it contains, for this death is no longer death; it is an illusion of Art. Death has started to hide. In spite of the apparent publicity that surrounds it in mourning, at the cemetery, in life as well as in art and literature, death is concealing itself under the mask of beauty.⁴

Here is how someone might summarize this passage. The summary would require a footnote or an endnote.

---

³New York, McGraw-Hill, 1985, p. 113.
⁴Philippe Ariès, *The Hour of Our Death,* tr. Helen Weaver, New York, Vintage Books, 1982, p. 473.

>   In the nineteenth century the attitude toward
> death turned into a cult of the beautiful. People
> gathered around the deathbed to participate in an oc-
> casion that was supposed to be exalting. In fact, such
> rituals were a way of hiding death, of granting an
> artistic illusion to the moment of life's end. The
> thought seemed to be that if people could put a beau-
> tiful mask on death, it would cease to be death.

Because the thought in the paragraph depends on the material in the source, the writer should indicate her indebtedness. One might do so with a footnote at the end of the paragraph. It would be even better to write a statement like this:

>   Philippe Ariès has said that the attitude toward death
> in the nineteenth century turned into a cult of the
> beautiful.

You could go on then with the paragraph as it was written in the first version, putting a footnote at the end.

3. Acknowledge any significant ideas that you have picked up from reading that you have done. Sometimes you can make this acknowledgment in your text. Sometimes you need to add a footnote. You might say something like this:

>   Richard Lanham feels that the <u>Book of the Courtier</u>,
> frequently called an aristocratic book, is in reality
> a bourgeois creation.

The important tasks are always to let people know where you have found your ideas and where they should go to find further information in your sources.

4. Do not footnote common knowledge or common expressions or allusions.

Common knowledge includes information that is so widely known that it would seem foolish to mention its source. You do not have to give footnotes to the information that Franklin Roosevelt was elected president in 1932 or that the Japanese attacked Pearl Harbor on December 7, 1941, or that Thomas More wrote the book *Utopia,* or that Columbus discovered America. Nor do you have to footnote common expressions. You do not have to tell people that the sentence, "Pride goeth before destruction," comes from the Bible or that "To be or not to be" and "to paint the lily" come from Shakespeare.

Sometimes you may not know what knowledge is common in the area of history in which you are writing. You can usually decide by looking at several books or articles to see if they have the information. Innumerable books list the popes or the monarchs of England. Therefore you need not footnote the information that Pope Clement II ruled the Catholic Church from 1046 to 1047. But the medieval gossip that he was poisoned because he was a German and not an Italian would have to be footnoted to acknowledge the scholars who have studied Clement's life.

Sometimes you can write notes within your text in parentheses. If you are writing about only one book, as you might be in a thoughtful report about the book, some teachers will ask that you give the full bibliographic information about that book in a special appendix at the end of your paper. Then you can put the page numbers in parentheses.

Ladurie believes that men in medieval Montaillou were more likely to be able to marry for love than were women (p. 189). He means that men had choice in the matter, but the women they chose often did not.

In some papers you may use several sources, all fully described in your bibliography. If you do not then wish to use footnotes or endnotes, you may refer to the works by citing their authors.

Medieval women seemed to marry while they were still adolescents, but young men remained single until they

```
were twenty-five or even older (Ladurie p. 262). But
some evidence suggests that the numbers of marriages
fluctuated. People tended to marry with greater fre-
quency in time of plague as if to make up for the
population carried off by illness (Braudel p. 71).
```

If you cite two or more books by the same author, you may
have to add a short title within the parentheses to let readers know
that you are quoting from first one book and then the other. Suppose you wish to use Fernand Braudel's books, *Wheels of Commerce*
and *Structures of Everyday Life*. You might write a paragraph like
this with abbreviated titles set within your parenthetical annotation:

```
Both Columbus and the Vikings learned that the cur-
rents and the winds of the Atlantic Ocean will easily
carry ships both east and west (Braudel, Structures
p. 409). But for a very long time the largest seagoing
commerce was carried in small ships that traded along
the coastlines of Europe and never ventured far out
into the great and dangerous ocean (Braudel, Wheels
p. 362).
```

Notice that the abbreviated title is underlined or set in italics,
just as one would set off the full title of the book.

FOOTNOTES AND ENDNOTES

Parenthetical annotation gained in favor among history teachers and publishers for a long time. Such notes are easy and therefore
inexpensive to write and to set in type. They are, however, distracting. With computer word-processing programs that make
footnotes easily, the footnote may be coming back.

As the names suggest, footnotes are placed at the bottom or
foot of the page on which the reference to a source is made; end-

notes are placed at the end of the paper. The advantage of the foot-note is that the reader can look down easily from the text to the footnote. Some readers and editors find footnotes distracting, though, because they break up the eye's run across the page. The reader seeing a footnote number feels compelled to glance down to the note to which the number refers, thus breaking the train of thought created by the reading. To some, footnotes are as distract-ing as commercials that break the flow of a movie on television. Endnotes are less obtrusive. As might be expected, the complaint that some people make against footnotes is reason for others to extol them: the source is immediately available to the reader.

Follow the procedure required by your teacher or your pub-lisher. That advice also holds for the forms of the notes, whether they be footnotes or endnotes. Historians have never adopted a standard footnote form such as that used by the Modern Language Association. The main requirements most teachers and editors specify are that the notes provide enough information to allow readers to look up the sources for themselves. For a book, that means you should provide the name of the author, the title of the book, the place where the book was published, and the year of publication. Most editors and teachers like to have the publishing company listed, too.

Books sometimes migrate from publisher to publisher. A first edition may be published by one company, a second edition of the same book by another. The publisher of a book in hardcover often sells to another firm the right to bring the book out in paperback. Page numbers may change from edition to edition as pages are added or deleted or as the typeface is changed so that the contents of the book take up more or less room. A book may be published by one company in the United States and by another company in Great Britain in the same year, and the two editions may be slightly different. Adding the name of the publisher to the footnote or end-note may reduce some of the confusion caused by this migration. The publisher's name usually goes between the city where the book is published and the date of publication.

An article in a journal should have the author's name, the title of the article, the date of publication, and the page numbers in the journal. Many editors and teachers like to have the volume number of the journal, though others find this information redundant. The

February 1988 issue of *American Historical Review* happens to be volume 93 of that journal. In a few libraries the volume number may be stamped on the outside of the binding without additional information about the month and the year, and so in looking at a dimly lit library shelf, you may find volume 93 more easily than if the only reference you had was "February 1988." In my experience the year of the volume is stamped on the spine of most bound periodicals in nearly all libraries. To my mind the volume number in a bibliographic reference is an unnecessary complication. But again, consult your teacher or your editor, and follow the directions.

Here are sample footnotes or endnotes for various kinds of publication. I prefer the simple method of setting off every part of the note with commas and using a period at the end, and no publisher of mine has ever objected. Notice that the number at the beginning of the note is slightly elevated above the line in this style—an elevation easily performed by word-processing programs and computers these days. I use the abbreviation "p." for "page" because it clearly sets off the page number from other data in the entry. Some editors and teachers omit it, especially after parentheses.

[1]David McCullough, Mornings on Horseback, New York, Simon and Schuster, 1982, p. 183.

It is probably somewhat more common to place the publication data within parentheses:

[1]David McCullough, Mornings on Horseback (New York: Simon and Schuster, 1982), p. 183.

or

[1]David McCullough, Mornings on Horseback (New York, 1982), 183.

Many publishing houses omit the name of the publisher of books listed in footnotes and bibliographies. It is unlikely that two publishing houses in New York City would have issued David

McCullough's *Mornings on Horseback* in the same year. The place of publication is therefore enough to locate the edition of the book that you have used.

In the footnote or endnote, the first name of the author is given first. In the bibliographic note, which we will quickly come to, the author's last name is given first.

A book that has been translated into English from another language usually has the translator's name after the title:

> ²Jacob Burckhardt, <u>The Civilization of the Renaissance in Italy</u>, tr. S. G. C. Middlemore, Greenwich (Conn.), Phaidon, 1965, p. 14.

or

> ²Jacob Burckhardt, <u>The Civilization of the Renaissance in Italy</u>, tr. S. G. C. Middlemore (Greenwich, Conn.: Phaidon, 1965), 14.

The city of publication, "Greenwich," has the abbreviation for Connecticut after it to show that the book was not published in Greenwich, England.

When a book has more than one author, list the authors in the order in which they appear in the book itself.

> ³Joseph R. Strayer and Hans W. Gatzke, <u>The Mainstream of Civilization</u>, 4th ed., San Diego, Harcourt Brace Jovanovich, 1984, p. 146.

or

> ³Joseph R. Strayer and Hans W. Gatzke, <u>The Mainstream of Civilization</u>, 4th ed. (San Diego: Harcourt Brace Jovanovich, 1984), 146.

The edition number in this citation appears after the title. Books often go through several editions. You need not give an edition number for the first edition; do refer to the number of later editions.

A work in more than one volume may be cited in several ways:

⁴Jaroslav Pelikan, <u>The Christian Tradition</u>, vol. 4, <u>Reformation of Church and Dogma, 1300–1700</u>, Chicago, University of Chicago Press, 1984, p. 155.

or

⁴Jaroslav Pelikan, vol. 4, <u>Reformation of Church and Dogma, 1300–1700</u>, Chicago, University of Chicago Press, 1984, 155.

This work is the fourth volume in a series called *The Christian Tradition*. Volume 4 has its own title. Many writers would omit the series title *The Christian Tradition* and give only the title of volume 4 as though it were an independent book. Anyone looking in a card catalogue under the name "Pelikan, Jaroslav" would find the title easily even without the series name.

Some books are collections of essays, and you may wish to cite one of the essays. Give the author of the essay you wish to mention, put the title of the essay in quotation marks, and give the title of the book, the editor of the book, the publication data, and the page number.

⁷J. H. Baker, "Law and Legal Institutions," <u>William Shakespeare</u>, ed. John F. Andrews, New York, Charles Scribner's Sons, 1985, vol. 1, p. 43.

An article in a standard reference work is cited without page or volume numbers, though the title of the article is placed within quotation marks. It is assumed that those looking for the article will know to look it up in the alphabetical order in which such articles appear in such works. The year of the edition does appear in the note because articles are revised from edition to edition.

"Charles V," <u>Encyclopaedia Britannica</u>, 1974.

An article in a scholarly journal may be cited in one of these two ways. The first is without the volume number of the periodical:

[8]Natalie Zemon Davis, "History's Two Bodies," <u>American Historical Review</u>, February 1988, p. 6.

The other method of citation uses the volume number and places the date within parentheses:

[8]Natalie Zemon Davis, "History's Two Bodies," <u>American Historical Review</u>, 93 (February 1988), 6.

In citing a book review, you give both the author of the review and the title and author of the book being reviewed. In your citation of the review, you do not have to give the publication data on the book that is reviewed.

[9]Elizabeth G. Gleason, review of <u>Venetian Humanism in an Age of Patrician Dominance</u> by Margaret L. King, <u>Sixteenth Century Journal</u>, 18 (Winter 1987), 611.

Often, as in the paper on Woodrow Wilson and segregation, you may use a footnote or endnote to add information that you do not wish to place in the body of your paper. You may add bibliographic material to that information, or you may let the information stand by itself.

Cite manuscript materials as simply as possible. If you use letters, you can give the writer, the person to whom the letter was sent, and the date.

[10]Jones to Smith, September 3, 1873.

When you cite a book or an article for the second time, you need include only the author's name and the page number. Readers will assume that you are referring to the same work that you have previously footnoted.

[11]Davis, p. 10.

If you have used several books by the same author, you may devise a short title referring to the book you intend to cite in an additional reference to the work.

[12]Braudel, <u>Wheels</u>, p. 140.

In multivolume works you can sometimes use the volume numbers with an abbreviation of the work. The *Yale Edition of the Complete Works of St. Thomas More* is usually abbreviated *CW*. For a paper in which you cited many works by More scattered throughout the volumes of the edition, you might use the abbreviation thus, especially for notes after the first reference to the work:

[13]More, <u>CW 8</u>, p. 731.

Notice that both the abbreviation and the volume number are usually placed in italics or underlined.

BIBLIOGRAPHIES

The bibliography, an alphabetical listing, by author, of works cited in your paper, is placed at the end of your work. You have seen the bibliography for the paper on Woodrow Wilson and segregation. If the author is not given, the work is alphabetized according to the first word in the title. Just as variations appear in footnote and endnote style, so do they also appear in bibliographies. Some editors and teachers require periods setting off the author from the title and the title from the publication data.

Breen, Quirinus. <u>John Calvin: A Study in French Hu-</u>

<u>manism</u>. Chicago, 1931.

Or, you could make the bibliographic reference like this:

Breen, Quirinus, <u>John Calvin: A Study in French Hu-
manism</u>, Chicago, University of Chicago Press,
1931.

In both instances, the body of the reference is indented under the
first line. This style allows readers to spot the author's name
quickly, and on a page it clearly sets off each bibliographic entry.
Notice, too, that in both styles for making a bibliographic entry,
the parentheses around the publication data are omitted.

Here are some sample bibliography entries.

For a book with more than one author, the last name of the first
author is placed first, and the other names are left in their natural
order.

Strayer, Joseph R., and Hans W. Gatzke. <u>The Mainstream
of Civilization</u>, 4th ed. San Diego, Harcourt Brace
Jovanovich, 1984.

or

Strayer, Joseph R., and Hans W. Gatzke, <u>The Mainstream
of Civilization</u>, 4th ed. San Diego, Harcourt Brace
Jovanovich, 1984.

For a multivolume work:

Skinner, Quentin. <u>The Foundations of Modern Political
Thought</u>, 2 vols. Cambridge, Cambridge University
Press, 1978.

<u>Commonwealth History of Massachusetts</u>, 5 vols., ed.
Albert Bushnell Hart, New York, States History
Company, 1927, 1928.

Notice that this entry for a collection of essays composed by many authors begins with the title and puts the editor after the title.

For an article from a journal:

> Savage, Gail L. "Friend to the Workers: Social Policy
>
> at the Ministry of Agriculture Between the Wars."
>
> <u>Albion</u>, 19 (Summer 1987), pp. 193–208.

For articles, you give the page numbers in the periodical where the article is found. This information will help your colleagues find the article easily.

For an article from a collection of essays:

> Baker, J. H. "Law and Legal Institutions," <u>William</u>
>
> <u>Shakespeare</u>, ed. John F. Andrews, New York,
>
> Charles Scribner's Sons, <u>1</u>, 1985, pp. 41–54.

Notice that this article appears in the first volume of a three-volume set. The italicized *1* indicates volume 1. You might place the abbreviation *vol.* before the *1*.

7

Book Reviews

Students and working historians regularly write book reports and book reviews. A book report is a simple summary of a book. Historians write reports on books for annotated bibliographies or to serve as a general guide for other readers. These reports are, in effect, short abstracts. It's useful to write a report because the writer engages the book seriously, and the report itself provides an enduring record that may serve as a later note for research. A file of short book reports will help you refresh your recollection of your reading.

Book reviews are more complicated and demanding. Reviewers report on the content and evaluate the book, discussing matters such as the author's logic, style, evidence, conclusions, and organization. The reviewer may also compare the book with others whose authors have treated the same material. A good way to learn how to write reviews is to study examples in professional journals and in popular magazines. If you read a dozen or more book reviews, you will begin to know something about the general form that reviews take.

Always report the theme of the book. Remember the term "theme," which is not quite the same as the subject. The subject of the book may be the biography of Winston Churchill, prime minister of Great Britain during World War II. The theme may be that Churchill was a great wartime leader but a poor interpreter of the postwar world. A book may have several sub-themes, but a good book has a primary theme or thesis, the author's main purpose in writing it. That theme organizes the information the author presents and gives it meaning.

A book may be a narrative of events. It would be mindless in a textbook to present events without an effort to interpret them, to tell what they all mean. A good narrative lets readers know why the author tells us these things, and a good review will convey this purpose. Bruce Catton wrote his narrative history *The Coming Fury* to show how the United States fell into the Civil War. Barbara Tuchman wrote *Guns of August* to show how World War I began and how the combatants fell into the bloody stalemate that lasted four years.

How do you find that theme or purpose? Read the book thoughtfully. Always read the introduction or the preface, if the book has one. Students in a hurry may skip the introduction, thinking they are saving time—a serious mistake. Authors use introductions to state the reasons that impelled them to write their books. In the Introduction to his *The Classical Heritage and Its Beneficiaries,* R. R. Bolgar comments on recent attacks made by educators on the old classical curriculum. Having called attention to this hostility to the Greek and Latin classics, Bolgar gives us the theme of his book in a paragraph:

> This book has been written in the hope that it may contribute, within the narrow boundaries of its specialised approach, to the work of reevaluation which all these changes have rendered necessary. The classical heritage has played a distinctive part in the shaping of European culture. The long unbroken tale of its quickening influence stretches from Columba to E. M. Forster and Jean Anouilh. In every age, from the first to the last, the categories of European thought and the common institutions of European life have all borne to some degree the imprint of antiquity. In every age, we can find writers and men of action who benefited from their contacts with the Graeco-Roman past. We may expect therefore the history of the last fifteen hundred years to shed some light on the educational potentialities of the Greek and Latin literatures. It is not unreasonable to assume in view of Europe's long affiliation to the ancient world that an historical enquiry may prove as efficacious as psychological experiment or personal reminiscence to illuminate the manifold problems that face the classics teachers of today.[1]

[1]R. R. Bolgar, *The Classical Heritage and Its Beneficiaries,* New York, Harper and Row (Harper Torchbooks), 1964, p. 2.

Any reviewer of Bolgar's book would be obligated to begin with Bolgar's own estimate of what he thought he was doing when he wrote. Did Bolgar succeed? That is for the reviewer to judge. Bolgar's statement gives a place to start.

The first sentence in the preface to *Return to Camelot* by Mark Girouard (Yale University Press, 1981), is: "This book describes how the code of mediaeval chivalry, and the knights, castles, armour, heraldry, art, and literature that it produced were revived and adapted in Britain from the late eighteenth century until the 1914–18 war."

Here is Girouard's purpose. He expands it in the rest of the paragraph:

> Once one starts looking for the influence of chivalry in this period one finds it in almost embarrassingly large quantities. Knights in armour by the thousand are described in literature, depicted in painting, sculpture or stained glass, or actually appear live, jousting (or attempting to joust) at the Eglinton Tournament. Modern castles are everywhere, and so is the heraldry to go with them. Less obvious, but of equal if not greater interest is the part which the revival of chivalry played in creating ideals of behaviour, by which all gentlemen were influenced, even if they did not consciously realize it. In this respect chivalry had, in fact, a continuous if waning history from the Middle Ages; but from the late eighteenth century onwards it acquired a new intensity and new characteristics. The result was the chivalrous gentleman of Victorian and Edwardian days, who can be watched at work from the public schools to the Boy Scouts, and from Toynbee Hall to the outposts of the British Empire.

Now a reviewer is able to understand why Girouard wrote the book and is prepared to decide whether he succeeded.

I advise students reviewing books to turn at once to the last chapter in the book. This practice seems odd and even perverse to some. Shouldn't a book be read as the author presented it? The answer is, "Not necessarily." You may ruin a novel for yourself by reading the last chapter first. Nonfiction books present a different opportunity. If you read the last chapter first, you will know where the author is taking you from the beginning. Authors usually review their purposes in their conclusions. If you know the author's conclusion, you can keep it in mind when you go back and read the book from start to finish, and that knowledge will help you understand what you read.

Few writers can bear to leave their books without a parting shot: they want to be sure readers get the point. Reviewers should take advantage of that impulse. We will not reproduce here the entire last chapter of Girouard's book; a few paragraphs at the end convey the idea clearly enough. He has carried his story to World War I, the horrible carnage from 1914 to 1918. Here is his conclusion on the fate of the chivalric ideal:

> The increasing contrast between what was actually happening and how journalists, poets, politicians and clergymen preached or wrote about it at home filled those at the front with derision, amusement or disgust—according to their character. For, although the euphoria of the opening months of the war gradually faded away, those at home still doggedly rolled out the language which depicted the war as glorious, heroic or chivalrous. When it became increasingly hard to apply this kind of language to war in the trenches, they looked for other aspects of fighting which bore (or could be made to bear) more resemblance to war in the story-books. The activities of the Royal Flying Corps were one of them. Inevitably, Henry Newbolt weighed in: "Our airmen are singularly like the knights of the old romances," he wrote in his *Tales of the Great War* (1916); "They go out day by day, singly or in twos and threes, to hold the field against all comers, and to do battle in defence of those who cannot defend themselves. There is something especially chivalrous about these champions of the air; even the Huns, whose military principles are against chivalry, have shown themselves affected by it." Chivalry at home in literature or journalism was combined with chivalry in images. All through the war, and in the years that followed it, St. Georges, St. Michaels, and knights in armour continue to appear in memorial windows, in cartoons, in statues, in posters and even occasionally on postcards. Watts's Sir Galahad was transformed into stained glass in at least six different places; in Grahamstown in South Africa his Happy Warrior appeared alongside Sir Galahad in the same window.
>
> In retrospect such symbols of chivalry seem a little pathetic, for they were in fact swamped by the mass of other images and mementoes produced by the war, and moreover the values for which they stood were beginning to crumble round them. The sheer weight of numbers involved in the Great War is staggering. It is not

the occasional St. Georges that move one or even the memorials to the golden boys of the upper classes so much as the endless rows of headstones in the war cemeteries, the long lists of names of ordinary people on memorials in village after village. So many deaths, such vast movements of people, such huge expenditures of money could not but have cataclysmic effects on the structure of society. Among much else, gentlemen were never going to be the same again. Their qualifications to lead had been brought into serious doubt, even if not entirely discredited. Much of their self-confidence had gone. War conditions had brought a new level of wages and independence to the working classes. The absence of so many men at the front had put women in a position of responsibility which made many of them distrust chivalry as a form of concealed slavery.

Eight and a half million people had been killed. The concept of total war had been established. The government of Russia had collapsed, and been replaced by a Bolshevik regime. Germany was left impoverished and resentful, a breeding-ground for future trouble. In the circumstances Newbolt's triumphant celebration of the Armistice, "Think of the Fleet going up the Dardanelles—Think of the centuries—Think of the centuries—Think of chivalry victorious," seems inapposite.[2]

From these paragraphs you can infer several things about Girouard's major theme: chivalry was a romantic code for the upper classes—the code of "gentlemen," it came out of reading about the past, it produced a huge literature and a large imagery, but like so many other things, it faded in the horror of World War I when its gallant forms could not comprehend the carnage of industrialized and impersonal slaughter.

When you do go through the book the first time, skim it quickly. Read the table of contents, look at the first and last paragraphs in every chapter, look at the illustrations (if there are any) and the legends under them, dip in here and there. This sort of reading helps you absorb the meaning of the book and the author's point of view; it does not take long. Then you will be ready to think about the theme of the book. When you do start the more methodical reading, you will usually find that following the book

[2]Mark Girouard, *The Return to Camelot: Chivalry and the English Gentleman,* New Haven, Yale University Press, 1981, pp. 291–293.

is easier than it would have been had you not made this preparation.

This kind of reading also helps you remember things better. Few frustrations are quite so painful as the forgetfulness that overtakes all of us after we read something. Approaching a book in several ways helps memory, and thus makes your review better.

Your teacher or the editor requiring the review will give you a word limit. Professional journals usually ask for the book to be reviewed in 800 to 1,000 words—three and a half to four and a half pages. Sometimes a teacher or an editor will want a much longer review. Whatever the limits, stay within them.

The theme of the book usually comes first in the review. You may begin with a quotation from the book that spells this theme out. Then you may wish to define it further. The quotation need not be a complete sentence. If you were reviewing the book by Mark Girouard on English ideals of chivalry before World War I, you might quote part of the opening sentence like this:

Mark Girouard's Return to Camelot "describes how the code of mediaeval chivalry, and the knights, castles, armour, heraldry, art and literature that it produced, were revived and adapted in Britain from the late eighteenth century until the 1914—18 war." Girouard, an English architectural historian, gives much attention to architecture in this book, but his main purpose is to reflect on the spirit of the age as revealed in art, in books, and in the often-bizarre things people said and did.

Define essential words in your opening. Make these definitions early to avoid confusion. Identify the author as quickly as you can. Who is this person? Professor of history at the University of Tennessee? The author of a book on witchcraft? A Wall Street lawyer who has turned his hand to writing history? A citizen of Ithaca, New York, who has devoted her life to studying the archives? A doctor who has done vital cancer research and who has decided to write a history of attitudes toward cancer? Try to identify the author soon after first mentioning his or her name. Identifying the writer is a sort of definition. For Girouard's book you should also quickly define chivalry as he uses the word. You will have read the book by the time you start to write your review. Your definition can take advantage of your knowing everything the author has said.

What was chivalry? In the middle ages chivalry was the code of the noble knight. The chivalry died out with knighthood itself, a casualty to gunpowder and the modern age. But by the end of the eighteenth century, Girouard says, chivalry made a comeback, stirred by the love of the middle ages among English romantics. A resurrected code of chivalry provided the English aristocracy with justification for their privileged position in a world in which most people were miserably poor and in which the notion of aristocracy itself seemed out of date. How could aristocrats survive? They could claim to embody the values that they believed had been the best of medieval England—loyalty, courage, fair play, self-reliance, tenderness toward women, and above all, self-sacrifice. Their example could uplift all England.

Their notion was contagious. Not only the aristocracy but businessmen adopted the code of chivalry, and even the working classes found themselves fascinated by the possibility that they, too, could take part in the great masquerade of the times, a masquerade that for millions became a grand idea, painted in the rose colors of medieval splendor.

Having introduced the thesis of the book, you can develop
Girouard's ideas. Avoid the temptation to summarize each chapter,
to say, "First Girouard does this, and then he does this, and then he
does the next thing." Don't try to report every interesting detail in
the book. If you like the book, you assume that your review will
make others read it. Leave something for them to discover on their
own. Recount some interesting incidents. Tell a story or two from
the book. Quote a line or two here and there in your review to give
the flavor of the text.

> Early in the nineteenth century, Sir Walter
> Scott's wildly popular novels and poems extolled
> knighthood. Wealthy aristocrats built castles across
> England and Scotland, where, Girouard says, "comfort
> and modern upholstery usually reigned supreme, and
> chivalric symbols seldom got much further than the
> halls and staircase."
>
> Even more influential than Scott was the English
> eccentric Kenelm Henry Digby, whose Broad Stone of
> Honor, later expanded to four volumes, became the bi-
> ble for those whose nostalgia for the middle ages
> swept England like a contagion. Digby wandered all
> over Europe on foot, sketching castles, arguing pas-
> sionately for the superiority of the middle ages over
> modern times. He attacked "atheists, deists, ration-
> alists, Radicals, Americans, Utilitarians, and sup-
> porters of both dictatorship and democracy," Girouard
> says. The lower classes, Digby held, were eager to
> serve gentlemen. His ideal of the gentlemen had some
> flexibility: "natural gentlemen" could be found among
> the lower classes, and some of these could rise by

ability and energy to take their places among the recognized gentlemen in the ruling classes.

Many others wrote in the chivalric mode. Girouard summarizes Charles Kingsley's "muscular Christianity" and his Christian socialism, aimed at raising the working classes to security and dignity. Thomas Hughes's Tom Brown's Schooldays made the connection between chivalry and games played by schoolboys. It was not so important for Tom to do well in Greek or Latin as it was to be "A-1 at cricket and football and all the other games." Sir Robert Baden-Powell wrote his Scouting for Boys and founded the Boy Scout movement to discipline boys to be brave and to serve well.

The most vivid relics of this cult of chivalry are its works of art that remain in funeral monuments, stained-glass windows, war memorials, and Victorian Gothic. Girouard's book is lushly illustrated, and we may feast on the absurd but somehow touching painting of Sir John Everett Millais, "The Knight-Errant," showing an English-looking knight in heavy armor releasing with his sword a rather heavy naked woman tied to a large birch tree in some unnamed wood, her back to the trunk. Of course the knight errant has approached her from the rear. After reading Girouard's book, one can never approach the nineteenth century again without thinking of how much the preoccupation with chivalry dominated English culture.

As a reviewer, you are expected to make some judgments. If you know the field well, you can comment on the accuracy of the book or on the responses others have made to it. It may be helpful to look up reviews written by others about the book you have chosen to review. The reference librarian can help you find the periodicals in which such reviews are likely to appear. (If you use any of the ideas from these reviews, be sure to give credit in your text.)

Even without specialized knowledge, you can say some useful things about the book. Above all, examine your own feelings about the book as you read it. Do you like it? Mistrust it? Do you find it interesting? Are you bored by it? These feelings, though not definitive, are clues to thoughts you might develop about the book. You can go from the feelings to analyze why you have them. Why do you like the book? Why do you mistrust it? What is interesting about it? Don't say, "It's interesting because these stories are all bizarre." Be more analytical than that. Tell yourself something like this: "The notion that well-educated, modern people could see themselves as knights on horseback seems strange. It must have indicated boredom with their lives in an industrial age or a desire for vindication. They must have thought that the people with the noblest thoughts were the people who deserved most to rule their society. What did that mean about their attitudes toward the lower classes? The lower classes must have been scum because they were not chivalrous." This sort of informal reasoning and questioning can provide the foundation for more formal writing about your subject. It is an example of inference at work.

Listen to your intuitions and analyze them. Try to understand them. Try to make others understand them. It is never a shame to dislike a book; it is a shame for an educated person not to be able to put the reasons for that dislike into words. You don't accomplish anything in historical writing by saying, "I didn't like this book because it was boring, and I don't see how anybody can like it. I hated it from the beginning to the end." Someone reading your unsupported tirade against the book may be forgiven for believing that the fault lies not in the book but in you.

Your reflections on the book can take many forms. Naturally most of them will depend on material you take out of the book itself. It is always impressive when you can bring information from the outside, whether that information be knowledge you have of the special field the author investigates or more general knowledge derived from other reading.

Yet much about chivalry was sham and more than a little ridiculous. Many of the expensive enthusiasms of the chivalrous set took place against the background of dislocation and suffering caused by the Industrial Revolution. The England that we read about in the novel Hard Times by Charles Dickens hardly counted in these romantic dreams.

Girouard shows how important ideals of chivalry were in making Englishmen believe in their innate superiority over all the peoples of earth—one of the fundamental convictions that created British imperialism. Despite talk of chivalry for the lower classes, the cult favored the upper classes and fostered the notion that the poor were naturally inferior. The lower classes were supposed to accept their inferior position. When Titanic struck an iceberg and sank in April 1912, English and American gentlemen stood back and let women and children go into the lifeboats first. First-class women and children passengers, that is. The poor women and children traveling down in steerage with others immigrating to the United States went down with their men and the gentlemen on the upper decks.

Girouard makes the point that the passion for chivalry often overcame good sense. In World War I, that passion proved to be catastrophic. Girouard gives us a stark photograph of the football kicked off by Captain Wilfred P. Nevill when the British army went over the top on the first horrible day in the Battle

```
of the Somme in 1916. Nevill was cut down by the Ger-
mans.
```

```
    Girouard does not think it was all foolishness.
"Many will remember that particular mixture of
gentleness, courtesy, sweetness, lack of guile, and
unbending sense of honour which characterised old-
fashioned gentlemen of a certain kind. One says old-
fashioned, because the type scarcely survives; it was
the product of a particular set of circumstances which
no longer exist." His book provokes us to wonder and
amusement and at times to indignation--but stirs up
sadness of nostalgia for beliefs that despite every-
thing did sometimes create men almost as noble as
their extravagantly costumed professions.
```

Here are some points to remember in writing a book review:

1. Always give the author's major theme.

2. Always give some of the evidence that the author gives to support this major theme.

3. Identify the author, but do not waste time on needless or extravagant claims about him or her. It is a cliché to say that the author is "well qualified" to write a book.

4. Avoid lengthy comments on the style of the book. It's fine to say that the style is good or bad, interesting or tedious. Don't belabor the point.

5. Avoid generalizations such as, "This book is very interesting," or "This book is very boring." If you do your job in the review, readers should be able to see whether the book is boring or interesting without your having to tell them so.

6. Avoid passionate attacks on the book. It is always a mistake to launch an emotional attack on a book merely because you do not like it. Scholarship is not always courteous, but it should

be. Reviewers who launch savage attacks on books usually make fools of themselves. They may even win friends for the book they are seeking to demolish.

7. Do not feel *compelled* to say negative things about the book. Sometimes reviewers feel that they have not done their job unless they have had something bad to say about the book. If you do find significant inaccuracies, say so. If you disagree with the writer's interpretations here and there, say that, too. But do not feel that you are obliged to say something bad about the book if you do not find something obvious to criticize. Petty complaints may make you look foolish or unfair. Don't waste your time by pointing out typographical errors unless you think they change the meaning of the text.

8. Judge the book the author has written. You may wish the author had written a different book. But *this* is the book the author has written. If the book did not need to be written; if it adds nothing to our knowledge about the field; if it makes conclusions unwarranted by the evidence, say so. But don't review the book as if it should be another book.

9. Always remember that every good book has flaws. The author may make some errors in fact or some questionable judgments; even so, the book may be extremely valuable. Don't condemn a book outright because you find some mistakes. Try to judge the book as a whole.

10. Try to bring something from your own experience—your reading, your thoughts, your recollections—to the book review. Use that independent knowledge to explain the book and your attitudes toward it.

11. Avoid writing as if you possess independent knowledge of the author's subject when in fact you have taken all you know from the book itself. Reviewers sometimes deceitfully write with a tone implying that they have studied the material independently of the author and are thus equally expert in the field. The tone conveys a dishonest impression, and you should not fall into it.

12. Whenever possible, bring some of your own knowledge to bear on the book—something you have learned in class or something you have read in another course. Try to apply a broad part of your education when you write a review. If you know other books,

or if you have thoughts about some facts the author may have over-looked, mention them in your review.

13. Quote selectively from the book you are reviewing. Quotations give some of the original's tone, and they may express thoughts in a sharp and pungent way. The prose crafted by the author whose work you are reviewing could help spice up your own review.

14. Avoid long chunks of quotation. You must show your readers that you have absorbed the book you are reviewing. If you give them too many long quotations, they may think you are asking them to do the reflection and analysis you should have done yourself.

Here is a short review of the type you may write in a history class. Like the reviewer of *Return to Camelot,* this reviewer deals with cultural history. Study it with the checklist in mind. The review is reprinted as it appeared in *Smithsonian* magazine:

> *Deadly Encounters: Two Victorian Sensations.* Richard D. Altick. University of Pennsylvania Press.
>
> While they ate their breakfasts on Saturday, July 13, 1861, Londoners read two fascinating items in the *Times.* One reported THE CHARGE AGAINST THE BARON DE VIDIL. The other, in the very next column, recounted in breathless and horrified detail a FRIGHTFUL ENCOUNTER IN NORTHUMBERLAND-STREET. From that beginning, Richard D. Altick, an authority on Victorian literature and taste, dates the growth of a "public appetite for the improbable and perilous" that gave rise to an Age of Sensation in both newspaper reportage and literature. In *Deadly Encounters,* he thoroughly details the two cases as covered and commented on in the London press and draws some interesting conclusions.
>
> The Baron de Vidil was a French nobleman, an intimate of London clubmen and on friendly terms with the French royal family living in England. One afternoon in a wooded Twickenham lane near London, the Baron, it was alleged, struck with intent to kill his own son. The son brought charges and then, as an avid public followed the case from Magistrate's Court in Bow Street to the Old Bailey, refused to testify against his father, hinting at some still darker secret. The public read on eagerly as a mysterious inheritance and motivations of greed came to light, and the whole case raised questions of class and the place of foreigners in English society.

In the other case, a Major Murray was assaulted and fired upon with a pistol in the rooms of a Mr. Roberts, a small-time moneylender in Northumberland Street, near the Strand. From the appearance of the rooms and the wounds of both—Roberts' injuries soon proved fatal—the encounter was indeed "frightful." The press had a field day. The *Times* called it "a contest where strong and angry men struggle to tear and beat each other down with whatever weapon they can seize in their frenzy." The *Daily Telegraph* called it a *"horrible slaughter-house mystery"* and opined that there was a woman at the bottom of it. And there was. The Major's illicit romance with a young woman named Anne Marie Moody came to light and the existence of her child was revealed, together with a tale of her borrowing money from Roberts and of his frustrated passion for her and consequent jealousy of Major Murray. The horrified public watched it all unfold in a "spirit of morbid wonder."

Altick quotes extensively from press accounts, and his book is a treasury of overheated prose and outraged Victorian morality. Much of the underlying interest in the Murray case centers on the uncertain and dependent position of women, but the two cases together bring to light the fears beneath the surface of an apparently secure society. Violent criminal cases such as these, Altick makes clear, drove home to mid-Victorian society that "beneath their feet were dangerous unplumbed depths, uncontrollable forces that constantly threatened the peace and stability of their social system. In a direct, stark confrontation, middle-class respectability evidently was no match for remorseless passion. . . ."

Less certain, however, is Altick's thesis that these two cases of 1861 and the press coverage of them, brought about an Age of Sensation. Charles Dickens and Wilkie Collins were already being read at that time, and the hugely popular and horrific *Varney the Vampyre,* which Altick doesn't mention at all, had been published in penny parts from 1847 to 1849 and was several times both reprinted and acted on the stage. In real life, the Constance Kent case, an especially gruesome and shocking tale of murder, which Altick mentions only once and briefly, had captured the public fancy a year or so earlier.

Even so, Altick's book vividly preserves an important and fascinating element of daily Victorian life. As such, it is the best sort of historical scholarship: the kind that puts us in close touch with a lost world and with people very much like ourselves.

—Alan Ryan[3]

8

Suggestions about Style

"Style" refers to the way we express ourselves in our writing. Style in writing varies from writer to writer, and general agreement on style is hard to come by. Thousands of readers have loved the style adopted by the late Garrett Mattingly, whose book *The Armada* remains a standard work on the defeat by the English of the Spanish Armada in 1588. Here is Mattingly in a typical passage, describing the battle of Coutras in 1587, when Catholics and Protestants (called Huguenots) fought each other during the French Wars of Religion:

> Across the few hundred yards of open ground, the opposing horsemen had time to eye each other. The Huguenots looked plain and battle-worn, in stained and greasy leather and dull gray steel. Their armor was only cuirass and morion, their arms mostly just broadsword and pistol. Legend was to depict Henry of Navarre as wearing into this battle a long white plume and romantic trappings, but Agrippa d'Aubigné, who rode not far from Navarre's bridle hand that day, remembered the king as dressed and armed just like the old comrades around him. Quietly the Huguenots sat their horses, each compact squadron as still and steady as a rock.
>
> Opposite it the line of the royalists rippled and shimmered. It billowed out here, shrank back there, as its components jostled each other and jockeyed for position like riders at the start of a race, curvetting their horses and now and then breaking ranks to exchange a greeting with a friend or an insult with a foe. The flower of the court had accompanied M. de Joyeuse on his journey to Poitou. More than six-score lords and gentlemen served as troopers in his first rank, most of them accompanied by their own armed servants. So the lances with which the duke had insisted they be armed were gay with pennons and bannerets and with knots of colored ribbon in

193

honor of noble ladies, and there was a great display of armor, as much armor as anyone ever saw in combat any more, even to cuisses and gorgets and visored casques, and every conspicuous surface chased and inlaid with curious designs, so that d'Aubigné wrote afterwards that never was an army seen in France so bespangled and covered with gold leaf.[1]

Others find Mattingly's style too dramatic, too much like a novel. Edward Gibbon's *Decline and Fall of the Roman Empire,* written in the eighteenth century, has been extravagantly praised for its style ever since it appeared. Yet it is not much read today, and my students have usually found it tedious. Here is a celebrated paragraph with a famed declaration by Gibbon about history:

Titus Antoninus Pius has been justly denominated a second Numa. The same love of religion, justice, and peace, was the distinguishing characteristic of both princes. But the situation of the latter opened a much larger field for the exercise of those virtues. Numa could only prevent a few neighbouring villages from plundering each other's harvests. Antoninus diffused order and tranquillity over the greatest part of the earth. His reign is marked by the rare advantage of furnishing very few materials for history; which is, indeed, little more than the register of the crimes, follies, and misfortunes of mankind. In private life, he was an amiable as well as a good man. The native simplicity of his virtue was a stranger to vanity or affectation. He enjoyed with moderation the conveniencies of his fortune, and the innocent pleasures of society: and the benevolence of his soul displayed itself in a cheerful serenity of temper.[2]

Most writers work hard all their lives to develop a style they find both natural and attractive, one that others can understand and enjoy. No writer ever finds a style that pleases everybody. You do best to begin forming your own style by making it as readable as you can, trying at the same time to avoid monotony of expression.

We know a lot about readability—the qualities in a style that can be read without undue confusion. Specialists in rhetoric have done research about what makes a text reasonably clear. Some of this research has been incorporated into computer programs de-

---

[1]Garrett Mattingly, *The Armada,* Boston, Houghton Mifflin, 1959, pp. 154–155.
[2]Edward Gibbon, *The Decline and Fall of the Roman Empire,* New York, Modern Library, n.d., vol. 1, pp. 68–69.

signed to measure a text's readability. But readability and style are not identical. Few books are clearer than the primers used to teach children how to read in the first grade, but such a style quickly becomes tedious to adult readers. A good style combines readability and elegance.

The following suggestions take much of this research on readability into account. Keep them in mind as you write. They are not carved in granite; you can violate them now and then. But if you violate them too often, the readability of your work will suffer.

1. Write in coherent paragraphs.

Paragraphs are groups of sentences bound by a controlling idea. You have been reading paragraphs throughout this book, taking them for granted because they are familiar to any English reader. Indeed you have been reading paragraphs since grade school.

Paragraphs are useful aids to readability. Indentations break the monotony built by long columns of type. They help readers follow the text with greater ease, providing special help when we lift our eyes from the page and then must find our place again. They signal a slight change in subject from all that came before. They announce that the paragraph to follow will develop a thought that can usually be expressed in a simple statement.

Paragraphs vary greatly in length. Newspaper and magazine paragraphs are much shorter than paragraphs in books. Editors, teachers, and readers differ widely in their tastes about paragraph length. Some like long paragraphs, some short ones. There are no firm rules. The paragraph was not defined until the second half of the nineteenth century; those who did the defining could not agree on length, and the disagreement persists today.

Long paragraphs may become disorganized. Even a well-organized long paragraph may create eyestrain. Short paragraphs may give an appearance of choppiness, of shifting from subject to subject without giving readers time to adjust. A good rule of thumb is to have one or two indentations on every typed manuscript page. It is only a rough rule, not a divine command.

The first sentence in any paragraph shows the direction the paragraph will take. Here is a paragraph by William Manchester, who in this part of a book on recent American history describes political figures who became popular immediately after World War II.

> Joe McCarthy, late of the Marine Corps, was reelected circuit judge in 1945. He immediately began laying plans to stump his state in the following year under the slogan "Wisconsin Needs a Tail Gunner in the Senate," telling voters of the hell he had gone through in the Pacific. In reality McCarthy's war had been chairborne. As intelligence officer for Scout Bombing Squadron 235, he had sat at a desk interviewing fliers who had returned from missions. His only wartime injury, a broken leg, was incurred when he fell down a ladder during a party on a seaplane tender. Home now, he was telling crowds of harrowing nights in trenches and dugouts writing letters to the families of boys who had been slain in battle under his leadership, vowing that he would keep faith with the fallen martyrs by cleaning up the political mess at home—the mess that had made "my boys" feel "sick at heart." Sometimes he limped on the leg he broke. Sometimes he forgot and limped on the other leg.[3]

The first sentence in this paragraph, *Joe McCarthy, late of the Marine Corps, was reelected circuit judge in 1945,* sets the topic—Joe McCarthy, later Senator from Wisconsin who gained worldwide notoriety (some would say infamy) for his reckless charges that communists had infiltrated government, universities, and even churches in America. In the second sentence, Manchester picks up the main thought in the first sentence by using the pronoun "He" and by telling us something else about McCarthy. In the third sentence he continues the subject by telling us about "McCarthy's war." And so he continues through the paragraph. We could summarize this paragraph by saying, "Here is a collection of facts about the political rise of Joseph McCarthy after World War II."

In any paragraph you can draw lines between connectors, words like the pronoun "He" in the paragraph about McCarthy, repeated throughout the paragraph. Sometimes the connector will be a word in one sentence that is repeated in the next sentence. The connectors are important because they tie your sentences—and therefore your thoughts—together. They help keep your ideas and information in an orderly framework. You can often test paragraph coherence by seeing if every sentence has a connector word that

---

[3]William Manchester, *The Glory and the Dream,* Boston, Little, Brown, 1973, p. 394.

joins its thought in some way to that of the preceding sentence, all the way back to the first sentence in the paragraph.

In structure the paragraph is usually either serial or listing. In the serial pattern of paragraph development, the second sentence will develop a word or thought in the first sentence; the third sentence will develop a word or thought in the second sentence; the fourth sentence will develop a word or thought in the third sentence, and so on to the end. In the list pattern, sentences in the paragraph make in essence an interchangeable list of items that support the general statement made in the first sentence. In the serial paragraph, the order of the sentences cannot be rearranged because each sentence depends on the one immediately before it. In the list paragraph, the order can be rearranged after the first sentence because the sentences that come after all have an equal relation to that first sentence.

Here are three short paragraphs that illustrate these principles. The first two are serial paragraphs. The third paragraph is a listing paragraph, beginning with a general sentence that is then supported by sentences relatively independent of each other. The other sentences form a list that helps expand the first sentence. The paragraphs are about the assassination of Ngo Dinh Diem, dictator of South Vietnam, killed by his own troops in November 1963 during the Vietnam War. The first two paragraphs are straight narratives; the third is an explanation.

At Saint Francis Xavier, a French mission church in Saigon's Chinese district of Cholon, the early morning Mass had just celebrated All Souls' Day, the day of the dead. A few minutes later, the congregation gone, two men in dark gray suits walked quickly through the shaded courtyard and entered the church. South Vietnam's President Ngo Dinh Diem and his brother Nhu, haggard after a sleepless night, were fugitives in the capital they had once commanded.

A few hours earlier, rebel soldiers had crushed the last of their loyal guards. The remote church was their final haven. They prayed and took Communion, their ultimate sacrament. Soon their crumpled corpses would be sprawled ignominiously across the deck of an armored car that rumbled through the streets of Saigon as the people cheered their downfall.

Diem, though dedicated, was doomed by his inflexible pride and the unbridled ambitions of his family. Ruling like an ancient emperor, he could not deal effectively with either the mounting

Communist threat to his regime or the opposition of South Vietnam's turbulent factions alienated by his autocracy. His generals—some greedy for power, others antagonized by his style—turned against him. His end, after eight years in office, came amid a tangle of intrigue and violence as improbable as the most imaginative of melodramas.[4]

The order of sentences in the first two paragraphs cannot be changed. That is a characteristic of serial paragraphs. Because each sentence depends for its meaning on the sentence that comes immediately before it, you cannot change the sentences around without changing their wording. But the order of sentences in the third paragraph could be changed after the first sentence. Every sentence in the last paragraph reaches back to the first sentence with its controlling word "Diem." You could write the paragraph like this:

> Diem, though dedicated, was doomed by his inflexible pride and the unbridled ambitions of his family. His end, after eight years in office, came amid a tangle of intrigue and violence as improbable as the most imaginative of melodramas. His generals—some greedy for power, others antagonized by his style—turned against him. Ruling like an ancient emperor, he could not deal effectively with either the mounting Communist threat to his regime or the opposition of South Vietnam's turbulent factions alienated by his autocracy.

The simplest and most readable paragraphs are like these two models, the serial paragraph and the listing paragraph. They are the two fundamental structures of the English paragraph.

Now and then the two structures are combined in one paragraph. The first sentence has a word or words that are repeated in the next sentence. Words or thoughts in that second sentence are repeated in the third sentence. But then the fourth sentence—or a later sentence—may go back not to the sentence immediately before it but to the first sentence in the paragraph. The following

[4]Stanley Karnow, *Vietnam: A History,* New York, Penguin Books, 1984, p. 277.

paragraph shows a mixed character. Some of its sentences cannot be rearranged because they pick up ideas in the sentences immediately before them. Some of them can be rearranged because they look back beyond the previous sentence to an earlier thought. The paragraph deals with Greek colonization around the Mediterranean Sea in classical times:

> South Italy and Sicily became known as Magna Graecia—Great Greece. By the sixth and fifth centuries the cities of this area were larger, wealthier and more populous than those of mainland Greece. The Greeks who settled there became the *nouveaux riches*. Everything they built was "bigger and better." Their temples were larger and more ornate. Culturally, however, they lagged behind mainland Greece. Like colonial Americans, they were anxious for "civilization" from the homeland. They imported creative men of all sorts, from artists to poets and philosophers, from Pindar, who wrote victory odes for the tyrant of Syracuse, to Plato, who tried to establish his ideal state under a philosopher king in Sicily. They regularly sent competitors in splendor to the Olympic Games, and if its contestants were victorious the entire city rejoiced in celebration. When a certain Exaenetus of Acragas was a victor in the ninety-second Olympiad, he was conducted into the city in a procession consisting of three hundred chariots, each drawn by two white horses. Two stories, though probably apocryphal, well portray how ravenous the Sicilian Greeks were for culture. In 413 B.C. survivors of the catastrophic Athenian campaign against Syracuse were given aid and shelter by the hostile Sicilian population in return for recitations of the verses of the playwright Euripides. Another story tells of a Caunian ship fleeing from pirates which once tried to sail into Syracuse but was forbidden entry until the sailors recited songs from Euripides.[5]

The repetition of the word "they" or "their" in sentences four through nine holds the paragraph together. The tenth sentence, beginning "When a certain Exaenetus . . . ," supports the statements made in the preceding sentences about the pride of the Sicilian

---

[5]Robert J. Littman, *The Greek Experiment: Imperialism and Social Conflict, 800–400 B.C.*, New York, Harcourt Brace Jovanovich, 1974, pp. 47–49.

Greeks. The next sentence builds on that idea. The last two sentences develop thoughts in that sentence, the one beginning "Two stories. . . ." The sentences that tell the stories could be easily transposed as long as the word "another" was used to introduce the second story. The paragraph combines serial methods and list methods of writing a paragraph.

A paragraph like this one on the Sicilian Greeks is readable because the word "Greeks" or pronouns referring to "Greeks" are repeated throughout. Although it does not strictly conform to one of the two patterns I have mentioned, it does follow the pattern of repetition that holds all good paragraphs together.

All paragraphs include some repetitions that make each sentence recall something that has gone before it and at the same time prepare readers for something that comes after it. Repetition holds all prose together. Every sentence after the first sentence in an essay refers both to something that has come before it and to something that comes after it. Some word (or words) in every sentence picks up a thought from a preceding sentence and some word (or words) in every sentence points to something that follows in a later sentence. The paragraph is a convenient way of joining sentences in a visual unity, but each sentence within the paragraph is connected by some idea picked up from a preceding sentence and then expressing some idea that can be picked up by the next sentence. We can see this principle operating serially in the paragraph on the facing page from historian Eugene D. Genovese, writing about religion among black slaves in the antebellum South. The lines drawn through the paragraph to circles around words demonstrate the patterns of repetition that hold the paragraph together.

Narrative paragraphs like this one seldom have a topic sentence. Even without the topic sentence, they, like expository paragraphs, develop unity by repetition. They relate events one after another, connecting one sentence to the next by some sort of repetition of words or ideas. Here is a paragraph from Wallace Stegner's *Gathering of Zion,* his story of the Mormon trail and the travel of Brigham Young's early group of Mormon immigrants to Utah. The "Revenue Cutter" in the paragraph is the name of a small boat the Mormons found operating on the river when they arrived at the crossing. Stegner calls the Mormons "saints" because that is what they called themselves.

The slaves' religious meetings would be held in secret when their masters forbade all such; or when their masters forbade all except Sunday meetings; or when rumors of rebellion or disaffection led even indulgent masters to forbid them so as to protect the people from trigger-happy patrollers; or when the slaves wanted to make sure that no white would hear them. Only during insurrection scares or tense moments occasioned by political turmoil could the laws against such meetings be enforced. Too many planters did not want them enforced. They regarded their slaves as peaceful, respected their religious sensibilities, and considered such interference dangerous to plantation morale and productivity. Others agreed that the slaves presented no threat of rising and did not care about their meetings. Had the slaves been less determined, the regime probably would have been far more stringent; but so long as they avoided conspiracies and accepted harsh punishment as the price for getting caught by patrols, they raised the price of suppression much too high to make it seem worthwhile to planters with steady nerves.[6]

[6]Eugene D. Genovese, *Roll, Jordan, Roll,* New York, Random House (Vintage Books), 1976, p. 236.

Travelers late in the season often found the North Platte here clear and shrunken and shallow enough to be waded, but in June it was a hundred yards wide and fifteen feet deep, with a current strong enough to roll a swimming horse. (It did in fact drown Myers' buffalo horse.) The Revenue Cutter could carry the wagons' loads, but the wagons themselves were a problem. While some of the saints brought down poles from the mountain and worked at making rafts, others experimented with swinging wagons across the river on a long rope tied to the opposite bank. Two wagons tied together keeled over on striking the far shore, breaking the reach of one and the bows of the other. Four lashed together proved to be stabler, but too heavy to handle. One alone, with an outrigger of poles to steady it, was caught by the current and the strong southwest wind and rolled over and over. The best system appeared to be ferrying one at a time on a clumsy raft. A backbreaking day of that, up to their armpits in icy water, and they had crossed only twenty-three wagons. It rained and hailed on them, and the wind blew. The river was rising so fast they were afraid of being held up for days; and thinking of themselves, they also thought of the great company crowded with women and children who would soon follow them. Brigham put a crew to hewing two long dugout canoes from cottonwood logs and planking them over to make a solid ferryboat.[7]

The internal connections of this paragraph are made of the repetition of words having to do with the river, the wagons, and the people. Were there a topic sentence to this paragraph, it would be something like this: "These were the problems the Mormons had in getting their wagons across the North Platte River." Such a sentence is not necessary because the action, built sentence by sentence by a careful pattern of repetition, is clearly understandable.

Although narrative paragraphs seldom have topic sentences, analytical paragraphs usually do have them. Analytical paragraphs explain information. We explain documents or people or events by paying attention to the details that make up a text, a personality, or a happening. We look at the relation of those details to one another. We try to see how they came about. We see what they contribute to the whole. A general statement at the beginning of an analytical paragraph usually states the issue that is to be explained. Here is such a paragraph, discussing the political climate in the United

[7]Wallace Stegner, *The Gathering of Zion,* New York, McGraw-Hill, 1964, p. 148.

States during the 1920s, the decade before the Great Depression and the New Deal of Franklin D. Roosevelt. The topic sentence is in italics:

> *Even the most hopeful advocates of liberalism began to feel discouragement toward the end of the decade.* The margin of the Hoover victory in 1928 was a blow. When Paul Douglas organized the League for Independent Political Action in 1929 as a means of fulfilling Dewey's *The Public and Its Problems,* he found meager response. The suspicion was spreading, even among liberals, that the theorists of the New Era might be right—that business leadership was not only stronger but wiser than ever before, that the next step might really be, as Mr. Hoover had promised, the abolition of poverty. "The more or less unconscious and unplanned activities of business men," wrote Walter Lippmann in 1928, "are for once more novel, more daring, and in general more revolutionary, than the theories of the progressives." By 1929 even Steffens, who a decade earlier had reported that he had seen the future and it worked, moved to reconsider. "Big business in America," he wrote, "is producing what the Socialists held up as their goal: food, shelter and clothing for all. You will see it during the Hoover administration." And the once bright hope of Communism? "The unconscious experiment this country is making in civilization and culture," declared Steffens, "is equal to that of Soviet Russia. The race is saved, one way or the other and, I think, both ways."[8]

The first sentence in this paragraph makes a general statement that everything else in the paragraph supports. When you are explaining an idea or an event in history, you will often help readers see where you are going if you present a generalization in the first sentence and develop that thought through the rest of the paragraph. Such sentences help readers understand the information in the body of the paragraph. Without such general statements, clearly expressed and carefully related to the following sentences, readers can easily lose the thread in an explanation, become frustrated, and refuse to continue reading.

Such sentences help especially in paragraphs where you answer the question "Why?" Why did something happen? Why did someone write this text? Why did people believe what they did at

---

[8]Arthur M. Schlesinger, Jr., *The Crisis of the Old Order,* Boston, Houghton Mifflin, 1957, pp. 142–143.

the time you are writing about? Topic sentences are also helpful in sentences that explain the meaning of ideas or events. Here are three consecutive paragraphs, each beginning with a general statement, a topic sentence that introduces an explanation, an answer to questions that might begin with "Why?"

> *One of the great blows to American scholarship took place on February 1, 1770, when a modest upland plantation burned to the ground.* At the time, it was an entirely personal tragedy. The young master of Shadwell, Thomas Jefferson, was absent, and his mother was with him, so no lives were lost. But time would reveal what the world had lost: It had lost a world. Except for a few papers he carried with him—his account book, mainly, and two books of his private "florilegia"—this compulsive writer and record keeper lost everything he had composed to the age of twenty-seven, along with the library he had been assembling with great care and cost for over a decade.
>
> *The loss is easily put in concrete terms.* Though the great Boyd edition of Jefferson's papers promises to stretch out to the crack of doom, only twenty-five pages of the first volume are devoted to his writings before the fire occurred—letters saved by their recipients (mainly John Page), one advertisement in the newspapers, one draft of a public paper.
>
> *That accident goes far toward explaining one of the odd things about Jeffersonian scholarship.* Despite the fact that the Declaration of Independence is Jefferson's most influential composition, studies of his intellectual world tend to pick him up after 1776, when he wrote it. Daniel Boorstin, for instance, tries to reconstruct the "lost world" of Jefferson's thought around the Philadelphia activities of the American Philosophical Society, which Jefferson did not even join until 1780, and where he was not active for another decade—not, that is, until his Philadelphia years as Secretary of State and Vice President, the years when he turned fifty.[9]

The author here carefully leads us step by step through an explanation, giving us the subject of each paragraph by making a generalization at the start. Then he supports that general statement with details supplied by successive sentences. As he was writing, he probably organized his own thoughts and directed the flow of his prose by using those generalizations. You will find that writing

---

[9]Gary Wills, *Inventing America: Jefferson's Declaration of Independence*, Garden City, N.Y., Doubleday, 1978, pp. 167–168.

a good general sentence at the beginning of a paragraph will help you think of the details to support it. A clear general statement at the beginning of a paragraph will also help you eliminate interesting details irrelevant to the general statement.

2. Illustrate your major generalizations by specific references to evidence.

Evidence is any supporting information that helps readers believe any general statement you make. If you are trying to prove that people in the sixteenth century were unusually fearful, mention the horrifying representations of death in art, the hundreds and hundreds of fearsome paintings depicting the last judgment, the predictions of the end of the world, the magic and astrology cults, and the common fear of ghosts and other apparitions. Give the sources of this information. Be detailed enough to help your readers believe you know what you are talking about.

If you say that Woodrow Wilson had racist ideas, quote from his works to demonstrate these ideas. Flat generalizations or assertions following one on the other may seduce the writer into believing that he has proved a case when in fact he has only stated a case that remains to be proved.

The following paragraph includes a general statement, that death rates in the seventeenth century were so high that many survivors married several times. We have the general statement at the beginning of the paragraph (a typical topic sentence), followed immediately by confirming evidence. Peter Laslett, author of the book from which this paragraph is taken, has compiled the raw data for his conclusions by studying the parish records of English churches, the books in which church officials kept records of births, marriages, and deaths. Some town records preserved rough census figures that also became a part of his book.

> The heavier mortality of that age made for more frequent remarriage. Records of the number of times people had been married unfortunately only rarely survive, but it so happens that the listing of the people of Clayworth in 1688 was carried out with such care that this information can be worked out from it. There were at that date 72 husbands in the village, and no less than 21 are recorded as having been married more than once: 13 of them had been married twice, 1 a number of times unspecified, 3 three times, 3 four times and 1 five times. Of the 72 wives, 9 had been previously married; 1

of the 7 widowers and 1 of the 21 widows are known to have been married more than once. This is spectacular confirmation for one single community of a law which seems to obtain for the whole pre-industrial world, that once a man reached the marriage age he would tend to go on getting married whenever he found himself without a wife. At Adel in Yorkshire one old man married his sixth wife in 1698 and his seventh in 1702. The law holds for women too, but is weaker in their case, because widows found it more difficult to get husbands than widowers to get wives. Together with the much-marrying majority of the older people there may also have been a small community of persons who did not marry at all.[10]

3. To test the coherence in your papers, see if the first and the last paragraphs have some obvious relations.

In most published writing, the first and the last paragraphs in a book, a chapter in a book, or an article have such coherence that you can read them without reading the intervening material and have a fairly good idea about what comes between. Now and then you will find a piece of writing in which the first and last paragraphs do not have a clear relation. Writers who wish to be sure that their work does hold together can help their efforts by seeing to it that each of their papers ends in a paragraph reflecting some of the words and thoughts appearing in the first.

Try to avoid the easiest way of achieving this consonance—starting with a summary stating what the paper will be about and concluding with a summary paragraph on what it has been about: "In this paper I am going to examine the controversy over General James Longstreet's actions at the battle of Gettysburg." "In this paper I have examined the controversy over General James Longstreet's actions at the battle of Gettysburg." Such beginnings and endings are tedious, and all readers, including your teachers, expect essays that come after such introductions to be boring.

Here are the first and last paragraphs from an essay on the education given England's unfortunate King Edward V, the twelve-year-old child who with his younger brother, the little Duke of York, was pushed aside by Richard III in 1483 and later vanished. It has generally been assumed that Richard had him killed, though

[10]Peter Laslett, *The World We Have Lost,* New York, Charles Scribner's Sons, 1971, p. 104.

a few vehement "Ricardians" still maintain Richard's innocence. Study in the final paragraph the repetitions of key words and thoughts expressed in the first paragraph and see how they suggest a binding together of the essay, a coherence that makes reading easier, more comprehensible.

First paragraph:

> The childhood and education of Edward V necessarily make up the whole of his biography, for he was only twelve when he was overthrown as king in 1483 and died, almost certainly, before he was thirteen. They are also worth studying, however, because of the careful and well-recorded arrangements which were made by his father, Edward IV, for bringing him up. The education of previous heirs to the English throne, of course, had been careful, too. Special households were organized for them to live in; nurses, mistresses and masters were assigned to care for them and teach them; and they were trained in a wide range of knowledge, skills and activities. The education of Edward V conformed to this tradition, but seems to have differed in being more deliberately and formally planned in advance. Written ordinances were drawn up to regulate the prince's education in 1473 when he was nearly three, and reissued ten years later with appropriate revisions as he entered upon his adolescence. It is in the formulation of these ordinances, where hitherto princely education had been mainly informal, that the particular interest of Edward's childhood lies. The article which follows is centred on discussing them and placing them in context.[11]

The last paragraph:

> The arrangements of Edward IV for his son look paradoxical today. They brought an almost unprecedented formality to the prince's education, yet they allowed him to become too closely associated with a single group of important, yet unpopular men. This had not been true of the upbringing of earlier royal princes, to nearly such an extent. Their household officers had usually been lesser men uninvolved in high politics, or respected men holding equable relationships with the royal uncles and other great magnates. Henry VII, in the bringing up of his own two sons, was to revert to this older less dangerous tradition. In the case of Edward V, his close associa-

[11]Nicholas Orme, "The Education of Edward V," *Bulletin of the Institute of Historical Research,* November 1984, p. 119.

tion with the Wydevilles and the Greys proved disastrous. Their un-popularity stimulated and enabled Richard III to seize and remove them from power, and then left Edward V as a defenceless remnant of their party. Richard could hardly feel safe after robbing Edward of men so close to him, and to whom he was probably sincerely attached: the removal of Rivers and Grey must have helped to dictate the elimination of Edward. Sadly, the education which was intended to build him into a great king became, instead, a principal element of his downfall.[12]

You can see the relation of these two paragraphs in their rep-etition of thoughts about Edward V's education. The word "edu-cation" is repeated, and thoughts about it are expressed in both paragraphs.

Something more is needed, obviously, than mere repetition of words. That repetition should indicate a circling of thought back to its origins at the start of the paper. The words must have content if they are to do the job of making the beginning and the end of the paper coherent.

Sometimes the connections between the first and the last paragraph are subtle. Sometimes they are clear. But we can believe from seeing the close consonance of these two paragraphs that the article presents a coherent statement of the author's case. You can help coherence by seeing to it that some thought expressed in the first paragraph has some valid conclusion in the last. If you can see no connection between your first and your last paragraphs, you may do well to check your essay to see if indeed you develop one major thesis throughout. You may have gone off the track into a digression so that your essay does not hold together.

4. Begin most sentences with the subject.

Sentences are statements about subjects. In published Amer-ican English, about three-fourths to four-fifths of the sentences and independent clauses within sentences begin with the subject. This principle is often undermined by well-meaning writing teachers who tell their students to vary sentences by inverting them; that is, by putting the verb before the subject. Or they tell them to begin with a participle or to do something else. Yet examining published

---

[12]Orme, p. 125.

English in widely read books and articles shows the proportion of openings with the subject that I have mentioned here.

Each year when I teach a graduate seminar in the teaching of American English, I have my doubting graduate students take any magazine of their choice and make this count for themselves. They have so often been taught that sentence variety arises from changing the beginning of the sentence that they can scarcely believe that our best writers follow no such advice. They invariably discover that the writing they enjoy reading follows the same pattern that rhetorician Francis Christensen discovered years ago.[13] Only about one-fourth or one-fifth of sentences by almost any American writer begin with something other than the subject; these other beginnings or "openers" are usually some sort of adverb—a word, a phrase, or a clause. A few sentences begin with conjunctions. Now and then a sentence begins with a participle or a participial phrase. But most sentences begin with the subject. You will help keep your thinking clear if in writing sentences you think first of the subject, then of what you want to say about it.

The main point in this advice is that our natural way of composing sentences, whether we speak or write, is to name a subject and then to make a statement about it. Sometimes inexperienced writers are paralyzed by the thought that they begin too many sentences with the subject. They feel a laudable desire to vary their sentences and try to change the beginnings. They often then write amazingly complex and difficult sentences that are a strain to them and their readers. Let nature take its course; begin most of your sentences with the subject.

This suggestion is more important than it may seem at first. Many sentences go astray and become hopelessly confused because the writers do not know clearly what they want to say. They put words down, hoping for some sort of inspiration, and keep writing without order, winding and winding until at last they come on the period like swimmers struggling to save themselves from drowning.

Be sure that you write each sentence to make a clear statement about a subject. Don't bury your real subject, the most important

---

[13]Francis Christensen and Bonnijean Christensen, *Notes Towards a New Rhetoric,* 2nd ed., New York, Harper and Row, 1978, pp. 61–73.

element in the sentence, in a dependent clause. Indeed, most readable writers use dependent clauses only once or twice in every three or four sentences. The main action in your sentence should be in the main clause, and in that clause you should identify the subject as the most important element about which a statement is to be made.

Here is a paragraph that demonstrates the common English and American practice of beginning most sentences with the subject. It is from a book by an English scholar on social life in France under King Louis XIV. The subjects are in italics.

> *We* have examined in some detail the three kinds of surgeons practicing in France 300 years ago. *We* must not, however, overlook the surgeon-dentists, who in some ways were an even cruder body of technicians. *Charlatans and quacks* abounded in dentistry, since its practitioners were quite prepared at any time to turn their hand to a dozen related trades. *Some progress towards modern techniques* was, of course, being made at this time. About the middle of the long reign *it* became possible to secure a set of dentures, which, though almost useless for eating, at least filled up the gaps when the wearers went into polite society; and *we* read of the fair Mademoiselle de Gournay who removed her upper set before a meal, but restored them to their proper place when conversation demanded. On the whole, however, *we* must pity the unfortunate victims of Grand-Siècle dentistry, who were often bled for toothache. Indeed, *it* is with no surprise that we read that, like the king, some preferred to treat themselves with cotton wool soaked in oil of cloves, whilst others resorted to the old wives' method of stuffing the cavity with a mixture of earthworms and wax.[14]

Four of these sentences begin with the subject. Three of them begin with various kinds of adverbs—two prepositional phrases acting as adverbs and one with a simple adverb, "indeed." Here it is easy to see the tendency of a readable writer to place the subject either at the very beginning of the sentence or shortly thereafter, following some sort of fairly simple adverbial construction.

Always consider the subject as the linchpin of your sentence.

---

[14]John Laurence Carr, *Life in France Under Louis XIV,* New York, G. P. Putnam's Sons, 1970, pp. 83–84.

Everything revolves around it. It should be simple and clearly stated. It should also come at the beginning of the sentence most of the time.

When you do not begin with the subject, usually begin with some sort of adverb, either a word or a phrase.

> While other cities exhausted themselves in foreign and domestic wars "through the din and thunder of shot," Amsterdam had flourished.[15]

The sentence above begins with an adverbial clause modifying the verb *had flourished*.

A prepositional phrase with an adverbial sense may also begin some sentences.

> By this time the rancher probably would have decided on a brand to use for his cattle.[16]

The prepositional phrase "*By this time* acts as an adverb answering the question *when*. Other adverbial prepositional phrases may answer the questions *where, why,* and *how*.

You may also begin some sentences with a conjunction. Some sentences may be inverted. That is, the verb may come before the subject: "Gone forever was the dream of a united Europe under a French Empire."

Don't begin many sentences with participial openings. They can be confusing.

> Looking for gold and silver in ancient tombs, most nineteenth-century archaeologists were hardly more than grave robbers.

The participial opening is *Looking for gold and silver in ancient tombs*. Such an opening must modify the subject of the sentence, and this one correctly modifies the subject *archaeologists*. But it is easy to go astray with such openings:

> Digging up graves for treasure, we can see now that the nineteenth-century archaeologists were hardly more than grave robbers.

---

[15]Simon Schama, *The Embarrassment of Riches*, New York, Alfred A. Knopf, 1987, p. 300.
[16]David Dary, *Cowboy Culture*, New York, Alfred A. Knopf, 1981, p. 145.

Here the participial opening modifies the subject, but the meaning of the sentence is now distorted. Did we dig up the graves for treasure? That is what the sentence says. Readers speeding along in that text will have to stop and hesitate a moment before deciding that you have made a mistake. Such pauses are irritating.

If you must use a participial opening, make it modify the subject it should modify in the sentence. The wrong word used as a subject will confuse readers momentarily even if by application they can discover your meaning. You should never create needless work for your readers.

Good writers much more commonly begin most of their sentences with the subject but change the predicates to add variety. The next several points in this list will help you change your predicates.

5. Keep subjects as close to their verbs as possible.

The most readable writers seldom interrupt the natural flow of their sentences by placing a dependent clause after the subject. Like the general principle that most sentences begin with the subject, this is another that you can verify by reading almost any popular (and therefore readable) prose. Here is a paragraph of readable English by historian A. L. Rowse. Notice that every subject stands next to its verb:

> Towns and manor-courts, and therefore villages, had some sanitary arrangements, though they varied very much. Principally private enterprise prevailed: people were supposed to keep their bit of street or lane in front of their own houses clean, as in the more backward parts of Europe today, where one can see it operating, smells and all. People were not supposed to leave their household refuse in the street, though it was not always possible to avoid doing so. In 1552 John Shakespeare was fined at the manor court leet for making a muckheap in Henley Street; others fined were Adrian Quiney and the deputy steward of the manor himself. It was a very common offence. More important was to keep waters, streams, and wells clean—especially where the water was used for drinking or brewing. One finds continual regulations against people washing clothes in or near waters used for drink, or against washing the entrails of beasts after slaughter. Naturally regulations were stricter in towns; it is ev-

ident from innumerable documents how frequently they were broken.[17]

Here is another paragraph from Garrett Mattingly's *The Armada:*

> If the English fleet owed its escape from the shore guns to the enemy's poor weapons and poor marksmanship, it owed its preservation from the galleys and fireships to its own seamanship and alertness. No matter how they dodged and circled, the galleys were always driven off before they could close the range. (Properly laid out anchors, and crews that haul in and pay out smartly can swing a sailing ship through a wide arc in a short time.) As for the worst menace, the fireships, skillfully handled boats towed or fended them off to drift away and burn out in the shallows. Meanwhile the admiral's joke that tonight the Spaniards are doing our work for us and burning their own ships was bawled from one end of the fleet to the other. The English got as little sleep on Cadiz Bay on Thursday night as they had the night before, but they seem to have ended by enjoying themselves. After those twelve hours none of them would ever be much afraid of shore batteries, or galleys, or even fireships again.[18]

In this paragraph only one sentence separates its subject from its verb with a clause: "Meanwhile the admiral's joke that tonight the Spaniards are doing our work for us and burning their own ships was bawled from one end of the fleet to the other." The separating clause is *that tonight the Spaniards are doing our work for us and burning their own ships.*

We could multiply examples of this principle endlessly: subjects are usually followed immediately by their verbs. You can prove the principle to yourself by studying any prose, historical or otherwise, which you enjoy reading. Readable writers now and then use a clause or a phrase between the subject and the verb. But if you separate your subject from your verb in every second or third sentence, you make your prose more difficult than it should be.

---

[17]A. L. Rowse, *The Elizabethan Renaissance: The Life of the Society,* London, History Book Club, 1971, p. 137.
[18]Mattingly, p. 107.

6. Use an occasional rhetorical question.

The rhetorical question is one that you, the writer, ask so that you may define a problem you wish to pursue or an issue that seems pertinent to your discussion. You ask the question in order to answer it yourself. Sometimes you ask the question to show readers how obvious your answer is. Here is the English historian Charles Ross writing about Richard III and the death of the little princes in the Tower of London in 1483. Having recounted many incidents in which English kings and noblemen had been murdered in the century previous to Richard III, Ross asks a rhetorical question:

> Why, then, should it be supposed that Richard, as king, would depart from this established pattern of *raison d'état,* especially given that his position was more insecure than that of his predecessors, and the legality of his claim seems to have been generally disbelieved?[19]

Notice the way in which Rebecca West uses the rhetorical question to make a point about the French at the turn of this century.

> Meanwhile the French had endured the Franco-Prussian War of 1870–71 and come out of it fairly well because the Germans had been unable to handle the large monetary penalty they had exacted from the defeated nation and had let it disorganize their finances. But the French were now faced with the prospect of another war with Germany.
> How did they spend the time given them to put their house in order? More foolishly than anybody could have supposed. . . .[20]

7. Use an occasional metaphor or a simile to make a vivid statement.

Metaphors and similes appeal to us with some familiar experience or perception to illustrate an experience that may not be so familiar. Here is Civil War historian Shelby Foote, speaking of the danger sharpshooting snipers posed to troops in the line, even during lulls in the fighting:

---

[19]Charles Ross, *Richard III,* Berkeley, University of California Press, 1983, p. 99.

[20]Rebecca West, *1900,* New York, Viking Press, 1982, p. 94.

Because of them, rations and ammunition had to be lugged forward along shallow parallels that followed a roundabout zigzag course and wore a man down to feeling like some unholy cross between a pack mule and a snake.[21]

The simile, "like some unholy cross between a pack mule and a snake," vividly expresses the discomfort felt by the men Foote is describing.

The comparison of real people to characters in literature often becomes a simile in the writing of history. Here is a passage from Frank Brady's *James Boswell: The Later Years*, in which he compares, by a simile, Margaret Caroline Rudd with Becky Sharp, a self-seeking and manipulating character in William Makepeace Thackeray's nineteenth-century novel *Vanity Fair*. "Mrs. Rudd was the feminine sensation of the year. Like Becky Sharp, she had to make her own way in the world and, like Becky, she was not fastidious about the means she used."[22]

Sometimes metaphors can be expressed by a single word. Arthur Schlesinger, Jr., writes, "As Michigan banks closed, an infection of panic began to spread across the country."[23] Calling the panic an "infection" is a metaphor that conveys the idea that the panic was like a disease, spreading relentlessly.

Such metaphors and similes enliven writing. Don't carry them to excess. Used discreetly, they can be a great help.

Avoid clichés, the tired old expressions that we have heard again and again. The essence of the cliché is its predictability. When we hear the beginning of the expression, we know what the end will be. We know that a bolt is always from the blue, though we seldom think that the person who speaks of the bolt from the blue is speaking of lightning striking on a clear day. We have heard the expression so often that we think only that it is supposed to indicate a surprising happening. We know that unpleasant facts are often "cold, hard facts" and that people who are foiled by their own ma-

[21]Shelby Foote, *The Civil War: A Narrative,* New York, Random House, 1974, vol. 3, p. 297.

[22]Frank Brady, *James Boswell: The Later Years,* New York, McGraw-Hill, 1984, p. 133.

[23]Arthur M. Schlesinger, Jr., *The Crisis of the Old Order,* Boston, Houghton Mifflin, 1956, p. 476.

nipulations are "hoist by their own petar," though we do not know why unpleasant truth should be cold and hard, and we may have no idea what a petar is. The expression begins and ends without requiring any thought from us or from our readers.

But the fear of clichés should not make us shun occasional figurative language.

8. Avoid the passive voice whenever possible.

In sentences using the passive voice, the verb acts on the subject. In the active voice, the subject acts through the verb. Here is a sentence in the active voice:

> John F. Kennedy made the decision to invade Cuba.

Here is a sentence in the passive voice:

> The decision was made to invade Cuba.

You see at once the problem with the passive voice: it often hides the actor in the sentence. In the active voice, we know who made the decision. In the passive voice, we do not know who made the decision unless we add the somewhat clumsy prepositional phrase "by John F. Kennedy," which makes the sentence read like this: "The decision was made by John F. Kennedy to invade Cuba."

Readable historians seldom use the passive voice. Here is David McCullough, writing about young Theodore Roosevelt's work in the New York state legislature shortly after the death of his first wife and his mother. The only passive verb is in italics.

> Now week after week, on into March and April, he did little but work, shunting back and forth from Albany to his hearings by night trains. He reported a flood of bills out of his City Affairs Committee—seven, nine, fourteen a day. His outpouring of work, of words printed and spoken, of speeches delivered, of witnesses grilled, of interviews, of inspection tours (of conditions at New York's infamous Ludlow Street jail), of headlong, concentrated energy was utterly phenomenal, surpassing anything he had ever done before and causing those close at hand to wonder how much longer he could maintain a hold on himself. One day in March he reported fifteen bills out of committee, then six more at a night session, and even then his work for the day had only begun. Dissatisfied with a report on his hearings that *had been drafted* by counsel for the com-

mittee, he wrote an entirely new version at a single sitting, working through until morning.[24]

Use the passive if the subject is acted upon and is much more important than the actor. In the following excerpt, the passive is in italics. Historian Eli Sagan is discussing the practice of human sacrifice in the South Seas in times gone by. His focus is on the victims when he uses the passive. The agent in making the sacrifices has been identified already as the tribe itself, acting through representatives chosen by the chief. Here the passive is justified because it keeps the focus on the victims:

> Buganda has a class system based upon differences in wealth and political power, but *there was no pariah class set aside* for unusual contempt, nor was there a certain group of people *from whom human sacrifices were chosen,* as was the case in Mangaia. On Tahiti the victims were war captives kept alive for that purpose, or people of political importance who had become anathema to the ruling powers, or anyone from the lowest class, called *manahune.* Once a Tahitian *victim had been taken* from a particular family, *the members of that family were marked* to end their lives in the same manner. *When ritual homicide was called for,* such people fled and hid themselves until the drum announced *that a suitable man had been taken.*[25]

When you do not have such a clear reason for the passive, use the active voice. We usually want to know who does things, and the active tells us.

9. Keep sentences short enough to be manageable.

Sometimes writers lose control of their sentences and end with long, involved coils of words. Long sentences can be difficult. They slow readers down and hide your meaning. They may make you lose the thread of your thought. They can be hard to tie into other sentences.

Always keep in mind the most important statement you want to make in every sentence. That is the statement which can be con-

---

[24]David McCullough, *Mornings on Horseback,* New York, Simon and Schuster, 1982, p. 285.
[25]Eli Sagan, *At the Dawn of Tyranny,* New York, Alfred A. Knopf, 1985, p. 125.

nected to a preceding sentence and joined to a sentence you have yet to write. Don't entangle that statement with other information which you cannot develop or which is not a development of some previous information.

One way to keep sentences manageable is to avoid multiplying dependent clauses. Dependent clauses act as adjectives or adverbs and modify other elements in a sentence. In the next example, the dependent clauses are in italics. The paragraph describes the opening of the battle of Manila Bay in 1898, when the American fleet defeated the Spanish navy. The *Olympia* and the *Baltimore,* also italicized, were American warships.

> The squadron was now within a mile or so of the city's waterfront, *which lay almost directly to the west.* Shortly after five o'clock, *as the growing early light revealed more of the coastline,* a lookout sighted ships about five miles to the south, *where a hook of land protruded into the bay.* Calkins swung around and thumbed the knob on his binoculars, bringing Sangley Point and the Cavite naval station into sharp focus. A line of gray and white vessels stretched eastward from the point. Above them flew the flame-colored flags of Spain. Dewey turned and spoke an order to the *Olympia's* commander, Captain Charles V. Gridley. The flagship swung to starboard. The *Baltimore* following astern did the same, and in a few moments the six warships of the squadron were bearing south, the distant Spanish fleet on their starboard bows. The pulse of the warships quickened *as their speed was increased to eight knots.*[26]

The entire paragraph has four dependent clauses in nine sentences. Only one sentence includes two dependent clauses; none has three. Six sentences have no dependent clauses at all.

Writing cannot be reduced to a numerical formula. The ratio of dependent clauses to sentences varies from writer to writer. Some writers use more, some fewer. If you think your writing is stiff and difficult to follow, count the dependent clauses in your sentences. You may be able to make your writing more readable by devising ways to reduce the number of such clauses.

[26]G. J. A. O'Toole, *The Spanish American War: An American Epic, 1898,* New York, W. W. Norton, 1984, p. 183.

10. Don't overuse adjectives.

Adjectives modify nouns; that is, they change the meaning of the noun somewhat. They can also weaken nouns. A good adjective, well used in a necessary place, can brighten a sentence and help readers see the action better. Too many adjectives thicken and slow down the flow of prose. If you use few adjectives, you leave the action of your sentences where it ought to be—in the verbs and nouns.

Study the adjectives in the next paragraph and consider the number of adjectives in proportion to the number of other words:

> As the year 1587 drew to a close, a shudder of apprehension ran across *western* Europe. In part it was perfectly *rational* apprehension. As the closing in of winter made it less and less *likely* that the fleet gathering at Lisbon would sail before the year's end, it became increasingly *certain* that come spring it would sail—against England. In fact, although Philip still wrote to his ambassadors that the armada's destination must remain a secret closely kept, although at Paris Mendoza maintained an *enigmatic* silence, meanwhile trying every *security* and *counter-espionage* device he could think of, although Parma attempted misdirection by putting it about that the *obvious* aim at England was only a blind for a *sudden* descent on Walcheren, the shape of Philip's plan was becoming *unmistakable*. Lisbon was always *full* of foreigners and the least *experienced* observer could tell that this *vast* mobilization of ships and seamen, soldiers and cannon was not meant just to protect the commerce of the Indies or stir up trouble in Ireland.[27]

The paragraph has thirteen adjectives, a ratio of about one adjective to every thirteen words. Notice that Mattingly does not pile up adjectives before nouns. He uses many adjective complements, adding to the description of the subject by placing an adjective modifying the subject after the verb.

The proportion of one adjective to every twelve or thirteen words is fairly constant among writers in history or in any other publication in America. Like everything else in this list, the proportion is not absolute. Some writers may use more and some may use fewer. But if you think of that ratio and count your own use

---

[27]Mattingly, p. 172.

of adjectives relative to the other words in your writing, you may have some reason to check your prose and to work at reducing the number of adjectives.

11. Don't write long strings of prepositional phrases in your sentences.

Prepositional phrases allow nouns to be used in sentences in an adjectival or adverbial sense. We say, "I can drive home *through Lexington*" to give an adverbial sense of where we can go driving home. We cannot say, "I can drive home Lexingtonly." We say "the nation required encouragement by its leader." We cannot say idiomatically, "The nation required leader encouragement."

Too many prepositional phrases in a sentence can be distracting. Now and then we will all write sentences with three or even four prepositional phrases. Do not write *every* sentence like that; you will blunt your meaning. See how hard this sentence is to follow:

```
The prohibition movement of the nineteenth century
among liberals and progressives in the large cities
and in the Midwest and among certain church groups was
part of a reform sentiment directed against immigrants
with strange ways in contradiction to the values of
Protestants in a rural America.
```

12. Write about the past in the past tense.

Often, inexperienced writers striving for dramatic effect will shift into the historical present. They will write something like this:

The issue as Calvin Coolidge sees it is this: the government has been intervening too much in private affairs. He is now the head of the government. He will do as little as possible. He takes long naps in the afternoon. He keeps silent when people come to ask him favors. He says things like this: "The chief business of the American people is business." He means that anything contrary to business interests is bad. Within a year after Coolidge leaves office, we have the Great Depression.

Such writing quickly becomes tedious because it is unnatural. In English, we use the past tense in talking about past events.

13. Use the present tense in referring to the content in writing or art.

A piece of writing or a work of art is always assumed to be present to the person who reads it or observes it. Therefore you can use the present tense when you report its content unless you are talking about it in a historical context.

> The Fourteenth Amendment to the Constitution gives to the citizens of the various states all the rights guaranteed under the Constitution itself.

> In *Moby Dick* Melville portrays an obsessive madness in Captain Ahab.

Sometimes it may be better to use the past tense, even if you are speaking of a text either spoken or written. Use the past especially when you do not intend to give an extended summary of the work.

> In his "Cross of Gold" speech, delivered at the Democratic National Convention in 1896, William Jennings Bryan took the side of impoverished farmers who thought that inflation would help raise the prices they received for their crops.

CONCLUSION

Style is a difficult matter. Not only is there little agreement about what makes a good style; the sentiment is common among historians that style does not matter. Often these same historians wonder why their books are not read. Students may wonder why their papers don't receive better grades.

This book is not intended to be a style manual. Yet these suggestions will help you if you take them to heart. They will not in themselves make you a great stylist. They may make you think about the clarity of your style, and from clarity may flow eloquence or at least elegance. These suggestions may make you think more specifically about historians whose work you like; they may also help you understand why some works of history bore you or make you read them again and again to see what the authors may have meant. Learning to read is part of learning to write. You learn to read and write best not by consulting a book on grammar and syntax but by noticing carefully the devices good writers use to woo readers and the flaws that make some prose unreadable. Your own style will be better for that growing awareness.

9
Conventions

Historians make up a broad community, and like most communities they have their conventions, their ways of doing things. The conventions are not laws; people are not arrested and put in jail for violating them. Even so, members of the community notice when the conventions are violated—just as they notice when someone blows his nose on a linen table napkin at a formal dinner or wears a formal gown to a football game. As a writer you want to woo your readers, to make them respect you, believe your evidence, and accept your point of view. It's a good idea to follow the conventions followed by other members of the group you are trying to influence.

All of us follow conventions in every community to which we belong. Historians' conventions are not unlike the others. It violates the conventions of going to the theater when someone in the audience decides to play the harmonica while on stage Hamlet is delivering his soliloquy on whether it is better to be or not to be. It violates the conventions of weddings if the father of the bride starts selling candy bars in the church as the minister is about to pronounce the vows. It violates the conventions of courtesy if when we are introduced to a perfect stranger we suddenly howl with laughter and tell him that he is the ugliest person we have ever seen—even if he is.

Conventions may not be logical, but they are necessary. They provide forms that allow people to get along with each other, to understand each other, and to work together. Historians' conventions allow them to communicate with one another and to add to the total of what we know about history. They help us engage in a dialogue that keeps our minds alive as we pursue our discipline. If you habitually violate the conventions, you run the risk of not being taken seriously. Your readers may even turn hostile. It makes no sense to irritate them in that way. Irritate them for important matters of substance if you must; deliver a new interpretation based on the evidence, and deprive your readers of some of their cherished prejudices. Don't irritate them out of carelessness.

MANUSCRIPT CONVENTIONS

Many of you will be using computers with word-processing programs. Take advantage of the marvelous ability the computer gives you to generate clean copy. You can set the format of a computer to fit any manuscript style required by your teacher. You can mark up a printed copy of your work, write the corrections onto your disk, and print out a clean copy. Computers make things much easier for writers and readers alike; use them when you can.

The appearance of a manuscript tells readers many things about the writer. A slovenly, scarcely legible manuscript makes some readers think the writer cares little for the subject or for them. The writer may care deeply—just as the parent who screams at children may love them. Still it is not pleasant for the children to be screamed at, and it is not pleasant for readers to be forced to read the almost illegible.

The presentation of your paper in some respects resembles the presentation of food in a fine restuarant. You would be irritated if your waiter in an expensive restaurant served your main course on a plate that he snatched out of a pile of dirty dishes, wiped off with his apron, and banged down on the table in front of you. A sloppy paper can irritate the people who should enjoy it.

Formats vary. Your teacher may give you a format to follow. If not, these general principles represent common sense and generally accepted forms.

1. Use 8½ × 11-inch white bond paper. Twenty-pound bond is best. It is heavy enough to handle easily and to make a nice contrast with the type or the ink you use. Teachers reading three dozen research papers appreciate such favors. Do not turn in your final draft on yellow-pad paper or on paper otherwise colored. If

you use a computer, most word-processing programs allow you to feed bond paper one sheet at a time to the printer. If you use continuous-roll computer paper, be sure that it is reasonably heavy. Always separate the pages for your teacher and tear off the perforated edges that have carried your paper through the tractor feed of the printer.

2. Write on one side of the page only. If you type or use a computer, always double space. Use a fresh ribbon. A faded ribbon makes typewriter print difficult to read; a faded ribbon on a computer-driven dot-matrix printer makes the words almost illegible.

If you submit a handwritten copy, use lined white paper and write, in dark blue or black ink, on every other line. Do *not* use red, green, purple, or brown ink. Besides looking tacky, such inks tire your reader's eyes.

3. Put your name and class or course number in the upper right-hand corner of the first page, one inch from the top and flush with the left margin. Put your teacher's name on the paper, too. If you are in a large course divided into sections, always put your section leader's name on the paper. You may also want to include the time at which your section meets. Number the pages. Put your last name before the page number in the upper corner of each subsequent page so that the reader can easily reassemble your essay if somehow a page gets mixed in with other papers. If you use a computer, you can put a header or a footer with your last name and the page number on every page of your text. Be sure to separate headers and footers enough from the body of the text to let readers easily tell the difference at a glance.

4. Double-space after the name or number of the course, and center the title of your essay. Capitalize the first letter of the first and last words of your title, and capitalize the first letter of all the other words except articles, conjunctions, and prepositions. Here is an example:

```
Luther's Ideas for Church Reform in his

Commentary on Romans
```

Notice that the title is neither underlined nor enclosed in quotation marks. Here the title of the paper includes the title of a book, Luther's *Commentary on Romans*. *That* title is underlined, indicating italics if the paper should be printed. If the title runs to more than one line, double-space between the lines.

5. Begin the essay by double-spacing *twice* below the title. If your instructor prefers a title page, begin the essay on the next page.

6. Except for page numbers, leave a margin of an inch and half at the left side of your page, a margin of at least an inch on the right side of your page, and a margin of an inch at both top and bottom of your page. Usually these margins will result if you set your computer for a 60-line page for double-spaced text including the header or footer.

7. Fasten the pages of your paper with a paper clip or with a staple in the upper left-hand corner. Stiff binders are a nuisance to the instructor, adding bulk and making it awkward to write comments in the margins. Don't use them.

8. *Always* make a second copy of your paper, either by photocopying it or by printing out a back-up copy from your computer. Papers do get lost. Computers go down. Always make a second copy just in case something happens to the original. If you use a computer, make a back-up disk with a copy of your essay on it.

CORRECTIONS IN THE FINAL COPY

You should revise your paper enough to catch most casual errors—typos, misspellings, words left out, words duplicated, and so on. Even so, you may find a few others just as you are ready to hand the paper in. Or you may want to change a word or two here and there at the last moment.

Additions should be made above the line with a caret (^) below the line at the appropriate place:

```
Luther's idea of reform in his Commentary on Romans
                                      to
was almost entirely limited improving the morals of
                           ^
the clergy and ridding popular piety of superstition.
             little
It had to do with doctrine.
       ^
```

Changes in wording may be made by crossing through words and rewriting just above them either on the typewriter or by hand in ink.

```
Luther's idea of reform in his Commentary on Romans

     was almost entirely limited to improving the morals of
   of the clergy
 ⋀ priests, monks, and nuns, and in ridding popular piety

of supersition. It had little to do with doctrine.
```

Transpositions of letters may be made thus:

```
Luther's idea of reform in his Commentary on Romans

was almost entirely limited to improving the morals of

the clergy and ridding popular piety of superstition.
```

Deletions are indicated by a horizontal line through the word or words to be deleted. Delete one letter by drawing a vertical or diagonal line through it.

```
Luther's idea of reform in his Commentary on Romans

was almost entirely limited to improving the morals

of the clergy and ridding popular piety of supersti-

tion.
```

Separation of words accidentally run together is indicated by a vertical line drawn between the letters that should be separated by a space. You may close up an accidental space by making a couple of curved lines connecting the letters to be joined.

```
Luther's idea of reform in his Commentary on Romans

was almost entirely limited to improving the morals

of the clergy and ridding popular piety of supersti-

tion.
```

Paragraph beginnings can be indicated by the paragraph mark ¶ set before your intended indentation.

```
Luther's idea of reform in his Commentary on Romans
was almost entirely limited to improving the morals of
the clergy and ridding popular piety of superstition.
He mentions faith frequently, but his comments about
faith lack the intensity that his later works on the
subject possess.
```

USING QUOTATIONS

You will frequently quote from both primary and secondary sources. These quotations (Don't call them "quotes") will give authority and style to your papers. Here are some things to remember.

1. Always use the American system of quotation marks. The primary American quotation mark is made with two apostrophes set together like this:

```
"History is the essence of innumerable biographies,"
Thomas Carlyle said.
```

Quotations within quotations are set off with single apostrophes like this:

```
Bingham declared, "I entirely reject Carlyle's state-
ment that 'History is the essence of innumerable bio-
graphies' because history is both more and less than
biography."
```

2. Periods and commas used at the end of a quotation always go within the quotation marks.

"We learn from history that we learn nothing from history," Hegel said.

Voltaire said, "The history of the great events of this world is scarcely more than the history of crimes."

3. A comma, a colon, or a semicolon used before a quotation to introduce it is placed before the first quotation marks.

Thomas Jefferson said this: "Blest is that nation whose silent course of happiness furnishes nothing for history to say."

In worrying about predestination, Thomas Aquinas said, "Man has free choice, or otherwise counsels, exhortations, commands, prohibitions, rewards and punishments would be in vain."

Mrs. Carter H. Harrison, wife of a former mayor of Chicago, denounced the film Birth of a Nation in unambiguous terms; "It is the most awful thing I have seen."

4. A question mark at the end of a quotation goes within the final quotation marks if the quotation itself is a question; it goes outside the final quotation marks if the quotation is not a question but is being used within a question.

Question mark that is part of the quotation:

Professor Buttram posed this question: "Why was a blatantly racist movie such as Birth of a Nation so popular?"

Question mark not part of the quotation:

> What did Francis Hackett, writing of the Rev. Thomas
> Dixon in the March 20, 1915 New Republic, mean when he
> said, "So far as I can judge from this film, as well
> as from my recollection of Mr. Dixon's books, his is
> the sort of disposition that foments a great deal of
> the trouble in civilization"?

5. Semicolons and colons always go outside the final quotation marks setting off a quotation:

> "He is yellow because he recklessly distorts Negro
> crimes, gives them a disproportionate place in life,
> and colors them dishonestly to inflame the ignorant
> and the credulous"; such was the judgment of Francis
> Hackett of The New Republic on the "yellow journalism"
> of the Rev. Thomas Dixon, author of the book made into
> the movie Birth of a Nation.

> "I am tired of being dependent on men I despise from
> the bottom of my heart": so spoke General George B.
> McClellan, commander of the Union Army of the Potomac
> in July 1862 when he was angry and disgusted with
> Abraham Lincoln and his Secretary of War, Edward M.
> Stanton.

6. It is nearly always better to use shorter quotations than longer ones. You can often incorporate a phrase or a clause from a source and give the flavor and the information you want to convey.

> Bruce Catton called the battle between the ironclad
> ships Monitor and Merrimack a "strange fight," for, he
> said, "Neither ship could really hurt the other."

7. Always be sure that you incorporate quoted material into your writing so that the grammar and syntax are correct.

Don't do this:

> "The major spiritual autobiographies in English," says
> Jerome Buckley, has some of the qualities of an ac-
> count of a religious conversion experience.

But do this:

> "The major spiritual autobiographies in English," says
> Jerome Buckley, have some of the qualities of stories
> about religious conversion.

8. For any quotation longer than four or five lines, indent the entire quotation five spaces and set it up as a block within your text. Double-space the block quotation, and do not enclose it with quotation marks. (Some teachers prefer that block quotations be single-spaced. Ask your teacher about that preference. In preparing manuscript for print, block quotations should always be double-spaced to make life easier for hardworking typesetters—and also to ensure fewer typographical errors. Because double-spacing of block quotations in manuscripts is an accepted standard in publishing, you should use it in your papers—unless your teacher objects.) Use quotation marks for any quoted material within the block quotation. General practice places a colon at the end of the sentence that introduces the block quotation, but this practice is not always observed. Here is an example of a block quotation appearing after an introductory sentence by the writer of a paper:

> Robert Caro's biography of Lyndon Johnson is unre-
> lenting in its account of how many people who knew
> Johnson as a college student disliked him. But Johnson
> had power with the administration. Caro tells the
> story of what happened when the student newspaper at

the University of Texas at San Marcos was about to run
an editorial that criticized Johnson:

> Sometime during that term—the month cannot be de-
> termined—<u>Star</u> editor Mylton Kennedy wrote an edi-
> torial satirizing Lyndon Johnson's "relationships
> with the faculty" and with President Evans. But
> the editorial never appeared—because, Kennedy
> says, Johnson "went to Dean Speck." The newspaper
> had been set in type, and the presses at the Buck-
> ner Print Shop were just beginning to roll, when
> over their rumble, Kennedy heard the telephone
> ring. When Kennedy answered it, Speck was at the
> other end. "Have you got an editorial in this is-
> sue about Lyndon Johnson?" he asked. And when Ken-
> nedy admitted that he did, the dean shouted, "Stop
> the presses!" (Those were literally the words
> Speck used, Kennedy says.) He demanded that Ken-
> nedy bring him the editorial. And after he read
> it, he ordered Kennedy to remove it from the paper
> and confiscated the few copies already in print.[1]

9. Use ellipsis marks to indicate words you leave out between the quotation marks with which you enclose quoted material. To make ellipsis marks, write three periods, placing a space
separating each period from whatever comes before and after it.
Ellipsis marks . . . are made like this. Notice that there is a space
between the word *marks* and the first period that comes after it, a
space between that period and the next, a space between the second
period and the third, and a space between the third period and the
word *are*.

[1]Robert A. Caro, *The Years of Lyndon Johnson: The Path to Power,* New
York, Alfred A. Knopf, 1982, p. 197.

Here is an example:

Original source:

> The Rosenbergs were not, prior to their arrest anyway,
> prominent national figures.

Quotation with some words left out indicated by ellipsis marks:

> In his history of political murder, Franklin L. Ford
> remarks of the Rosenbergs, executed for spying in
> summer 1953, "The Rosenbergs were not . . . prominent
> national figures."

Do not use ellipsis marks at the beginning of a quotation. Some writers and editors have taken to beginning quotations with ellipsis marks to indicate that the quotation does not include all of a text. But the quotation marks themselves indicate that part of a text is being separated from its context.

What not to do:

> Rebecca West says that Archduke Franz Ferdinand of
> Austria Hungary ". . . was a superb shot, and that is
> certainly a fine thing for a man to be, proof that he
> is a good animal, quick in eye and hand and hardy un-
> der weather. But of his gift Franz Ferdinand made a
> murderous use."[2]

10. Change capital letters to lower case or lower-case letters to capitals in quoted material when your purpose is to make the quotation fit into your own sentence.

Suppose that you wish to quote this sentence from Richard Ellmann's biography *James Joyce,* in which Ellmann comments on

---

[2]Rebecca West, *Black Lamb and Grey Falcon,* New York, Penguin Books, 1984 (first printed 1941), p. 334.

the city of Trieste in 1920 when, in consequence of World War I, it has passed from Austrian to Italian rule:

> "Under Austria the city had been full of ships; now
> its harbor was almost deserted."

Here is one way to use the quotation:

> Ellmann, writing of Joyce's return to Trieste in 1920,
> says that "under Austria the city had been full of
> ships; now its harbor was almost deserted."

Do not use brackets to indicate that you have changed the capitalization of the *u* in "under." Do not do this:

> Ellmann, writing of Joyce's return to Trieste in 1920,
> says that "[u]nder Austria the city had been full of
> ships; now its harbor was almost deserted."

The practice has taken hold among some editors of putting brackets around a letter that has been changed from capital to lower case or from lower case to capital in a quotation. The practice distracts us from reading, and you should not do it.

OTHER CONVENTIONS ABOUT MECHANICS AND GRAMMAR

Most people feel anxious about grammar, supposing they do not know it well and imagining that they make mistakes all the time. In fact most of us know grammar well enough to use it reasonably well. We learn grammar from our families and others with whom we regularly speak, and we know it well enough to communicate. The written language is more formal than the spoken language, and writing is much more difficult than speaking. Sometimes in the physical labor of writing our minds wander, and we make errors. That is, we violate conventions. Most people can spot their errors in grammar by reading their work aloud. You can usually trust your ear. When something you have written doesn't sound right, check it in an English handbook or ask a friend. (Writers collaborate all the time in real life; they should do so in school, too.)

The grammar we use in writing is set by editors and writers themselves. It has not changed much in the last century. You encounter it in your textbooks, in magazines, in the daily newspapers, and in your own writing. It is a part of mass literacy, the general expectation in the modern world that most people can read. Mass production of any sort requires standardization, and mass literacy has brought about some standardization and simplification of grammar. By following the standards, you increase the ease by which readers follow your work.

The following are some sources of common difficulties that come up in writing papers. The list is not a complete summary of English grammar. If you have other problems, buy a good English handbook and study the areas that give you most difficulty.

1. Form the possessive correctly.

The possessive shows ownership or a particular relation. We speak of John's pen or Prizzi's honor. In both, the apostrophe and a final-*s* form the possessive. Here are some examples:

Jane's computer	Lee's family
Mike's house	Churchill's policy
Napoleon's plan	

Some writers and editors will add only an apostrophe to singular nouns ending in -*s*. Thus the possessive may be, Erasmus' works, Chambers' book. But the preferred practice is to make the possessive of these words in the same way that we make the possessive of other singular nouns.

Erasmus's works; Chambers's book; Jesus's teachings

For plural nouns that end in -*s,* add the apostrophe to form the possessive.

the Germans' plan	the neighbors' opinion
the writers' consensus	the philosophers' view

Plurals that do not end in *-s* form the possessive like singular nouns.

women's history   men's fashions   children's rights

The possessive pronouns used before the thing possessed are *my, our, your, his, her,* and *their.*

my book	his complaint
our house	her drill
your case	their position

Possessive pronouns used in positions other than before the thing possessed are *mine, ours, yours, his, hers,* and *theirs.*

The idea was mine.
He liked ours better than yours.
The decision was his.
The money was hers.
The thoughts were theirs.

2. Always make the plural of nouns ending in *-est* and *-ist* by adding *-s* to the singular form.

Singular	*Plural*
guest	guests
nest	nests
scientist	scientists
socialist	socialists

3. Distinguish between *it's* and *its.* The contraction "it's" stands for "it is." The possessive pronoun "its" stands for "belonging to it."

He said, "It's almost impossible to guarantee safe travel."
This doctrine had lost its power by 1900.

4. Use the objective case of pronouns correctly.

The nominative or subjective case of pronouns includes forms such as "I," "we," "he," "she," "they," "who," and "those." The objective case includes forms such as "me," "us," "him," "her," "whom," and "them."

The nominative case is used as the subject of a sentence or a clause.

I read Huizinga's books.

It was said that *he* was not the king's son.

Successive Russian leaders have believed that *they* were threatened by a strong Poland.

The objective case should be used for the object of a preposition. Therefore you should say, "It was a matter between *him* and *me*," and "Between you and me, I would say that the policy was wrong."

The objective case should be used as a direct object.

Bryan's campaign lifted *him* to sainthood among American farmers.

The objective case should be used as an indirect object.

The president gave *her* a cabinet position.

The objective case should be used as the subject or an object of an infinitive. The infinitive is a verb form that includes the infinitive marker "to" and the dictionary form of the verb. Thus "to go," "to be," "to dwell," "to see" are all infinitives. The subject of the infinitive is a noun or pronoun before the infinitive that does the action the infinitive expresses.

King Leopold wanted *him* to go at once to Africa.

In this example the person designated by the objective pronoun *him* will go to Africa. Because he will do the going, the action expressed in the infinitive "to go," the pronoun *him* is the subject of the infinitive and is in the objective case.

The prime minister supposed both Russell and *me* to be damaged by the report.

In this example the pronoun before the infinitive receives the action of the infinitive—here an infinitive phrase.

Do not use the objective case as a subject. Do not say, "Both Queen Elizabeth and *him* believed in going to war in the Netherlands." The idiomatic English way of expressing such a thought would be to say, "Both he and Queen Elizabeth believed in going to war in the Netherlands."

5. In *who* or *whom* clauses, the case of the pronoun is determined by how it is used in the clause, not how the clause is used

in the sentence. (Many authorities now say that we should eliminate *whom* and use *who* for both the nominative and objective cases. Many others think the distinction should be preserved.)

Sometimes people eager to use *who* or *whom* correctly use *whom* where *who* is proper. The problem is especially acute in the use of the word *whomever,* a variant of *whom.* Some will write things like this: "In the late nineteenth century, women and children worked for *whomever* would pay them pennies an hour for a fourteen-hour day." The writer of this sentence knows that the object of a preposition is in the objective case. He writes the preposition "for" and puts *whomever* after it. But here the entire clause is the object of the preposition. The pronoun should be "whoever" because it is the subject of the clause. The pronoun in the clause is governed by how it is used in the clause, not by how the clause is used in the sentence. The sentence should read, "In the late nineteenth century, women and children worked for whoever would pay them pennies an hour for a fourteen-hour day."

The same principle applies in a common sentence form in which a parenthetical clause appears after the pronoun *who.*

You should not write this:

> The Indians whom *Custer* thought were only a small band, in fact numbered in the thousands.

You should write this instead:

> The Indians who Custer thought were only a small band, in fact numbered in the thousands.

The parenthetical clause "Custer thought" does not govern the clause "who were only a small band." The subject of the verb *were* is the pronoun *who,* which must be in the subjective case.

6. Use commas in these instances:
   a. Commas set off independent clauses from each other. Independent clauses can nearly stand by themselves as sentences.

> The McNary-Haugen bill would have provided subsidies for American farmers, but President Coolidge vetoed it in 1927.

The Plains Indians loved ceremony, and Francis Parkman recorded some of their rites.

The people of the United States decided that they must give up Prohibition, for Bootlegging and the gang wars that accompanied it were making cities run with blood.

b. Use commas to set off long introductory phrases and clauses.

Even after the transcontinental railroad was completed in 1867, some people still made the trip west by covered wagon.

After the American entry into the war in 1917, the victory of the allied powers was ensured.

c. Use commas to set off the items in a series.

President Franklin D. Roosevelt moved to solve problems such as unemployment, banking, and extremism.

William Jennings Bryan campaigned for the presidency in 1896 by traveling 18,000 miles, making 600 speeches, and attacking the "Monied interests."

d. Use commas to set off nonrestrictive clauses and phrases.

Nonrestrictive clauses and phrases define other elements in a sentence. You could remove the nonrestrictive clause or phrase and still have an intelligible sentence.

Horatio Alger, who was a graduate of Harvard, wrote stories that appealed to the poor who yearned to believe that they could become rich.

Henry David Thoreau, one of the greatest American writers, died of tuberculosis.

e. Commas usually separate two or more adjectives used before a noun.

Ralph Waldo Emerson was a tall, frail, elegant man.

f. Use commas to set off parenthetical words and phrases.

Education was, to be sure, not merely a private matter.

Roosevelt, however, died before the Yalta agreements could be put to the test.

g. Place commas before quotation marks when a clause such as "he said" introduces the quotation.

Editor William Allen White said of his fellow Kansan Alf Landon, "I have never been able to visualize him as President."

h. Place commas within closing quotation marks.

"I have never been able to visualize him as President," editor William Allen White said of Alf Landon in 1935.

7. Distinguish between restrictive and nonrestrictive clauses and phrases. Restrictive clauses and phrases are essential to the principal meaning in the sentence; nonrestrictive clauses and phrases are not. A nonrestrictive clause or phrase adds information that is interesting without being essential. Whether an element is restrictive or nonrestrictive depends on the author's purpose. Nonrestrictive clauses and phrases are set off by commas.

Here are some examples.

Restrictive clause:

The only candidate who could have beaten Thomas E. Dewey in 1948 was Harry Truman.

The clause *who could have beaten Thomas E. Dewey in 1948* is restrictive; it is necessary to the primary meaning in the sentence. If we wrote, "the only candidate was Harry Truman," we would have an entirely different meaning.

Nonrestrictive clause:

Theodore Roosevelt, who happened to be facing an election campaign, made a strong pronouncement.

Here we have a clause that adds information not essential to the main statement in the sentence. We know who Theodore Roosevelt was. The main statement in the sentence can stand alone. Theodore Roosevelt made a strong pronouncement. The nonrestrictive clause *who happened to be facing an election campaign* adds interesting detail to the sentence. But because it is nonrestrictive, we set it off by commas.

Sometimes changing a clause or a phrase from restrictive to nonrestrictive changes the meaning.

> In his novel, *Doomed by Grammar,* Weatherby treated sympathetically a corporate lawyer whose firm went bankrupt because of a dangling participle.

This sentence means that Weatherby wrote only one novel, and that it was entitled *Doomed by Grammar.* The commas indicate that the title provides additional but not essential information. If we leave out the commas, we have a slightly different meaning:

> In his novel *Doomed by Grammar,* Weatherby treated sympathetically a corporate lawyer whose firm went bankrupt because of a dangling participle.

Here we have a comma setting off the introductory phrase from the rest of the sentence. We do not set off the title *Doomed by Grammar.* Thus the sentence could mean that Weatherby wrote several novels but that we are talking about only one of them, and so we must give its title.

8. Be sure that clauses acting as adjectives clearly modify the noun they are supposed to modify in the sentence. Modification is usually clearest when the modifying clause comes immediately after the noun it is modifying. Very often confusions in modification result when a writer tries to put too much into one sentence.

Don't say this:

> Bismarck's response to the German Socialist movement, which was his own way of ensuring labor peace, effectively kept the Socialist Party from obstructing his aims.

Was the German Socialist movement Bismarck's own way of ensuring labor peace? No, though an uninformed reader might think so from this sentence. It would be better to make two clear sentences rather than one confusing one: Bismarck's response to the German Socialist movement effectively kept the Socialist Party from obstructing his aims. He gained the loyalty of German workers by giving them a generous welfare program.

Sometimes the problem comes when writers follow the admirable policy of keeping the subject and the verb close together but then decide to tack an adjectival clause on at the end and so confuse an otherwise excellent sentence.

Don't say this:

> The Dreyfus case weakened confidence in the French army, which unleashed furious passions in the French public.

The writer meant to say this:

> The Dreyfus case, which unleashed furious passions in the French public, weakened confidence in the French army.

9. Make your subject and your verb agree.

Problems may arise when you have a prepositional phrase with a plural object after a singular subject.

Not this:

> His statement of grievances *were* read to the assembly.

But this:

> His statement of grievances *was* read to the assembly.

Use singular verbs after indefinite pronouns such as "anybody," "everybody," "anyone," "everyone," "somebody," "someone," "either," "neither," and "none."

> Anybody in the group *is* likely to accept.
> Everyone *was* ready.
> Neither *was* possible.

None is occasionally used with a plural verb by some writers, though most still prefer to say, "None of the advantages *was* as great as the sum of the disadvantages."

Some collective words give problems. More traditional writers will say, "the majority of his followers was not convinced." But some writers will say, "The majority of his followers were not convinced," seeing "majority" as a collective noun that can take a plural verb. Here you must use your own judgment to decide which you will use.

10. Be sure that participial phrases opening a sentence modify the grammatical subject.

Betrayed by his trust of unscrupulous friends, Warren G. Harding died just in time to receive a respectful funeral.

Descending into Alsace, Louis XIV proclaimed it the "Garden of God."

You can make your prose incomprehensible and even ridiculous if you violate this rule.

Rocketing toward the moon, Americans stayed up late by their television sets to see the photographs sent back by our astronauts.

This sentence means that Americans rocketed toward the moon and sat up late by their television sets. But the writer meant to say that while the astronauts were rocketing toward the moon, Americans at home stayed up to watch television.

Avoid making an opening participle modify an expletive *it.* The expletive *it* is the pronoun without a referent and used as a subject. We say, "It will rain," without having the pronoun refer to another noun. We say, "It is hard to see what he wanted," using the pronoun as the grammatical subject.

Avoid constructions like this: "Steaming toward Europe, it seemed wise to him to hide from photographers on the ship." It is better to say, "Steaming toward Europe, he tried to avoid photographers on the ship."

11. When you use adverbs such as *only, even, hardly, nearly, almost,* and *just* to modify adjectives, place them just before the adjective. Don't say, "Edward VIII only ruled a few months." Say, "Edward VIII ruled only a few months." Don't say, "Germany did not even gain an acknowledgment that Austria-Hungary might also have had some responsibility for beginning World War I." Say, "Germany did not gain even an acknowledgment that Austria-Hungary might also have had some responsibility for starting World War I."

12. Use "hardly" as a negative in itself. Do not use it with another negative. Don't say, "Adams was not hardly ready to face the real implications of democratic government." Say, "Adams was hardly ready to face the implications of democratic government."

13. Do not break the parallel form of a series. English and American writers often use words or phrases in series, often in

units of three. We speak of exorcising a demon in the middle ages "by bell, book, and candle." We write sentences like this: "the moral principle of seeking the greatest good for the greatest number motivated Rousseau, Bentham, and Mill." The units in the series must stand as grammatical equals. Therefore you should not write sentences like this: "Richelieu wanted three things for France: authority for the king, an end to religious strife, and he also wanted secure "natural" frontiers." The first two elements in this faulty series are nouns modified by prepositional phrases, but the last element is a clause. The sentence should be rewritten like this: "Richelieu wanted three things for France: authority for the king, an end to religious strife, and secure 'natural' frontiers."

14. Use a colon only after a complete clause. Use the colon to introduce a statement that elaborates on the thought in the preceding clause. That elaboration may be a quotation, often a block quotation. Or it may be a list. Or it may be simply another clause. The colon before the block quotation is frequently illustrated in this book. Here is a sentence that uses the colon to introduce a list that elaborates the thought in the clause.

> Franklin Roosevelt faced a multitude of problems: catastrophic unemployment, daily failures of banks, and a demoralized American people.

Some writers substitute a dash for the colon: Franklin Roosevelt faced a multitude of problems—catastrophic unemployment, daily failures of banks, and a demoralized American people. The dash is more emphatic.

The colon may be followed by a clause elaborating the statement made in the first clause.

> President Harry S. Truman made one of the greatest advances in the fight for civil rights for American blacks: he desegregated the armed forces.

15. Do not join independent clauses with commas alone. Do not write:

> The Fugitive Slave Act required free states to return escaped slaves to their owners in the South, in effect it removed the boundary of safety for fleeing slaves from the Ohio River to the Canadian border.

You can use a semicolon to make such a division:

> The Fugitive Slave Act required free states to return escaped slaves to their owners in the South; in effect it removed the boundary of safety for fleeing slaves from the Ohio River to the Canadian border.

16. Observe the difference between *lie* and *lay*.

"To lie" means to recline; "to lay" means to put something down so that it reclines. We lie down to go to sleep; we lay our watch on the table beside the bed.

Most of the problems arise from the past forms of these verbs, for the simple past tense of "lie" is "lay." "The chief responsibility for the Confederate defeat at Gettysburg lay on the shoulders of Robert E. Lee."

The past tense of "lay" is "laid." "Many southerners, unwilling to acknowledge a flaw in their hero Lee, laid the blame on Longstreet."

The past participle of "lie" is "lain," and the past participle of "lay" is "laid." "The myth of Lee's invincibility has lain in the heart of the South for more than a century." "But modern students of the battle have laid the myth to rest."

17. Never use the apostrophe to form a plural. Do not say 1960's or "The Wilsons' were happy together." The apostrophe is used to form the possessive case in ways stated above. It is not used to make words plural.

18. Avoid vulgarisms such as "alot" and "alright." These are efforts to combine two words and make them one. You should speak about "a lot" of people and of Joseph McCarthy's view that it was "all right" if innocent people suffered by his public attacks.

19. Avoid confusion in making pronouns refer to antecedents.

Pronouns stand for nouns. Definite pronouns such as "he," "she," "it," "him," "her," "they," "them," and "their" stand for nouns that usually appear somewhere before them in a sentence or paragraph. Be sure to make the pronoun reference clear, even if you have to revise the sentence extensively. Don't do this:

> The Czechs disdained the Slovaks because they were more cosmopolitan.

To whom does the pronoun "they" refer? Were the Czechs or the Slovaks more cosmopolitan? You must rewrite the sentence:

> The more cosmopolitan Czechs disdained the more rural Slovaks.

20. Maintain parallel forms.

The coordinate conjunctions *and, but, or, nor,* and *for* must join grammatically equal parts of a sentence. You disrupt parallel forms when you join grammatically unequal parts of a sentence.

> Churchill told the English people that he had nothing to offer them but *"blood, toil, tears, and sweat."*

Appendix: Essay Examinations

Essay examinations are not like the other kinds of papers that I have discussed in this book. Nevertheless, as the name "essay exam" insists, they are essays—essays to be done within a given time in circumstances where you must rely entirely on your memory, without notes or the library reference room. Essay examinations test what you know and how you think about what you know. They are to some degree artificial creations; historians do not write under the strictures demanded by the standard essay-exam format. Such exams are, however, perhaps the best way devised to test how much you have learned in an academic course, and they are so much a part of the western academic scene that you doubtless already have much experience with them. The best examinations allow you to show your knowledge about the facts and some sources for those facts and to prove that you can make some judgments about the material.

Here is a sample question that you may find on an examination in the history of the Protestant Reformation:

> Trace the career of Martin Luther from the Indulgence Controversy of 1517 to his appearance before the Diet of Worms in 1521.

In this question you are asked for narrative. You must tell Luther's story from one important moment in his life to another. You are not asked for an explicit argument. It is assumed that you have read about Luther in your textbooks or in several other assigned readings, that you have followed his career in the lectures, that you have given his life some thought, and that you can repeat the major events relating to him in these years.

You are not being asked for a list of happenings. You are being asked to write an essay, to tell a story, to construct a narrative. An essay examination requires an essay! Although we may suppose that such a statement might be self-evident, many students defeat themselves in examinations and get lower grades than they should when they try to do something other than write an essay. They write a series of short answers without trying to tie those short answers into a coherent story, and they do not fulfill the assignment.

The question about Luther assumes that important changes took place between 1517 and 1521. You should sketch those changes in your answer. What was Luther in 1517? He was an obscure monk in a remote part of Germany who attacked the sale of indulgences supposed to release souls from Purgatory. What was he in 1521? He was known all over Europe as a rebel against church authority, excommunicated by the pope, and called to defend himself before the emperor of the Holy Roman Empire.

The differences in Luther between the first date and the last define your answer. What happened? Why? In an exam question calling for a narrative, try to answer both questions. Knowing what happened tells your teacher that you have learned the material; giving your argument about why it happened tells the teacher that you have thought about what you know.

Take a moment to jot down a few words outlining your answer. For this question you might write the following. (These words may make no sense to you if you do not know something about Luther; that is all right. I use them only to show a method.)

```
                    95 Theses

              Disputation at Heidelberg

                Meeting with Cajetan

               Justification by Faith

            Leipzig Disputation with Eck

                Babylonian Captivity

                Other writings of 1520
```

<pre>
             Papal Excommunication
       Appearance Before the Emperor in April
</pre>

You can expand each of these headings to a paragraph. The headings happen to refer to events in chronological order, each important to Luther's career. Any teacher would be pleased to have you recount them as the answer to the question phrased above. By pausing to write them in a brief outline (which could be even briefer than this version), you can work off the natural nervousness we all have at the start of an examination, you organize your thoughts, and you start thinking before you write. You will not then be writing blindly as the exam goes along. This scratch outline resembles the finger exercises musicians take before a concert or the athlete's limbering up before a game. A brief outline helps you include everything you should include and provide shape to your thoughts.

You may recognize some uncertainties about the events in these years. Even on an examination you should recognize those gaps in our knowledge and those confusions where they occur. Let your reader know that you recognize puzzles in the evidence. Scholars have argued vehemently over the date of Luther's "discovering" his major doctrine, justification by faith. You can't solve the problem in an exam; you can show that you know it exists. Teachers are impressed by such things. Neither in your essay exams nor your other writing should you try to grind off the rough edges of historical study. History does not hold together smoothly; don't pretend it does.

If your teacher is trying to get you to demonstrate some of your own thinking during an examination, you may get a question like this:

> Compare Luther's view of God and the church with that of Thomas More.

Comparison questions are popular in history courses. They force students to think about similarities and differences. (Your teacher may write, "Compare and contrast Luther's view with that of Thomas More." But any comparison requires us to declare not only the similarities but also the differences between two or more items.)

Above all, pick out the *significant* areas of comparison. Some comparisons are significant for this question. We know that More and Luther liked eggs but that although Luther usually drank beer, More usually drank wine. These items, though interesting, have nothing to do with the question.

If you have studied hard for an examination, you may be tempted to pour all your knowledge into the question. Avoid that temptation. Answer the question as it has been asked. A hard-pressed teacher will not have time in grading your paper to give you the benefit of the doubt. If you give no clear answer to the question, your teacher will assume that you do not know the answer, and you will get no special credit for the flood of confused knowledge that you pour out on your paper. Answer the question. Limit what you say to the job you are asked to do in the question.

Start your comparison with a brief outline:

```
Both More and Luther wanted reform in the church.

Both of them believed that God was all powerful and
mysterious.

Both believed that human beings had no worth in them-
selves except as God gave them worth.

Both of them feared hell.

Both demanded an infallible authority.

Luther's authority was the Word of God as revealed in
the Bible; More's authority was the tradition of the
Catholic Church.

Luther wanted reform in doctrine; reform in morals was
secondary to him.

More wanted reform in morals; he thought that if doc-
trines had been deemed essential to salvation by the
church, they could not be changed.
```

```
Luther wanted to cease veneration of the saints and to
rid worship of saints' relics; More wanted to keep
both.
```

```
Both believed religion was necessary if society were
to endure.
```

In the examination situation, when you may have only a half hour or perhaps an hour to write on such a topic, you would probably abbreviate your outline considerably. You could write for the topic above:

```
reform
God
hell
authority
Word of God/Church
reform in doctrine/reform in morals
saints and relics
religion/society
```

You could list many more items for comparison between Luther and More. Your quick jottings here can start you off on writing a good essay. It seems to be more natural in comparisons to begin with the similarities and then to pass to the differences. I have suggested here a means of concluding the essay with a sort of flourish, ending it on an important matter on which both men agreed.

Exams requiring arguments are both difficult and challenging. They may take several forms. Some teachers like to ask "what if" questions. Such a question requires you to demonstrate your knowledge of what did happen and the connections that you perceive between people and events. A teacher might ask you to speculate on what might have happened had the British won the American War for Independence. You might then argue that Napoleon would never have sold the Louisiana territories to the British, though he was willing in 1804 to sell them to the weak and distant independent United States. Other consequences would have followed. A question like this allows you to play in a serious way with some of the data and to see more clearly some relations that might otherwise have been obscure. Then, using your knowledge, you must argue your own point of view.

The point of an argument on an examination is not to prove one side or another beyond any doubt. Historians seldom prove anything beyond any doubt. You cannot resolve all doubts and eliminate all contrary opinions in the few minutes you have on an examination. You can, however, show that you know the material and that you can think about it intelligently. You will always impress your teacher if you can rapidly survey the arguments opposite to your point of view and show how you disagree with them.

Many kinds of arguments may come up in exams or in history papers. Your teacher may ask you to compare the two historians' opinions on a controversial matter and argue for the correctness of one of them. You may have to argue who was more guilty for beginning World War I, the Germans or the Russians. You may be required to argue whether Reconstruction following the Civil War was a success or a failure or whether economics or political influences contributed more to the emancipation of women. The subjects are endless. It is worth repeating that the aim in such questions is not to have you resolve the issues but to demonstrate that you know the material and that you can think about it. Asking you to do an argument is a good way of preventing you from merely repeating the information you have taken from your reading and the lectures.

Often teachers will ask you why something happened. "Why did France put up such a stiff fight against the Germans in 1914 only to collapse in a little over a month in 1940?" Your teacher will expect a carefully reasoned discussion about the possibilities that may be suggested by this question. You will have to consider the differences between 1914 and 1940, the arguments that the French people lost their enthusiasm for their own government between the wars, and the counterarguments that the Germans simply employed tactics that would have defeated any country that tried to use the French army's tactics in 1940. A "why" question always demands a discussion. It nearly always implies that several points of view are known and that you should demonstrate some acquaintance with those views and then arrive at your own conclusion.

To show that you do know the material, you must be specific. You should be able to mention books and authors and to give their points of view. You should by all means be able to give specific examples to illustrate your generalizations. Do not say, "Some people claimed they came on the Reformation consciousness without being influenced by Luther." Say, "Ulrich Zwingli in Zurich claimed he came to the Reformation without reading Luther; if he did, we have a further argument for the belief that the Protestant Reformation would have come if Luther had never been born." Specific information carries authority; vague generalizations do not.

Much of your success in examinations will depend on how well you prepare. Always read with a notebook beside your book. Jot down the main points of authors, points you can usually learn quickly by reading the introductions to books and the first and last paragraphs of articles. Write down names and next to them write their significance. Write down major events and use a few words to explain why they are important.

A good preparation for an examination is to make up questions of your own on the material. You will discover that you can be extremely successful in guessing what the questions may be if you have paid close attention to the teacher's emphases in lectures and discussions. Teachers come to questions in the same way you can: they ask themselves what they can ask you to make sure you have arrived at the main points they wish to emphasize. Rarely do teachers give questions on matters they have not covered in class. If you listen attentively and concentrate your reading on the things most important to the teacher, you will almost certainly be able to guess the general shape of the questions to come on the examination. If you write out your guesses, you will shape the information before you go to the exam. You will be pleasantly surprised at your ability to guess what you will see on the exam.

If you have time to write out some sketches of answers to those questions, so much the better. You will learn the extent of your knowledge. If you do not know things, you will learn your weaknesses, the gaps in your knowledge, and you can set yourself to learning. You will imprint what you do on your mind, and when the real exam comes, you will discover that this information will be there in your memory where you can retrieve it without the nervous strain that sometimes comes in exams.

Acknowledgments

Pages 13–14: From Colin McEvedy, "The Bubonic Plague," *Scientific American,* February 1988, p. 118. Copyright © 1988 by Scientific American, Inc. All rights reserved.

Pages 16–17: From Douglas J. Preston, "A Daring Gamble in the Gobi Desert Took the Jackpot," *Smithsonian,* December 1987, p. 94. © 1987 Douglas J. Preston.

Pages 48–49: From Sylvia Thrupp, *The Merchant Class of Medieval London,* University of Michigan Press, Ann Arbor, 1962, pp. 137–139.

Pages 56–57 and 204–205: From Peter Laslett, *The World We Have Lost,* pp. 84–85, 104. Reprinted with permission of Macmillan Publishing Company from *The World We Have Lost* by Peter Laslett. Copyright © 1965, 1971 by Peter Laslett.

Pages 62–63: Pages 34–36 from *Sacco and Vanzetti: The Case Resolved* by Francis Russell. Copyright © 1986 by Francis Russell. Reprinted by permission of Harper & Row, Publishers, Inc.

Pages 67–68: From *The Face of Battle* by John Keegan. Copyright © 1976 by John Keegan. All rights reserved. Reprinted by permission of Viking Penguin Inc.

Pages 69–70: Excerpts from pp. 82–83 and 70–71 from *The Spirit of Seventy-Six* by Henry Steele Commager and Richard B. Morris. Copyright © 1958, 1967, 1975 by Henry Steele Commager and Richard B. Morris. Reprinted by permission of Harper & Row, Publishers, Inc.

Pages 76–77: Excerpt from *The Book of the Courtier* by Baldesar Castiglione. Translation copyright © 1959 by Charles S. Singleton and Edgar de N. Mayhew. Reprinted by permission of Doubleday, a division of Bantam, Doubleday, Dell Publishing Group Inc.

Pages 94–95: From *The Progressive Historians* by Richard Hofstadter, pages 115–117. Copyright © 1968 by Richard Hofstadter. Reprinted by permission of Alfred A. Knopf, Inc.

Page 179: From R. R. Bolgar, *The Classical Heritage and Its Beneficiaries,* © Cambridge University Press, 1954.

Pages 181–182: From Mark Girouard: *The Return to Camelot,* Yale University Press (1981), Copyright: 1981 Pothecary Ltd.

Pages 191–192: From Alan Ryan, *Smithsonian,* March 1987, pp. 175–177. Copyright © 1987 by Alan Ryan.

Pages 193–194, 213, and 219: From *The Armada* by Garrett Mattingly. Copyright © 1959 by Garrett Mattingly. Reprinted by permission of Houghton Mifflin Company.

Pages 197–198: From *Vietnam: A History* by Stanley Karnow. Copyright © 1983 by Stanley Karnow. All rights reserved. Reprinted by permission of Viking Penguin Inc.

Page 199: From Robert J. Littman, *The Greek Experiment: Imperialism, and Social Conflict, 800–400 BC,* 1974, pp. 47–49. Reprinted by permission of Thames & Hudson, Ltd.

Index